ACE YOUR FIRST YEAR TEACHING

How to be an Effective and Successful Teacher

Anthony D. Fredericks, Ed.D.
www.anthonydfredericks.com

BLUE RIVER PRESS

Indianapolis, Indiana

Ace Your First Year Teaching
How to be an Effective and Successful Teacher

Published by **Blue River Press**
Indianapolis, Indiana
www.brpressbooks.com

Distributed by **Cardinal Publishers Group**
317-352-8200 phone
317-352-8202 fax
www.cardinalpub.com

ISBN: 978-1-68157-045-7

Author: Anthony D. Fredericks, Ed.D.
Editor: Dani McCormick
Book Design: Dave Reed
Cover Design: Scott Lohr
Cover Photo: Rawpixel.com / Shutterstock
Publication Date: 2017

Printed in the United States of America

Dedication

For **Morgan Lanzalotti** - the quintessential teacher!
May her constant effervescence, deep compassion,
and sincere dedication serve as models for us all.

Contents

Acknowledgements

There are many to thank for this book and I am appreciative of all their sharing that permeates these pages. That so many are involved is a testament to the concentrated wisdom of dedicated individuals earnestly seeking to make this profession dynamic and strong. I am fortunate to have had the opportunity of tapping into their minds and hearts. Their passion for excellence rings loud throughout this book.

A lavish "tip of the hat," generous genuflections, and long strings of "high fives" are extended to my colleagues in the Department of Education at York College of Pennsylvania. They have munificently supported my literary efforts and provided intellectual sustenance at every turn. They are to be honored, celebrated, and cheered (a standing ovation would be appropriate, too!). Here's to Stacey Dammann, Katie Beauchat, Josh DeSantis, Nicole Hesson, Leah Kocoronis, Kim Sutton, Becky Speelman, Amy Glusco, Leslie Trimmer, and Sherry Rankin. What a crew! What an experience!

I am equally honored to have worked with a most outstanding cadre of undergraduate students at York College—each of whom will make a magnificent difference in the lives of students for years to come. They are truly the "best of the best" and have distinguished themselves as educational leaders of the first order. Our profession is all the better for their sincere dedication, steadfast determination, and remarkable *joie d'vivre.*

To all the teachers (including several former students) around the country who answered my call for advice and counsel—all of which is liberally sprinkled throughout the pages of this book—I extend my eternal gratitude, appreciation, and thanks. Your "words of wisdom" are clear markers for what it takes to be an outstanding teacher and influential educator. I am forever grateful for your willingness to share. Thanks go out to Morgan Lanzalotti, Donna Cherry, Anita Meinbach, Becky Glatfelter, Mike McGough, Vicky Lynott, Jane Piepmeier, Parker Palmer, Donna Albertson, Amanda Cuff, Amy Glusco, Ashley Miller, George Severns, Darian Kiger, Nicole Hesson, Kim Dunlap, Phil

Monteith, Suzanne Barchers, Steph Crumbling, Dawn Ramos, Bryan Quibell, Ashley White, and Susan Fetner.

An enormous gold star (no, make that a bushel of gold stars) goes to my editor—Dani McCormick—who is not only a joy to work with, but a literary professional of the highest caliber. Her eyes are eagle–sharp, her editing pen light, and her editorial suggestions (specifically, a certain author's punctuation proclivities) consistently supreme. Other writers should be so fortunate!

To you, the reader, I offer my appreciation for including this book as a valuable resource in your professional library. I wish you the greatest of success in this exciting journey you are about to undertake. There will be much to experience and much to learn for both you and your students. May those times be filled with wisdom, adventure, and the joy of truly affecting a new generation of learners. Cheers!

Introduction

Let's begin this book with three eye-opening statements from a recent survey of new teachers conducted by the American Federation of Teachers (AFT):

1. *"Fewer than half of new teachers describe their [teacher] training as very good.*

2. *One out of every three new teachers reports feeling unprepared on her or his first day of teaching.*

3. *The top problem experienced by new teachers in their own training was a failure to prepare them for the challenges of teaching in the "real world."*[1]

You may read the words above and think to yourself, "Yes, that sounds just like me!" Or, you may be more inclined to shout, "OMG, I'm one of those new teachers and **I DON'T HAVE A CLUE** as to what I'm doing!!!"

Not to worry!

While many new teachers feel underprepared and insufficiently trained on the skills, strategies, and procedures necessary to be an effective and successful classroom teacher; you, on the other hand, will be able to approach your first day and your first year with a heightened degree of confidence, positive attitude, and critical training designed to ensure your success both now and well into your teaching career. That's because, with this book

You will *ace your first year teaching*!

There may well have been some important things about teaching you didn't learn; significant elements of successful teachers and equally successful classrooms that may have been missing from your teacher training program. That's not to condemn your undergraduate

---

1 American Federation of Teachers. *Raising the Bar: Aligning and Elevating Teacher Preparation and the Teaching Profession* (Washington, D.C.: AFT, 2012), p. 7.

preparation; it's just to say that no two teacher training programs are ever the same. There is a wide range of variation between institutions in terms of program standards, philosophy, scope and sequence, and state regulations. Even institutions within a specific geographic region will vary significantly in how they approach teacher education. In short, depending on where you went to college the emphasis on selected teacher competencies may be quite different from that emphasized at other similar institutions.

But, there are some elements of teaching that hold true, no matter what institution you attended. One of those is the fact that as teachers, we have the capacity to touch our students in life-changing ways. Not only do we prepare them academically, but we have an impact on their social and emotional growth as well. In fact, I can't think of another profession that has such a significant influence on the lives of others as we do in education. It is both scary and exciting at the same time.

QUOTABLE QUOTE

"Teaching is not the filling of a pail, but rather the lighting of a flame."

– William Butler Yeats

Early in my teaching career I had a student I will never forget—one who made an indelible impression on me (and my teaching philosophy) in a very short amount of time. It was late October and the reds and golds of autumn were in clear display around the school. Shortly after the opening bell one day, the guidance counselor came into my classroom holding the hand of a tiny waif with a faded dress, hand-me-down shoes, and the saddest expression I'd ever seen. She stared at the floor as the counselor told me her name was Karen. I learned later that Karen's mother had gone through three husbands and three divorces and was now settling in to her fourth marriage. Karen, at eight years old, had experienced seven different schools in seven different cities in four different states. As a third grader, she didn't know how to read, couldn't write her name, and lacked simple social skills. She had experienced a lot of tough times and it was likely that she would continue to do so.

But, for some reason, she and the class connected.

I quickly learned that she was a fan of horses. Having gone to prep school on a working cattle ranch in the middle of Arizona, I too, was an admirer of horses. I brought in some of my daughter's horse books (*Misty of Chincoteague* and *Black Beauty*) and recorded them for her to listen to on a tape recorder. She would dictate horse stories to me, I'd type them up, and they became our literacy lessons (we tossed aside the reading textbook). She would dictate horse words to students who would write them on index cards for her own personal "Word Wall." Together we hunted up some horse books in the school library as well as the local public library. We talked about horses, we made models of horses, we wrote horse stories together, and we even visited a horse farm on a Saturday morning. The entire class jumped into our 'Horse Curriculum" with enthusiasm and camaraderie. We soon developed a reputation as the class that always "horsed around."

And, for the first time in her young life, Karen smiled. I suspect that for the first time in her life a group of people took a real interest in her; a teacher and a bunch of exuberant kids took the time to learn something about her. And she thrived! Oh, boy, did she thrive!! By February, she was just about on grade level in both reading and math. But, by February her mother's marriage was, once again, crumbling and she had to move on. And, so did Karen. On her last day, I gave her a special copy of *Black Beauty* and a letter signed by every kid in the room. As she walked out the door she turned and said, "Thank you everyone for helping me to learn."

And, I've never forgotten her.

You and millions of other teachers got into this profession for any number of reasons. For me, teaching has been, and continues to be, the most exciting profession I know. But, after more than four and a half decades as an educator, I also know there's lots to master and lots to learn. And so, I'm honored to share this book - hoping it will be your personal guide to a lifetime of teaching success. You'll quickly discover that this is a book based on the best ideas from the best teachers all over the country. When you finish you'll have everything you need to succeed as a classroom teacher. You'll be able to walk into any classroom with confidence and the assurance that both you and your students will shine.

Three bonus features are sprinkled throughout the pages of this book. These include:

A Word of Advice

For this book, I contacted scores of elementary, middle school, and secondary teachers from around the United States. I e-mailed requests, conducted phone interviews, and had many pleasant conversations with experienced teachers (including several former students) from a wide variety of schools. Their perceptions (they were all first year teachers at one time) will give you inside information about this all-important year.

What a Great Idea!

These sections include valuable and practical tips that will make your job more successful and less stressful. You'll get inside information available in no other resource.

QUOTABLE QUOTE

Throughout the writing process for this book, I've collected counsel from several leading thinkers (both past and present). Their sage advice and learned contemplations offer you (and all teachers) significant "words of wisdom" that can have a most positive effect on your growth as a professional educator.

You should know that the information in this book is not textbook information. You won't get lots of theories and pages of dull, dry research. What you will get are my experiences as both a secondary and elementary classroom teacher as well as teacher educator. You'll also get the insight of hundreds of other teachers from around the country that have been where you are now. I've interviewed them, visited them, and blatantly stolen their tips and ideas to share with you. Their wisdom is liberally sprinkled throughout these pages. Here, you will get support and encouragement from fellow teachers who have truly "walked the walk." Please know that every idea in this book has been classroom tested and teacher approved by educators in every section of the country. In short, my focus in writing this book was on three words: Practical, Practical, and Practical!

I sincerely hope you enjoy this journey. For here is a compilation of the best thinking, the latest research, and the finest teachers' advice available anywhere. I'm here to help you choose the strategies and procedures that will make you an unforgettable teacher - a teacher who inspires students and transforms lives.

And, along the way, I hope you discover lots of "Karens."

QUOTABLE QUOTE

"A teacher affects eternity; he can never tell where his influence stops."

– Henry Adams

Part I

◆

"Are You Ready?"

Chapter 1

"HELP! I'm a New Teacher!!"

August 24, 20___

Dear Diary:

OMG—I can't believe tomorrow's my first day! I'm a teacher—a real honest-to-goodness teacher. How did it happen so fast? It seems like just yesterday when I walked into my dorm room, met my roommate, and started my college career. Now, I've graduated and got that job I always wanted. And now I'm supposed to be that professional teacher all my professors kept talking about. I am so freakin' scared!

What am I supposed to do? Sure, I took all those courses, wrote all those papers, worked in all those classrooms... and now I'm supposed to be a qualified teacher. How did it happen so fast? I feel like I don't know a thing. I feel mentally naked. Next week I'm supposed to be a smiling, happy teacher with all my lesson plans in place and my classroom all arranged and everything ready for twenty-four happy, smiling students. I don't have any idea where to start or what to do. This is crazy. Me, a teacher! Who would have thought? OMG!!

This is so unbelievable! I'm so freakin' scared!!

You're about to set out on one of the most incredible journeys of your life. It will be an ongoing series of adventures, discoveries, tribulations, mistakes, experiences, tragedies, escapades, exploits, encounters, breakthroughs, laughter and wisdom that will change you as a person and as a professional educator. You will be a far different person thirty or forty years from now than you are today. You will change just as you will change the lives of your students. You will grow in character, wisdom, and self-discovery and become someone absolutely different from who you are today. You will know a hundred times more stuff about life than you ever thought possible. You will be smarter, better, and more confident. You will have influenced one or two generations (or more) of young people in ways that few individuals on this planet ever do.

You're beginning your life as a teacher. And you're scared!

Guess what? You're in good company! I, too, was scared—scared witless—when I started four and a half decades ago. And, so were all my fellow "newbies." And so are 150,000 other teachers this year who are starting down this incredibly exciting career path - a path with so many promises, and a path with so many possibilities.

For now, it's you on the other side of the desk. Now you're the one giving directions, checking assignments, creating lesson plans, establishing classroom management plans, integrating technology into your lessons, wiping up spills and drying tears, settling disagreements and building friendships, and a thousand other things that real-life classroom teachers have to do every day, and no two days are ever the same. You could teach for a million years and no two terms, two groups of students, two classrooms, or two lessons will ever be similar. And, yes, you're the one in charge.

You bet it's scary!

But, you got this book to help allay those fears, to give you some guidance and comfort in the face of all those decisions and choices and judgements you will soon make. This book will help answer your questions and give you the professional strength and courage to truly make a difference in the lives of students without losing your mind! With this resource you will be prepared with confidence and assurance to "hit the ground running" with both the skills and attitudes that will make you shine. This book—in concert with all those courses you took in your teacher preparation program—will be both your staff and your standard for a most engaging first year, a first year filled with both promise and success!

QUOTABLE QUOTE

"The only thing that interferes with my learning is my education."

— Albert Einstein

"Hey, Doc, I have a Few Questions about Being a First Year Teacher"

Right about now you have some concerns and worries about this new year that is fast approaching. Yup, you and all those other beginning teachers have a ton of queries that you need answered. As I've chatted with beginning teachers around the country, here are some of their most frequently asked questions:

1. <u>What if my students don't like me?</u> Guess what, not every student is going to like you. By the same token, you won't necessarily like every single student who takes up residence in your classroom. Look back on your own educational career. Did you like every single teacher you had in elementary school, middle school, high school, or college? Most likely, no! The same will hold true in your own classroom. It's important to remember that good teaching is not a popularity contest - it is about changing lives for the better. If you go into education to be everyone's friend, then you're in it for the wrong reason. If you go into it to make a difference, then you've chosen the right reason. Face it, teaching has nothing to do with the number of "Likes" you have on your Facebook page; but it has everything to do with changing lives for the better.

2. <u>What if I make a mistake?</u> Terrific! That's what good teaching is all about. It's how you handle the mistakes that's more important than the mistakes themselves. You'll make lots of mistakes— hundreds or them, perhaps even thousands of them. Every teacher does. I've made a million or so and continue to do so. I even announce that to my classes, "If you want to be perfect, go into the ministry or accounting, not teaching." I recognize the fact that I'm imperfect and, in fact, I celebrate it. If I make a mistake in a class I let students know and then I set about to fix it. Perhaps I've shared some erroneous information, showed the wrong video with a particular lesson, or erred in computing a student's grade. I fully admit my error to students and show them I'm willing to correct the mistake and make things right. My teaching philosophy has always been based on one single maxim—something I discovered long, long ago when I was in the same exact place you are right now. That is:

> "The best teachers are those who have
> as much to learn as they do to teach."

I've been learning new things for a long time now—and will continue to do so—as will you. Please don't try to be the "perfect teacher" right out of the box. You'll frustrate yourself and pile more stress into your day than you need. Know that you might make a mistake or two on the first day, on your second day, on your one millionth day! That's O.K.—you're a human being and you're only being human by making mistakes, but you're being a teacher when you use those mistakes as learning opportunities—learning opportunities for you as well as for your students.

3. <u>What if I don't know the answer?</u> Great! You now have a most wonderful learning opportunity! When students ask me a question where I'm not sure of the correct answer or I simply just don't know, I usually respond with something like, "Hey, you know what, I'm just not sure of the answer to that question. Let's find out together." First, I admit that I'm not the fount of all knowledge. I want to send a positive signal to students that teaching, for me, is also a learning process. I know a lot of stuff, but it's not possible for me to know everything about everything. The same goes for you. Admit to some of your shortcomings, celebrate them, and you'll be creating a very positive bond with your students. But, it's the second part of my response that I encourage you to adopt ("Let's find out together."). Here is where you send a most incredible message to students: Teaching and learning is a partnership; it's a joint effort by two parties to satisfy a curiosity or discover an unknown. By letting students know that I'm by their side in this intellectual quest— that I'm willing to share part of the load—I can help solidify a partnership that can reap untold benefits later in the year. In many cases, I'll brainstorm with one or more students for ways in which we can work to find an acceptable answer - there's work to do for me and work my students need to do as well. We'll come together at a later date to discuss the results of our investigations until we arrive at a satisfactory response.

A Word of Advice

"Do not underestimate your need for colleagues. You should pick their brains, accept their help and advice and find a 'team' to join as soon as possible. Asking for guidance is a sign of wisdom, not weakness. You will find great solace with your new family for years to come."

—Donna Cherry, current secondary teacher

4. <u>What if I get a "bad" kid in my class? What if I get several "bad kids" in my class?</u> It's inevitable. Not every one of your students will be an angel. Some will try your patience. Some will push your buttons. Some will drive you crazy. And, some will make you pray, wish, hope, and pray some more that they just don't show up for class on Monday morning. It's inevitable. First of all, don't believe everything you might read in a student's record. There may have been a personality conflict with last year's teacher. There may have been some discord between a teacher and a student's parents. There may have been any number of misunderstandings, miscommunications, or misinformation. Bottom line, don't prejudge a student (or group of students) based solely on information recorded from previous teachers. Every child deserves a fresh start, a new beginning. By assuming that a "bad child" from last year will also be a "bad child" this year is unfair to that individual. You've prejudged someone based on another teacher's perception. That child, no matter what kind of reputation he or she carries into your classroom deserves the same attention and commitment to a good education as every other child in your room. In Part III of this book I'll share important classroom management procedures that will eliminate bad behaviors (permanently) and help you establish a classroom atmosphere that is equally respectful of each and every individual.

5. <u>What if a lesson "bombs"?</u> They will! Count on it! I've created lessons that bomb. I created some "bombed" lessons when I first taught and, guess what, I created some lessons that "bombed"

just this year. That's OK Not every lesson you write will be memorable, inspirational, or successful. Some just won't make it. But, that's all part of what makes teaching so exciting. If you set out to try and make every single lesson perfect you will only add to your level of frustration. You need to face this reality: some lessons will fall flat on their face because you forgot a simple ingredient, a critical piece of technology (like, say, your laptop), a necessary fact or slice of information or you didn't do something your professors told you in one of your college classes. But guess what, you will learn from that mistake. And, the next time you teach that lesson it will be much better and much more effective. Trying to write perfect lessons shouldn't be your goal; your goal should be to create learning opportunities to the best of your ability <u>at this point in time</u>. The longer you teach, the better your lessons will become. It's like playing the piano, the more you practice (over the years) the better you get. Unless you're a musical prodigy, you don't play Liszt's Hungarian Rhapsody #2 the first time you sit down at a piano, it takes many years of constant and sustained practice to play this most demanding piece. By the same token, it will take you lots of practice to perfect all the skills of an accomplished teacher. Don't expect to do it all in your first year. Just remember to practice, practice, practice! Learn from your mistakes; you'll be better next time. Trust me, you will!

6. <u>What should the first day of school look like?</u> Read Chapter 5.

A Word of Advice

"Create a challenging environment that encourages students' natural curiosity and love of learning. Use a variety of strategies to make learning relevant, dynamic, and appropriate for a wide range of learning styles and needs. Build a curriculum that empowers them to reach beyond their perceived potential."

—Anita Meinbach, former classroom teacher

7. <u>How do I know if I'm doing a good job?</u> For the past 30 years I've been doing something at the conclusion of every single class I teach. Before setting off down the hallway to the classroom I place a single 3 X 5 index card on my desk with the title of that class's lesson clearly printed on the top. As soon as I return from the class, I sit down at my desk and self-evaluate the lesson. I'll select a number from 1 (low) to 10 (high) and record it in the upper right hand corner of the card. Then I quickly write down some of the positives of the class, some possible areas for improvement, and any ideas I might have to use the next time I teach that lesson again. In all, this takes about 3-4 minutes.

Each semester I teach a course called "Teaching Elementary Social Studies." Somewhere in the middle of the course I address the topic of Multiple Intelligences (M.I.), a two-week overview of one of the critical components of effective instruction. My introductory lesson consists of an overview of M.I., a video of several classroom teachers using M.I. in the classroom, and a hands-on activity in which students begin generating their own M.I, activities for a specific piece of children's literature.

One recent semester I returned to my office and gave myself a "3" on that particular lesson. I pulled the index card from the previous semester and noted that I had given myself a "3.5" for that same lesson. Clearly, there was something amiss, but I just couldn't figure out what it was. My lesson objectives were sound, my explanations were clear, students were provided with visual examples of M.I. in the classroom, and everyone participated in the scheduled activity. But, something was obviously not "clicking" with students.

So, I decided to go right to my students and find out. I found a trio of them in the hallway outside my office and invited them in for a cup of coffee and a discussion. I asked the three of them what they thought of the M.I. lesson. They all looked at each other and smiled. Finally, Jennifer spoke up and said, "Listen, Dr. Fredericks, that lesson was so out of date." I asked her to be more specific. It was then that the three of them told me, "Your video was so ancient. Nobody wears clothes like that anymore. The teachers were using chalk on a blackboard—nobody uses blackboards any longer. And there wasn't a single computer to be found anywhere in the classrooms. It was an ancient video." That's when it struck me, as soon as students saw the video and all its "ancient" references they assumed that the topic I was sharing with them was also ancient; it wasn't current or up-to-date. The old guy was showing old stuff (A check of the copyright date on the video indicated that it had been produced four years before any of my students had been born, meaning the video was "older than dirt." Gulp!).

The following semester, when I was planning to teach that lesson again, I downloaded a video from YouTube (which had been filmed the year before) and used that as my introduction to M.I. When I returned to my office after that lesson I wrote an "8.5" on the index card. This time, students could "connect" to the teacher in the film and what she was sharing made a bigger impact. It was a most valuable lesson for me as well as my students.

8. <u>What's your best advice?</u> I've got three tidbits. First, don't be so hard on yourself. Remember that every teacher has a first year! This is yours! Celebrate it. Know that there will be some bumps in the road. You'll have a few hiccups, a few muddles, and a few gaffes. It's inevitable. We all did. Don't try to be perfect—you'll frustrate the hell out of yourself if you do.

    Second, beg, borrow and steal as many tips, ideas, and strategies as you can. Talk to colleagues, read other books (yes, you have permission to read books other than this one—my ego won't suffer), go to conferences, pour through teacher magazines, and scour the internet. Build up file folders full of innovative, creative and dynamic ideas to share with your students. Be a "packrat of ideas."

    Third, feel free to take risks. We don't make any progress as a teacher, a hairdresser, an architect, a horticulturist, a sailor, a doctor, an interior designer, or a handyman without taking risks. Sure, you may trip or stumble. That's OK. You and I and a few billion other people around the world tripped and stumbled (and fell) when we first began to walk. But, guess what? There were plenty of people around to pick us up and get us started again. And, guess what, that's how it is in teaching, too. You'll have lots of people (and this book) around you to pick you up and get you started again. Your first steps may not be perfect, but with a little practice you'll be walking, then jogging, then running. And then, someday, perhaps an Olympic marathon (Gold medal, anybody?)!

Are you ready? Let's go!

Chapter 2

What They Never Told You in College
(and what they did)

For a moment, think about all the courses you took in college—all the papers you had to write, all the lectures you had to sit through, all the classrooms you had to visit, and all the lesson plans you had to write during your student teaching semester. During the last four or five years of your life you were bombarded with tons of information, lots of advice, and a plethora of "do's" and "don'ts" about teaching. At times it was overwhelming; at times it was overpowering.

Wow—lots of stuff!

But, it's likely your professors didn't tell you everything. They may have (unintentionally) left a fact or two about teaching out of their lessons. So, let's rectify that situation right now. Let's fill in some of the blanks with practical advice shared by classroom teachers who have been right where you are now.

QUOTABLE QUOTE
"Education is what remains after one has forgotten what one has learned in school."
—Albert Einstein

1. You'll Have Many Roles as a Teacher.

As a teacher, you will wear many hats. You don't just teach; you are a multiple-personality-type person who satisfies many roles in the lives of your students and the school. Take a look at some of the multi-faceted responsibilities you'll assume as a teacher:

- Doctor/nurse (patching up bruised elbows and knees)
- Counselor (patching up bruised egos and personalities)
- Surrogate parent (explaining the facts of life)
- Paralegal/Legal assistant (interpreting school rules, issuing hall passes)
- Traffic cop (keeping the peace with bus duty and hall duty)
- Stock clerk (ordering copy paper, obtaining pencils/pens)
- Accountant (handling lunch money, field trip money, book and club money)
- Recreation worker (monitoring recess, supervising athletic events)
- Social worker (understanding family relations)
- Interior decorator (creating posters and decorations)
- Human resources manager (scheduling "Meet the Teacher" night, parent conferences)
- Architect (designing and laying out your classroom)
- Transportation coordinator (arranging field trips, bus duty)
- Librarian (organizing books and bookshelves)
- Information clerk ("Where do I put my homework?", "Who's got the bathroom pass?")
- Plumber (water spills, overflowing toilet)
- Secretary (dealing with paperwork, paperwork, paperwork!)

Suffice it to say, the roles and responsibilities of teachers are many. Some seasoned veterans will tell you that teaching is like a circus juggling act—you're trying to keep as many objects in the air as you possibly can without dropping a single one. Sometimes it's demanding; sometimes it's complicated, but it is never, ever dull!

2. Who you are is more important than what you know.

Students will not judge you based on the quantity of "stuff" you have in your head. Nor will they judge you by how smart you are, what your GPA was, or by your IQ. All that means very little to students. Your evaluation, in the eyes of your students, will be based primarily on how you made them feel. Did you go out of your way to make them comfortable in the classroom? Did you acknowledge their presence on a regular basis? Did you give them valid opportunities to make choices and follow through on those choices? In all the years I've been teaching there is one kind of teacher that students universally despise: the "My way or the highway!" teacher—the one who supposedly has all the answers and controls all the activities in a classroom. You've probably had those teachers in your educational career (and I know what you've said about them). Don't be one.

3. You learn to teach by working with kids; not by memorizing stuff in a textbook.

I know you're probably looking at the previous sentence and thinking to yourself, "Well if that's true, then why did I (or my parents) have to spend all that money on all those stupid textbooks?" Truth be told, all those "stupid textbooks" gave you the foundation and groundwork you needed to be an effective teacher. But, all those textbooks didn't know about the dynamics of your classroom, they didn't know about the demographics of your students, and they didn't know about your singular and unique personality. You have the "basics" (gleaned from all those "stupid textbooks"), but it is you and your students who will begin to put those basics into action and no textbook can do that for you.

I have often told my undergraduate students that they will learn more about teaching by actually being with kids than they will in all of the methods courses they take in college. Kids will present new teachers with an array of situations, experiences, and challenges that can never be recounted in the pages of a book (this one included). You learn to drive, not by reading a driver's manual, but by actually getting behind the wheel of a car, turning on the ignition, pulling out into traffic and driving. You learn to teach in the same way: working with students. The bottom line is this: the more you work with students, the better you will become as a teacher. Let your students be your ultimate instructors. They have much to share with you.

4. Good teaching does not come about overnight.

Kids learn to walk sometime around their first birthday (as did you and I). In many cases a parent or guardian will place a child at the end of the living room couch or a nearby coffee table. The child will slap her or his hands on the furniture and take a sideways step (lots of giggling by the child is optional as are lots of photos by the parents). Then there's another sideways step as the child begins to progress, very slowly and very methodically down the edge of the couch or table. Eventually the child will come to the end of the designated furniture, take one more step and fall down. A parent will rush over, pick the child up, and place her or him back at the starting point and the entire process will start over again. This may take some time (since several YouTube videos of little Johnny learning to walk are being filmed by the parents), but each time the child comes to the end of the couch or table and falls down there is someone there to lift her or him up, place her/him back at the beginning, and the process repeats itself. Eventually after some time (days, weeks), the child is able to walk on her or his own and a whole new learning curve begins.

You know what? Your first year of teaching is just like learning to walk. Your first steps will be tentative, your progress may be slower that you would have hoped, from time to time you may think you've reached the end of your rope, and from time to time you will take a step beyond your limits and (ta da) fall down. But, there will be a friend, colleague, or fellow teacher there to pick you up, set you back on course, and encourage you to start the journey anew. And after some time (weeks, months, years) you will become an accomplished teacher just like you became an accomplished walker when you were considerably younger.

A Word of Advice

"Go out of your way to connect with colleagues. Ask for help when needed. They will view you as a 'team player' and not as a 'newbie know-it-all'."

—Becky Glatfelter, current elementary teacher

Please remember this: Good teaching (and good walking) takes practice, practice, practice!

5. Kids don't learn everything you teach them.

You'll put together a dynamic lesson, pull in some really interesting videos, schedule some fascinating guest speakers, assemble some incredible "hands-on" activities, and design the most creative PowerPoint presentation ever seen by human eyes—and your students won't learn! It's a sad reality, but the truth of the matter is that output is not always equal to input. There is no guarantee that the time and effort you put into a lesson will result in students ready to craft a Pulitzer-prize winning novel or design a Nobel Prize winning physics experiment. No matter how excellent you think your lessons are, the reality is that there will be some kids that just won't get it. This is not the time to beat yourself up ("How can I get EVERY student in the class to learn this stuff?") simply because you will fret over something that may be completely out of your control. There may be family issues at home, a student may be afflicted with a certain disease or ailment, a child may be experiencing traumatic relationship issues, or they may simple be having "a bad day" (just like you and I do at times).

The harsh reality is that you may not reach each and every student with each and every topic. That's as true for your students as it was for you. There have been some days in your educational career when you just weren't up to learning very much. Things may have been happening outside the classroom that affected what you were doing inside that same classroom. And, you couldn't (or wouldn't) learn a whole lot. Guess what, your students will go through the same process, perhaps many times. Just know that you have put out your best lesson and evidenced your best attitude and done your best job. It just may be that not everyone is on the same (mental) page as you this one day. And, you know what? That's OK

A Word of Advice

"Here's something important to remember: you won't save every kid. You will do your best; you will craft dynamic and exciting lessons; you will have a classroom that students love; and you will be incredibly effective, humorous, and personable. But you just won't reach every single student. It's a tough reality, but one you need to acknowledge to maintain your sanity."

—Mike McGough, former classroom teacher

6.   Teaching is not your life.

One of the things you will want to do during your first year is to completely devote yourself to your classroom, your students, your lessons, and every other little thing that has to do with teaching. Big Mistake! One of the most powerful quotes I picked up from a friend was the following, "Keep in mind that this is not your life…it is your job… and there's a big difference!"

As a first year teacher you will want to devote all your time to learning how to be the best teacher possible. That's a fine goal to have, but keep in mind that it's just one goal, it's not your only goal. You will want to spend lots of hours developing intriguing lesson plans, grading homework assignments, attending teacher meetings and all the other minutia of detail that will consume your time, and yes, begin to slowly suck the life out of you. You'll turn down social engagements because there's a stack of papers waiting for you to grade, you'll rule out weekend excursions and journeys because you have to create dynamic and exciting lesson plans, and you'll forgo reading a trashy novel or seeing the newest blockbuster movie because you have to deal with a behavioral management issue with two of your students. Teaching will slowly and inexorably become, quite literally, a 24/7 consumption of your time.

Take it from the experts (and I say this with all due respect), you need to GET A LIFE. It's true, one of the things most teachers fail to do is to seek a balance between their professional life and their personal one. Pros will tell you that your very sanity is dependent on working toward and achieving that balance. Without the balance you will be adding to your stress and put yourself firmly on the road to burnout. Indeed, the research has shown that as much as 50 percent of all teachers "burn-out" before their fifth year and they leave the profession as a result. Remember that teaching is your career; it's not your 24/7.

7. Society will frequently blame you if students aren't learning.

They'll also blame you if your students don't get high scores on district or state tests, if the star quarterback doesn't throw a winning pass in the last seconds of the Homecoming game, or if Mrs. Anderson's little Susie (in the back row) isn't smiling in the class photo. It's a fact: teachers get blamed for a lot of stuff—much of which they might have little control over. It's not always easy to hear these things, but it's often part of the job.

What They Probably Told You in College (But, It's Still All Wrong)

There are any number of myths or untruths shared during the teacher training process. Some of these have been around since—well, since forever (I even remember hearing some of these misguided statements when I was an undergraduate student in the 1960s). Quite often, these "standards" are simply passed down from one generation to another without being vetted by the experts in the field—real classroom teachers.

It is quite possible you have heard several of these falsehoods during your teacher training program. They may have been shared in one or more of your methods courses, been lodged in the deep recesses of a college textbook (which has, by now, been sold back to the bookstore), or been part of the discussions you and your friends have had over the past several years.

But, here's the truth: These are all erroneous. Let's take a look!

1. **Good teachers never ask for help (Hey, you just graduated from college; you should know it all).**

Always ask for help. No one has all the answers. Heck, I've been teaching for considerably more than forty years and I still ask for help on: 1) integrating more technology into my classes, 2) more effective ways of assessing student progress, and 3) innovative ideas for beginning any class session—ways to get students "mentally excited" about a forthcoming topic (to name a few). Asking for help, particularly during your first year, can be one of the surest paths to teaching success. Please don't cocoon yourself from the larger teaching community. Know that when you approach someone and ask for help, you are showing trust; and through trust you are building community.

A Word of Advice

"Reach out to the greater community of educators. Attend workshops of interest – there you'll meet others who teach your subject/grade level and you'll share conversation and learn what it's like in their building."

—Vicky Lynott, former middle school teacher

2. **Your first year of teaching will be your worst.**

Whoever came up with this absolutely ridiculous piece of rubbish should be drawn and quartered (and then tortured). Your first year of teaching will be challenging—that's for certain. It will offer you some interesting trials, many of which you'll be facing for the first time. And just like any "first-time" event in your life (riding a bicycle, your first kiss, signing your first lease) there are always some uncertainties and some fears. That's just human! But, you've prepared yourself for some of those challenges by reading this book and becoming more schooled in some of the essential "ingredients" of good teaching and equally good learning. So, if someone tells you that your first year will be your worst just smile at them and say something like, "No way! In fact I'm going to *ace my first year teaching*!!"

3. Make sure you attend all the extracurricular activities your students participate in.

You will be tempted to attend a lot of the special performances, athletic events, and musical concerts of your students. You want to support them in every way possible and you want to show them that you care, not just about their life inside your classroom, but also about their lives outside your classroom as well. But, be careful because if you attend one student's solo event then you will feel obligated to attend every student's solo events. As a result, you will exhaust yourself and increase your stress level. Acknowledge each student's accomplishments outside of class, but be careful about getting caught in a whirlwind of engagements that will sap your energy and your time.

4. Volunteer for as many "extra assignments" as you can.

You want to be an active and enthusiastic member of your school's instructional staff. But that doesn't mean you should volunteer yourself for every committee assignment, extra-curricular event, or special celebration. Be cautious and careful here—you may find yourself spread too thin and thus unable to attend to all the responsibilities before you in the classroom. It's fine to volunteer, but also let folks know that your primary responsibility is to your students

5. Stay with the tried and true; don't try new things.

This is a time of discovery. Don't do something just because it was professed in one of your college courses or laid out in a teacher resource book. You grow by taking risks. Will every one of them work? Of course not! But trying new stuff keeps you mentally fresh and professionally curious. Just don't try to do 199 new things in one day.

6. Don't let learning stop - start a Master's program right away.

Let's face it—you just completed four or five years of college, you probably had to study for and take some certification exams required by your state, you went through hours and hours of field experiences as well as an entire semester (or more) of student teaching. By this point in your educational career your brain cells are fried and your mental endurance is at an all-time low. What you don't need is to complicate your life (and your new job) by taking on additional responsibilities that you may not be emotionally or mentally ready for. Take a break! There are thousands of ways you can keep learning (e.g. reading articles and books, attending conferences, visiting web sites, etc.), but enrolling in a Master's program is not one I recommend. Right now you need to concentrate on designing and creating an effective learning environment. That's Job #1. Signing up for a graduate degree only complicates matters by piling on additional responsibilities and additional tasks that you really don't need right now.

My advice: take two years before you sign up for any graduate program. You'll need those two years to get your classroom "up to speed" and your philosophy firmly in place. Then, and only then, will you be ready to take on the added challenges of a graduate program.

7.   Quiet classrooms are the most productive ones.

False…blatantly false! Quiet classroom are often sterile environments where people are not interacting, engaging, or conversing. There is often a lack of community in these classrooms resulting in a cadre of individuals working separately and individually. Relationships are not encouraged and dynamic instruction is often lacking. There is peace, but very little (educational) prosperity. There is very little correlation between the noise level of a classroom and the level of learning taking place in that same room. There is, however, a direct correlation between the level of interactions taking place in a classroom and the level of instructional success. Yes, you need to regulate the noise, but don't suppress it.

8.   Don't visit the teacher's lounge—it's a wellspring of negativity.

I know, I know—early in my career as an Education professor I used to share this maxim with all my student teachers. Since then, I've changed my tune! Sure, teachers do spend some time dissing their students or saying unkind things about the administration. In fact, it almost seems as though there is a small cadre of teachers in every school whose primary responsibility is to tear down and rail against anything and anybody they can. But, guess what, that happens in every business lunch room, corporate cafeteria, or off-site lunch spot, too.

However, that said, I would encourage you to spend considerable time, particularly during your first year, in the Faculty Room. This is a grand opportunity to become part of the larger school community. It's a wonderful chance to forge new friendships, share tips and ideas, and engage in conversations that can improve morale as well as classroom procedures. It's also a great opportunity to tap into the collective wisdom of those who have been in the profession for some time and can offer advice and counsel. Moreover, it's a wonderful way to build a coalition of advisors, tutors, and confidants you can turn to when a problem or challenge comes your way. Take advantage of the collective wisdom of your fellow teachers and your own career will grow exponentially.

A Word of Advice

"Good teaching cannot be reduced to technique; good teaching comes from the identity and integrity of the teacher."

—Parker Palmer, former teacher

9. Don't smile Until Christmas.

In ancient times (you know, when I first began my teaching career) new teachers were constantly told that they shouldn't smile before Christmas. The thinking was that being too human too early would surely lead to a breakdown in classroom management. Furthermore, it was believed that it was far easier to start off hard and then ease up than the other way around. If you were tough from the beginning of the school year you would create an absolutely perfect classroom environment. Smiling during those first few months would reveal an emotional weakness—an emotional opening that students would surely exploit.

Hogwash!

Fortunately, those days are far in the past. We now know that opening up any school year with a smile establishes a tone of emotional comfortableness in any classroom—an environment that is both invitational as well as engaging. A smile says I welcome you, I respect you, I am excited about this new year, and I am passionate about what I am doing and want to model those beliefs for you. It also says that I'm an approachable person—someone who wants to establish a positive relationship with you—one that establishes a joint responsibility for teaching and learning. A smile tells students I want them to succeed because I respect them and want to work with them, not because I'm older or more educated or the only one in the room wearing a tie. Start your year off with a smile and it will always pay dividends, big time!

10. The more I know about my subject, the better teacher I will be.

Let's fix this misconception very quickly: **The more I know about my students, the better teacher I will be.** The fact that you can name all the countries of Africa or list all the elements on the Periodic Table or can recite all the phonics generalizations from memory does not make you a good teacher. It does, however, make you a good candidate for the TV game show *Jeopardy!* You will not distinguish yourself as a teacher by sheer brain-power; you will, however, distinguish yourself by what you do with your knowledge. The fact that you may have achieved a perfect 4.0 GPA throughout all your college courses does not ensure teaching success. In fact, it has very little to do with teaching success. There are considerably more important factors, detailed throughout the pages of this book, that will contribute mightily to your effectiveness as an educator. Memorizing a lot of "stuff" is not one of them.

Becoming an accomplished teacher is a process—an evolutionary process. It doesn't happen the day you graduate from college, or the day after that, or the day after that. It comes about over time. A true belief in your potential will ultimately ensure your success. I'm with you all the way.

Are you ready? Then, let's get going!

Chapter 3

<u>Becoming an Effective Teacher</u>

I have long believed (and always practiced) that good teaching is not about how much you know, but rather by how much you care. Good teachers don't dispense lots of facts, figures, and data for students to memorize; rather, good teachers work hard to develop a partnership with students —a partnership that says, "We're in this together; let's work in tandem to ensure that what we can learn is based on a solid foundation of trust, confidence, sincerity, high expectations, and mutual respect." Good teaching is not telling students what they need to know, but rather it's constructing and sustaining a shared learning experience.

In a word (actually two), good teaching is all about <u>building relationships.</u>

Think about the best teacher you had. What did that teacher do that made you enjoy being in her or his classroom? What did that teacher do that made you enjoy her or him as a person? What did she or he do that causes you to have fond and lasting memories of that course, class, classroom, or topic?

That teacher undoubtedly expressed or displayed many features, characteristics, and qualities. In this chapter, we'll consider those attributes. Most important, you will learn how you can make those attributes your own - becoming a teacher your students will remember long after they leave your classroom.

What Students Think

What is it that makes some teachers good and others slightly less than memorable? That's a question I've been asking for a long time, so I decided to go to some experts: people who have been in school for a long time. I asked a class of freshman college students about their criteria for effective teachers. They completed the following sentence: "Good teachers _____." Here's a sampling of their responses:

Good teachers...

- "Ask good questions that make us think."

- "Get along with their students. They aren't 'buddies,' but they foster open lines of communication."

- "Have a discipline policy that is consistent, fair, and impartial."

- "Can explain a topic clearly and without a lot of big words."

- "Admit when they're wrong and are always trying to improve themselves."

- "Respect students; they never put students down or ridicule them."

- "Make learning fun and aren't afraid to laugh or make fun of themselves."

- "Roll with the punches - they don't let little things get the better of them."

- "Know what they are doing; their lessons are planned (rather than off the cuff)."

- "Like to teach; they make learning enjoyable because they are enjoyable people."

It's important to point out that your effectiveness as a teacher depends on much more than your knowledge of one or more subjects. In fact, your success will be driven by characteristics and dynamics that are as much a part of who you are as they are of your classroom behavior.

Conversations with hundreds of teachers around the country indicate that good teachers are effective because they believe in (and practice) five essential principles:

1. The teacher as an authentic person

2. A student orientation

3. An emphasis on learning

4. Positive classroom management

5. Learning as a lifelong process

I invite you to consider these roles in terms of your own personality dynamics as well as in terms of your reasons for becoming a teacher.

1. The Teacher as an Authentic Person

The reasons you are a teacher are undoubtedly many. Who you are as a person and how you would like to share your personality with students are significant factors in why you choose to be a teacher. So too, will they be significant in terms of your success in the classroom. My own experience with thousands of teachers has taught me that the personality of a teacher is a major and predominant factor in the success of students within that teacher's influence.

- Good classroom teachers are joyful. They relish in the thrill of discovery and the natural curiosity of students. They are excited about learning and transmit that excitement to their students. They are stimulated by the unknown and are amazed at what can be learned, not just at what is learned.

- Students consistently rate teachers high when humor is part of the classroom environment. This humor does not come from telling lots of jokes, but rather from the good-natured conversations and discussions carried on with students. Humor breaks down conversational barriers, establishes good rapport, and builds strong classroom communities.

QUOTABLE QUOTE

"To survive as a teacher you need three bones: a wishbone, a backbone, and a funny bone."

—Author Unknown

- Good teachers are good because they not only have a love for children, but they also have a passion for the subjects they teach. If you're passionate about teaching, your students will know immediately. If you're less than excited about what you're doing, students will be able to determine that very rapidly, too. Your passion for teaching must be evident in everything you do.

- Effective teachers are inquisitive. They continuously ask questions, looking for new explanations and myriad new answers. They serve as positive role models for students, helping them ask their own questions for exploration. They are content with not finding all the answers, but rather with developing a classroom environment in which self-initiated questioning (by both teacher and students) predominates.

- Good teachers are also creative. They're willing to explore new dimensions and seek new possibilities—never sure of what lies around the corner or down the next path. They're willing to experiment and try new approaches to learning—not because they've been done before but simply because they've never been tried before.

- Outstanding teachers seek help from others. They talk about new strategies with colleagues, seek input from administrators and education experts, read lots of educational magazines and periodicals, and access websites frequently. They don't try to go it alone.

A Word of Advice

"Seek the most enthusiastic person in the building and become friends with that person. He/she will motivate you on gloomy days."

—Donna Albertson, current elementary teacher

- Effective teachers are change-makers. They're not afraid of change and realize that change can be a positive element in every classroom. If something isn't working, these teachers are eager to strike out into new territories for exploration. They're never content with status quo; their classrooms are always evolving, always in a state of transition.

A Word of Advice

"The biggest thing I learned my first year teaching is to be confident in everything you do. The kids will see that in you and respect you more for it."

—Amanda Cuff, current elementary teacher

- As you well know, there's no such thing as an average or typical day in teaching. Students come and go, clocks and computers break down, parents drop in unexpectedly, meetings are scheduled at the last minute, printers become non-operational, you forget your lunch, the video you downloaded won't run, and a hundred other things can, and often do, go wrong. However, it's the flexible teacher—the one who doesn't let these inevitable "roadblocks" get in her or his way—who survives and teaches best in the classroom. Yes, there will be "surprises," unanticipated and unplanned events, and glitches along the way. But if you are flexible you will give yourself an incredible opportunity to succeed.

QUOTABLE QUOTE

"I believe that curiosity, wonder and passion are defining qualities of imaginative minds and great teachers."

—Kay Redfield Jamison

2. A Student Orientation

If you were to walk into the classroom of any outstanding teacher, regardless of her or his grade level, one thing will become immediately clear: students are respected, attended to, and clearly more important than the subject matter or the instructional materials used.

QUOTABLE QUOTE

"Effective teachers let students know that they are somebody, not some body."

—William Purkey

- The best teachers are those who truly care for their students. They exhibit empathy and try to see the world through their students' eyes. They know students have good days and bad days just like they do, and they adjust their instruction accordingly.

- So, too, are good teachers sensitive to their students' cultural backgrounds. They respect students' languages, customs, traditions, and beliefs. They never make fun of students who are different, but rather celebrate these new opportunities for enriching the learning experiences of all students.

- Students need to know that they will never be embarrassed or ridiculed nor will they be intimidated or shown excessive favoritism. The best teachers have positive attitudes about everyone in the school: students, custodians, secretaries, aides, librarians, cafeteria workers, and fellow teachers. High-achieving classrooms are supportive, warm, and accepting.

- Good teachers listen. They're aware of the "rule of two-thirds," which states that in traditional classrooms (regardless of grade or subject) two thirds of class time is taken up by talking, two thirds of that time is taken up by teacher talk, and two thirds of the teacher's talk is telling or demonstrating rather than interacting with students. These teachers know that students have much to contribute to the curriculum and to each other and provide numerous opportunities for them to do so.

- Effective teachers provide opportunities for students to get extra help. They are observant of students' needs and work to provide the instruction or materials that will help them succeed and flourish. Student progress is constantly monitored and adjusted as necessary.

- The finest teachers are those who have high expectations for their students. They continually challenge their students, engaging them in higher-order thinking activities, problem-solving, creative-thinking extensions, and other instructional activities that s-t-r-e-t-c-h their minds. I once worked for a principal who said, "Students don't fail, teachers do!" It was his belief that good teachers must take personal responsibility for their students' learning. Good teachers are sensitive to the instructional needs of every student and work for the success of each individual in the classroom.

- Good teachers know they can significantly increase student engagement in the learning process by incorporating students' ideas in classroom discussions by:

   o Rephrasing student ideas in teacher words.

   o Using student ideas to take the next step in problem-solving.

   o Drawing relationships between student ideas and information shared earlier.

   o Using what students say as a summary of important concepts.

3. An Emphasis on Learning

Good teachers are always task oriented. That is to say, effective teachers put a high priority on the instructional activities that cause learning to happen rather than on the procedural matters of running the classroom.

- Effective teachers are able to handle administrative and clerical tasks efficiently, quickly, and without disrupting the classroom atmosphere. They spend more time teaching and less time on distractions and interruptions.

- Good teachers present logical, clear, step-by-step lessons and include cycles of review, practice, and feedback. Lessons reflect the curriculum and are designed to help students master specific objectives. Time is not wasted.

- The best teachers conduct their lessons in a businesslike, task-oriented manner. They maintain a strong academic focus in their classroom and are effective in designing lessons that enhance student mastery.

- Good teachers are in control of their classrooms. They invest time and effort in the prevention of behavioral problems by developing positive student relationships and planning well-organized lessons.

- Effective teachers know what students need, and they know how to provide for those needs. That means good lesson planning. We'll look into effective lessons in greater detail in Chapter 13, but use some of these markers to evaluate the appropriateness of your lessons:

  o Students know the purpose of the lesson.

  o The students' background knowledge is assessed and used to help direct the lesson.

  o Structuring comments or advance organizers are at the beginning of the lesson.

  o The lesson is logical, clear, and understandable.

  o Examples, illustrations, and demonstrations are used liberally

  o Group and individual activities are provided.

  o Practice and feedback is regular and systematic.

  o Student questions and comments are incorporated into the lesson.

  o A variety of instructional activities and instructional materials are woven throughout the lesson.

  o Thinking skills are emphasized and higher-order questions are used.

4. Positive Classroom Management

Managing a classroom requires many tasks, however, it's important to remember that classroom management is not about achieving order for order's sake. It's about achieving order so productive learning can occur. The ultimate goal of classroom management is to promote learning.

- Effective teachers provide opportunities for students to make decisions and follow through on those decisions. Good classrooms are not teacher-dependent environments but rather independent student learning arenas. Teachers who provide students with multiple opportunities to make choices and accept the consequences of those choices are excellent instructional leaders. Students who come up to your desk and ask, "Is this what you wanted?" or "What do I do next?" are saying they aren't allowed to make their own decisions. Teachers who empower students in making decisions are facilitating independent and responsible learners.

- Good classroom teachers teach their students classroom routines such as what to do when they finish an assignment early, how to get extra help, how to move in to and out of the classroom, and how to take care of their personal needs. This provides students with a sense of responsibility and allows them to make decisions that should be theirs rather than the teacher's.

- Good teachers establish a set of expectations early in the school year. These expectations are clearly detailed and explained to students and are upheld consistently throughout the entire school year.

- Here's something to think about: It's been proven that more than 90 percent of the positive things students do go unrecognized in the classroom. Part of an effective and productive classroom management plan recognizes frequently—no, make that <u>daily</u>—the good things students do.

QUOTABLE QUOTE

"Bark less, wag more."

—Bumper sticker

---

5. Learning as a Lifelong Process

Good teachers are those who keep learning, who continually add to their knowledge base throughout their teaching career. My lifelong motto has always been, "Good teachers have as much to learn as they do to teach." Your education is a continual learning process. It doesn't stop just because you've graduated and have a teaching certificate. It means that if you are to provide the best possible education for your students, you need to provide yourself with a variety of learning opportunities, too.

- It would be erroneous to think that your four or five years of college were all you needed to be successful in the classroom. There are too many developments within the field of education to think your college degree is the summation of all the skills, talents, and knowledge you'll need for the rest of your career. What you learn throughout the remainder of your teaching career might be significantly more important than the courses you took in college.

- Good teachers keep current, stay active, and continually seek out new answers or new questions for exploration. Your desire to find out more about effective teaching methods and dynamic new discoveries within your field can add immeasurably to your talents as a teacher and can also add to your students' appreciation of education in their own lives.

- Many schools assign a teacher/mentor to novice teachers to help them through their first year of teaching. It would be important for you to discover an experienced teacher in your school— one who is excited, enthusiastic, passionate, eager, energized, motivated, dynamic (well, I could go on and on….). Schedule regular weekly meetings with your mentor. You might wish to discuss some of the following:

  o How to obtain teaching supplies

  o How to help students with special needs

  o How to evaluate students fairly

  o How to interpret the curriculum in a specific area

  o How to work with parents

  o How to locate equipment

  o How to use various computer programs

  o How to motivate certain students

  o How to differentiate instruction

A Word of Advice

"While you will learn a lot from all of your colleagues, it's nice to be able to find one or two 'go to' teachers. This person can be your support both professionally and personally. Invite him/her into your classroom for some feedback and consider spending at least some of your own planning periods in his/her classroom to observe."

—Amy Glusco, former classroom teacher

- Many teachers invite their students to give them feedback on how well their lessons are designed or how comfortable they are in the current classroom environment. Here are some possibilities:

  ○ Install a suggestion box in the classroom

  ○ Invite students to answer 3–4 reflection questions at the end of a lesson

- Use Survey Monkey (https://www.surveymonkey.com) to solicit student comments about classroom procedures.

- Distribute exit slips at the end of each week for student input.

- Invite students to contribute adjectives (about a selected lesson) to a word cloud generator (www.wordclouds.com; www.wordle.net; https://tagul.com).

- Engage in periodic reflection sessions with yourself. Effective teachers make these sessions a part of their growth and development as professional educators. They offer valid opportunities to examine your strengths and weaknesses. In so doing, you will begin to see patterns of behavior and instructional trends that might need improvement. But, to be effective, these sessions must be systematic and purposeful. In addition, they should be a regular part of your weekly activities (say, on Saturday mornings, for example). Here are some possibilities:

  ○ Write your thoughts and perceptions in a personal journal.

- Videotape yourself and do a self-analysis of the lesson.
- Create on online journal.
- Use social media to communicate and reflect with other teachers.

QUOTABLE QUOTE

"Education is a progressive discovery of our own ignorance."

—Will Durant

What a Great Idea!

Here's a quick and easy reflection tool you can use on a daily basis. You may wish to use this on each of the first 10 days of your first year and then, periodically after that. I've been using something similar to this for many years and I continue to discover areas for reflection and improvement. You will, too!

Date: _____

My Daily Reflection

3 — What are <u>three</u> successes I experienced today?

2 — What are <u>two</u> things I need to work on?

1 — What is <u>one</u> question I have about today?

Bonus: Where can I discover the answer to that question?

Here's something to keep in mind: good teaching is an evolutionary process; it's always a work in progress. It's one of the things I enjoy so much about this profession; that is, there is always something new to learn, experience, or investigate. I always find that exciting, how about you?

A Word of Advice

"Here's what I would tell my 'First Year Self': 1) Don't stress over things you cannot control, 2) value the opinions of those who value yours, 3) admit when you've made a mistake, 4) be reflective on what you do, and 5) never stop learning and trying new things"

—Ashley Miller, current elementary teacher

Part II

◆

Inviting Students to Learn

Chapter 4

<u>Establishing an Invitational Classroom</u>

Here are two classroom scenarios. As a college student, which one would you find to be most welcoming?

A.

You walk into the classroom the first day of the new semester. The professor is seated behind the desk. He doesn't say anything as you search for a seat (most likely in the back of the room, since the guy doesn't look too friendly). There is a stillness in the air as other students enter the room and find their seats. Most of the people don't know each other so conversation is stilted and somewhat uncomfortable. At the appointed start of class the professor (still seated) says something like, "Welcome to Introduction to Geography. This will be a tough course with lots of outside assignments and papers to write. I fully expect that all of you, as college students, will get your assignments in on time and that all your work will be exemplary. Attendance will be taken at every class and I expect all of you, without fail, to be here on time. Now, let's go over the syllabus for the course."

For the next 30 minutes of this first class the professor reads much of the syllabus to the class highlighting significant portions, assignments, procedures, and expectations. Finally, he asks, "Any questions?" No one responds. The class is excused and everyone quickly exits the room.

B.

You walk into the classroom on the first day of the new semester. As you take a seat, the professor comes up to you, shakes your hand, and introduces himself, "Hi, I'm Dr. Jones and I'd like to welcome you to Differential Calculus. What's your name?" You share your name and he asks, "Where are you from, Connie [which is your name]." You tell him your hometown and then he says, "That's a great place. My wife and I drove through there a few years ago and we really enjoyed the scenery. I look forward to learning more about you throughout the semester. Again, welcome to our class."

He repeats the same dialogue with each new student who enters the room—introducing himself, shaking hands, learning a name, asking something personal about the student, and engaging in an active dialogue. Throughout all these short conversations, there is a genuine smile on his face and a sincere attitude. After about ten minutes of walking around the room and engaging in conversations with every student, he walks to the front of the room and re-introduces himself to the class and share some facts about himself: where he grew up, the college he went to, why he decided to become a college instructor and a little about his teaching philosophy. He then says to the class, "Let's talk a little about Differential Calculus and why it is important in your life."

The emphasis here is clearly on developing a relationship with individual students as well as with the entire class. The tone is relaxed, respectful, engaging, and personal. Finally, as students begin to leave the room he passes out individual copies of the syllabus and says something like, "Let's get together again on Thursday and we'll talk about the syllabus."

I would imagine that for most readers of this book, the second classroom environment would be the preferred. It was evident that each of those two scenarios was different because each professor displayed a completely different philosophy:

Professor A: *"This is __my__ class and my subject. I am in charge! I am the boss! You are the students and are here to learn and I am the professor and am here to teach. End of story!"*

Professor B: *"This is __our__ class. I would like to invite you to join me as we work together to learn some things about _____. Our goal will be to establish a community of learners here—a community beneficial to everyone."*

QUOTABLE QUOTE

"I have come to a frightening conclusion.

I am the decisive element in the classroom.

It is my personal approach that creates the climate.

It is my daily mood that makes the weather.

As a teacher I possess tremendous power to make a child's life miserable or joyous.

I can be a tool of torture or an instrument of inspiration.

I can humiliate or humor, hurt or heal.

In all situations it is my response that decides whether a crisis will be escalated or de-escalated, and a child humanized or dehumanized."

—Haim Ginott

Here's a fact of life that will ensure your success in your first year of teaching: concern yourself less with the curriculum of your classroom and more with its learning environment. New teachers, such as yourself, often make the mistake of believing that their initial success will come primarily from well-crafted lesson plans, dynamic educational activities, engaging lectures and lots of technology. But if you take a look at the previous sentence you will note that it over-relies on curricular factors.

It short, there is a common belief that a teacher's control of the material will produce successful learners.

Welllllll…not quite!

True, you do need a solid background in the material you will be teaching, but a strong hold on the curriculum alone will not produce high achieving students any more so than an intimate knowledge of long distance racing tactics will result in an Olympic gold medal in the 3,000 meter steeplechase. The conditions that surround your knowledge and how your knowledge is put into practice will ultimately determine the success you may achieve in either a classroom or on a 400-meter track.

My own experiences, in concert with the experiences of tens of thousands of other classroom teachers, have proven that five essential components are necessary for a classroom to work. These five elements comprise what many educators refer to as "The Invitational Classroom." Make these part and parcel of every lesson you teach, every day you teach, and every student you teach and you will see some incredible and quite unbelievable results—very positive results in not only your students' academic achievement, but in the general atmosphere of the classroom itself. You, too, will be able to craft your own invitational classroom.

1. <u>Respect</u>

It has often been said that respect can never be demanded, it must always be earned. That is to say, we can't ask our students to respect us simply because we're the teacher, the oldest person, or the only adult in the room. By the same token, we can't establish a culture of respect in the classroom unless we model that respect in everything we do and everything we say. Take a look at the following two pieces of dialogue and determine which one is based on respect and which one is a "power play" on the part of the teacher:

> **Teacher #1:** *"How many times have I told you not to get up out of your desk without raising your hand? Do I need to tell you a thousand times or do you just don't want to listen? Well, what is it, Justin?"*

Teacher #2: *"Miranda, your question really got me thinking. I'm not sure of the answer, but I'm wondering if you'd like to work with me to see if we can find an answer together."*

The dictionary defines *respect* as "an act of giving particular attention or consideration; to consider worthy of high regard." In educational terms, here is what I have discovered about *respect* both personally as well as in my conversations with many outstanding teachers throughout the country. Please consider these as significant elements in your own classroom.

A classroom that values respect is one where...

a. Each and every student feels accepted.
b. Students receive encouragement and recognition for their efforts.
c. Students' cognitive and emotional needs are met.
d. The sharing of ideas by all is promoted and practiced.
e. Students are taught at their appropriate instructional levels.
f. Everyone is courteous, mannerly, and well-behaved.
g. Humor is a constant and laughter is ever-present.
h. Teacher and students talk with each other, not at each other.
i. There are procedures for behavior (and consequences for misbehavior).

Listening

Interestingly, your personal philosophy about the role of listening in the classroom will have a significant impact on the maintenance of an invitational classroom. Let's see if I can make this point through the use of some interesting facts:

- In most traditional classrooms, approximately 80 percent of the instructional time is taken up by "teacher talk' (time when the teacher is doing all the talking). Stated another way, most lessons are based on the teacher lecturing, giving instructions or directions, reminding, disciplining, or telling.

- According to at least one significant body of research, teachers expect students to listen 60 percent of the day solely to the teacher.

- Observations of beginning teachers reveal that they have a tendency to talk more than necessary. This is due in large measure to a sense of nervousness, unfamiliarity with the curriculum, and a desire to "get through the curriculum" in a timely manner.

The invitational classroom is one in which students recognize and know that they have an audience for their thoughts, views, and observations. One of the most important "audiences" they can have is you, the teacher. Make sure you engage students in daily and active dialogues in which they have your undivided attention as an active listener. Demonstrate and use appropriate eye contact, body language, and affirming comments to show you are hearing (and reacting to) what they say. In turn, you will be demonstrating respect.

One of the comments most often heard in faculty rooms goes like this, "Those kids just don't know how to listen. They just don't listen!" Many teachers (and I certainly did) make the assumption that students, at a certain age or grade, know how to listen. We often have this false idea that students come into our classrooms knowing how to listen. The fact of the matter is that very few students are skilled listeners. The reason for that is often two-fold: either they haven't been taught or they seldom have good models of listening.

Engendering respect in your classroom can be accomplished when you consistently model what good listeners do in social conversations. Here are some suggestions:

1. Move out from behind your desk. Never have a discussion or ask a question from behind a desk or behind a lectern. The desk and the lectern are both physical and psychological barriers to good communication.

2. Move in and among your students. You'll learn about how to establish a classroom design in order to facilitate this process in Chapter 8. A close physical presence is how we communicate best. Teach, share, and discuss in the midst of students, rather than just in front of students.

3. Whenever I have a conversation with a single student, I move over to that student and stand approximately three to four feet in front of the student. I direct my attention to that student and that

student only. I let the student know that I am focused directly on her or him.

4. Maintain close eye contact. Look directly into the eyes of whomever you are talking with. Let that person know that she or he is the center of your attention.

5. Display body language that is positive. Stuffing your hands in your pockets, folding your arms across your chest, not directly facing a student, and displaying a disinterested or bored expression on your face are all signs that you are not actively engaged in the conversation.

6. Smile. Frequently.

7. Don't interrupt a student when she or he is speaking. Interruptions are one of the most obvious signs of disrespect. You certainly know the feeling when someone continually interrupts you when you are talking at a social engagement. Your students certainly deserve the same level of attention.

8. I've always found it beneficial to pause slightly before responding to a student. That pause (or "wait time") signals a student that you are carefully contemplating their verbiage, rather than spouting off the first thing that enters your head. When you say that "first thing" you're essentially saying that you weren't listening and were more intent in getting your thoughts out than in considering the thoughts of the student.

9. As you'll learn in Chapter 15, one of the most powerful techniques you can use in any conversation (with any human being) is to paraphrase or use the student's words in your response. For example:

Teacher: "So, Bianca, what do you think was Shelley's essential theme in 'Frankenstein'?"

Bianca: "Well, the original subtitle of the book is 'The Modern Prometheus' suggesting that the author, in reference to Greek mythology, was describing Dr. Frankenstein as a devil—as someone evil, and someone unleashing a new evil on the world."

Teacher: "So, what you're saying is that the author believes that humans, when given the opportunity, would rather advocate evil rather than good?"

Bianca: "Yeah. But I also think there's another intension with that title."

Teacher: "I'd be interested in hearing about this other intension."

In this brief example, you'll note how the teacher gave clear and convincing signals that she was actively listening to the student. Not only does a mutual respect begin to build, but the opportunities for an active and extended dialogue are enhanced as well.

Take a look at the following statements and see if you notice a commonality:

- "Hmmm, I never looked at it in that way."
- "I really like your analysis. How did you think of that?"
- "Your answer shows a lot of thought and a lot of insight!"
- "WOW! What a neat way of looking at this!"

A quick analysis will reveal that these comments (to students) affirm their contributions to the class and place a value on their participation. When students know that there is a high likelihood that they will be the recipient of a positive response from you, then they will be more likely to want to assume an active role in the conversations that are an essential element of any lesson. Agreeing with your students as often as possible is an excellent way of building a strong community.

QUOTABLE QUOTE

"Educating the mind without educating the heart is no education at all."

—Aristotle

A Word of Advice

"Let your children see the real you. Let them into your life. Share your childhood memories and recent memories. The bigger connection you have with your class, the more you will grow together."

—Amanda Cuff, current elementary teacher

Reciprocity

Here's a question many novice teachers ask, "How should I deal with the 'bad' kids in my class on the first day of school?" My short answer is always, "Just like the 'good' kids." That is to say that if you believe that respect is an essential element in your classroom, then it behooves you to demonstrate that respect to each AND EVERY student in the room—"good students" as well as "bad students."

Psychologists tell us that, as humans, we have a natural and normal tendency to want to do something nice for someone who does something nice to us. If, for example, you give me a compliment I will want to return the compliment at some later stage in our relationship. On the other hand, if I say something nice about you in class, then you will probably be inclined to share something nice about me in some future conversation. This is what is known as the Law of Reciprocity. Not only is it the basis for good classroom management, it is also a fundamental foundation for engendering respect throughout the classroom.

Think about this: Every time you shout at a student, berate a student, admonish a student, reprimand a student, glare at a student, or simply stand with your hands on your hips (behaviors we tend to exhibit with our "bad students") you are fracturing a relationship—you are sowing the seeds of disrespect. The key to good classroom management is to treat everyone equally, everyone the same. I know it's a difficult concept given some of the "bad kids" who may inhabit your classroom, but it's a necessary one. If you sit a bad student near your desk on the first day of class or rebuke a bad student and let a good student "slide" on an issue or classroom rule you have essentially said, "I don't respect you."

I know it's tough and I know it's challenging, but extending the same positive behaviors and reactions to ALL students in your room will pay enormous benefits. Don't single out the bad ones—in doing so you are starting off on the wrong foot. You have psychologically segregated your students into two groups. And when you have two distinct groups you will always have conflicts and confrontations. Treat everyone positively and equally—from Day One—and you will be helping to establish an arena of respect that can pay scholastic dividends later in the year. You will be building an invitational classroom.

Responsibility

In several of my teacher resource books I've written about the issue of "irresponsible learners" or "irresponsible students." I don't mean these as negative terms or derogatory labels, but rather as a state of affairs in which there is often an imbalance in the classroom. That is to say, students often feel disenfranchised in many classrooms. The teacher makes all the decisions, is the sole determiner of the curriculum, and is in charge of maintaining order and motoring student behavior.

It's important to note that, on average, a typical classroom teacher will make more than 1,500 educational decisions every day. What happens is that students often fall into a pattern of "learned helplessness" —that is, they come to believe that what happens to them in a classroom is governed by someone else. They are powerless and compliant; someone else is in total control and no matter what they do, that "control" will always be in force. They don't have to take any responsibility for their work or their behavior, because that responsibility has been assumed by the adult figure in the classroom. That adult figure will make the decisions, all students have to do is blindly follow them. They're not involved, not engaged, and not responsible. They are irresponsible learners.

Helping students, of any age, assume a measure of responsibility in a classroom—any classroom—ensures a productive partnership: one in which everyone is working *together* towards common goals. As an example, here's something I've been doing for many years now with a considerable degree of success. This particular classroom activity has worked extremely well with students from grade three all the way through my undergraduate classes. It puts a premium on the concept of shared responsibility—that is, for an effective teaching/learning paradigm to be established in any classroom, both teacher and students needs to be cognizant of their shared responsibility. The creation of an atmosphere in which everyone acknowledges and accepts their individual and group obligation to work in concert towards shared goals is an essential ingredient in any invitational classroom.

On the first day of class I pose the following statement, "Please raise your hand if you would like to earn an 'A' in this class."[2] Not surprisingly, and no matter if the class is a group of rambunctious third graders, "been there, done that" tenth graders, or college freshmen from a diversity of majors, the response is always the same: everyone raises their hand. Then, I ask the following, "What are some of your responsibilities that will ensure you earn that 'A'?" I invite students to think about that question while I divide the class into about 5–6 random groups. I ask each group to appoint a recorder and to generate an individual list of student responsibilities.

After about 5–6 minutes I bring the class together and I invite each of the groups to share their lists which I record on the white board. We eliminate any duplicate entries and discuss all the remaining items. Eventually we arrive at a list everyone can agree to. The following is a list recently generated on the first day of the semester by a class of college freshmen:

What I need to do to earn an "A" in this class:

- Stay awake
- Do all assigned readings
- Show up
- Do work diligently
- Use good study habits
- Respect my peers
- Turn assignments in on time
- Read the textbook
- Work hard

2 The use of the word "earn" is quite intentional. Instead of saying, "Who would like to get an 'A'" (an implication that grades are determined solely by the instructor), I would rather let students know, early on, that grades are something to be worked on by all parties concerned. Earning a grade (as opposed to getting a grade) is something that denotes a shared responsibility.

- Study for exams
- Ask lots of questions
- Participate in class
- Be open-minded

After that list has been agreed to, I invite the small groups to reassemble and to generate a list of items in response to the following question, "What are **my** responsibilities as your teacher that will help you earn an 'A' in this class?" At first, most students are taken off-guard with this query simply because it is not something typically asked in any classroom. But, I want to make my intension very clear to them. I want them to know—from Day One—that learning is a joint responsibility between teacher and student. Just because I'm the designated instructional leader for the class doesn't mean I abdicate my responsibilities. I want them to know that I'm a co-partner in this journey we're about to take—I have to carry my fair share of the load.

After some hesitation (and lots of dazed looks) the groups begin generating some tasks and responsibilities for me. Again, these are then written on the whiteboard, sorted, discussed, and a final list is agreed to by everyone in the room. Following is a list of teacher/instructor responsibilities prepared by a recent class of college freshmen:

<u>What the instructor needs to do to help me earn an "A" in this class:</u>

- Show up for class
- Grade fairly
- Offer extra help when asked
- Avoid "Death by PowerPoint" [3]
- Clearly define what we need to do for each assignment
- Respect the fact that we have other classes
- Listen and engage students with respect
- Challenge and encourage us
- Provide different methods of teaching
- Be clear and concise with directions
- Be a good communicator
- Provide feedback; offer constructive criticism
- Don't "phone it in"
- Be flexible

3 This is my favorite!

- Be enthusiastic (and in a good mood)
- Understand we all learn differently
- Be open-minded

Before the next class, I type up both lists and duplicate them. I distribute the first list to everyone in the room and invite them to use it on a regular basis to self-assess their progress in the course. In other words, are they adhering to their self-selected set of responsibilities—responsibilities that will help them achieve a high grade in the course? From time to time I invite students to share their self-assessments with me (in one-on-one conferences) so we can share strategies and tips that might help them deal with persistent issues.

But, I also do something that surprises many students. Once or twice during a course I invite students to take the second list (The Instructor's Responsibilities) and to informally assess me. How am I doing? Am I living up to my responsibilities? Am I working in concert with individuals and the class to ensure high academic achievement? Am I upholding my end of the bargain? As you might imagine, when I announce this to any class there is a puzzled response from many students ("You mean, we're going to give you a grade instead of the other way around?"). But, my intent is serious. I want them to know that I have some responsibilities to adhere to, just like they do.

And, you know what, every time I teach a course, my students always point out a flaw or two (or three) that needs some attention—something I should be doing, but have forgotten or neglected. I will acknowledge my shortcomings—letting them know I haven't satisfied my stated responsibilities—as well as what I plan to do to rectify the situation.

And, I do it!

Something amazing happens when I go through this activity—something I can actually see on the faces of my students that first week—**we start to connect**. We start to connect as a class with a common purpose and we start to connect as a class trying to build a community of learners. It's a magical transformation and it underscores a basic philosophy of good teaching and good learning—we're all in this <u>together</u>.

What a Great Idea!

This strategy can be easily modified for younger students. Instead of preparing the two lists as checklists, work with students to create two separate series of statements, each statement followed by 3-5 cartoon faces that denote emotions from sad to happy.

Here's a brief example:

Student List

1. I do my homework every night. ☺ 😐 ☹

2. I ask questions in class. ☺ 😐 ☹

3. I help other students. ☺ 😐 ☹

Teacher List

1. The teacher listens to me. ☺ 😐 ☹

2. The teacher smiles at me. ☺ 😐 ☹

3. The teacher talks with me. ☺ 😐 ☹

More Ideas to Engender Responsibility

In the chart below you'll find several additional procedures you can easily integrate into your classroom to help develop a sense of shared responsibility in the room. This list is not meant to be an exhaustive one, but rather as a starting point for becoming a more invitational classroom.

Process	Value
Give infrequent praise. Ask students to evaluate their own work.	Students often become overly dependent on teacher recognition. They need to recognize the worth of their own efforts.

Process	Value
Describes features.	Describes your features + also provides the benefits of those features.
Point out the positive results of students' actions ("Your contribution was important in helping your group complete the task.")	Students recognize that their contributions are valued and necessary for the smooth functioning of the class.
Let students decide on various ways to approach an assignment or task.	Responsibility is ensured when students are given valid opportunities to make decisions and follow through on those decisions.
Let student know that you need their contributions and that you will be counting on them to decide on several courses of action with a lesson or unit.	A partnership between students and teacher and between students and students is fostered when "shared decision-making" is a regular feature of the program.
Don't just assign tasks and have students complete them. Work alongside students, encouraging, prodding, and stimulating them when necessary.	You've heard it before: Good teachers should not be "the sage on the stage; but rather the guide on the side!"
Let students teach you.	Don't assume that you are the repository of all knowledge in the classroom. Students need to know that they have something of value to be shared.
Solicit lots of student ideas.	When students know their ideas and/or experiences will become part of any forthcoming lessons they will be more motivated to learn

Process	Value
Encourage students to verbalize what they are doing and why.	Teach your students metacognitive strategies (thinking about their thinking) and ask them to share what is going on in their heads. Make sure you model these behaviors (in your own head) for students, too.
Allow students some degree of choice in selecting activities and projects.	The more choice students have, the more involved they will be. For example: "Should we do Activity A or Activity B to help us understand the role of women in the nineteenth century?"

QUOTABLE QUOTE

"Responsibility, motivation, and respect are not the same as obedience, compliance, and fear."

—Alfi Kohn

Relevance

There is a question in the mind of each and every student, regardless of what grade or subject they may be in. It's in the mind of every kindergarten student, every fifth grader, every ninth grade science student, every eleventh grade Trigonometry student, and each and every college student. It's a question that was in your mind for every college course you ever took. Sometimes the question was answered; but, more often than not, it wasn't. But, it still persists and it will be firmly lodged in the minds of every one of your students, too. It is so universal and so persuasive that it often dominates the mental reactions students have toward any new learning endeavor.

The question: Why do I have to know this stuff?

A Word of Advice

"Make it real! Students who personally connect to information or can see where the real-world application lies are the ones who achieve the greatest learning."

—Becky Glatfelter, current elementary teacher

For millennia, students (at every level of education) have been asking that question. And, you know what: One of our chief responsibilities as teachers is to make a connection between the world of the classroom and the real world outside that classroom. To do anything less is to give students a partial education - something less than complete.

Let's say you were the track coach at the local high school and were working with a group of prospective sprinters. You take them into a classroom and show them a couple of videos of Usain Bolt at the 2008, 2012, and 2016 Olympics, ask them to memorize the various components of starting blocks, and have them read a handout on the rules governing false starts. You give them periodic quizzes and several papers to write about the principles of good sprinting. Finally, one day, in complete exasperation, one of your athletes asks, "Hey, coach, when are we going to actually sprint on the track?"

Sounds silly, doesn't it? But, guess what, it happens every day in classrooms all across the country. Teachers spend a lot of time teaching the facts and figures of a subject to students, but not enough time on how those facts and figures can be used in "real life." There's little or no connection between what goes on in the classroom and what goes on in the outside world. If we teach students "stuff" they need to have opportunities to use that "stuff" to explore, examine, interact with, manipulate, and react to their environment. It must be relevant. It's that relevance that makes learning stick; it's that relevance that glues together what we do in a classroom and what we can do outside that classroom. Good teaching has nothing to do with students getting high scores on annual achievement exams, but it has everything to do with how they will be better able to exist in, and contribute to, the larger world. A test can't determine that.

QUOTABLE QUOTE

"Relevant learning is the ability of the student to acknowledge and align oneself with a purpose that's meaningful, one that will enhance their survival or success."

—Steve Revington

Truth be told, I'm a crusader for relevance! And, there's a considerable body of research to support the notion that when students can see the connection between a lesson in the classroom and an element in their everyday lives (present or future) they will be more motivated to actively engage in the learning of that material. In short, good teaching is all about making good connections.

So, here's the key: focus on the "Why" of a lesson, rather than just the "What." In designing meaningful and purposeful lessons you will be helping yourself as well as your students when you concentrate on the "why" of what you are presenting. Why do they need to know about the Protestant Reformation? Why do they need to know their multiplication table? Why do they need to know about the Darwin's Theory of Evolution? Why do they need to know the chemical symbol for salt (NaCl)? By focusing your attention on the "why" of a lesson you will be helping students relate that lesson to their own personal lives. If the only reason you're teaching a particular lesson is because it says so in the school's curriculum guide, then you are cheating both yourself as well as your students. You're doing it, not because it's something you believe in (or something you want your students to believe in), but because someone who has never met you or your students says that you have to teach it. Bottom line: If you don't believe in something, then you cannot teach it effectively. In fact, one of the pieces of advice I always give beginning teachers is to begin the design of any new lesson with the answer to one or both of the following questions: 1) why am I teaching this? And 2) why do students need to know this? If you can't come up with a satisfactory answer to either question, then there is a very good chance that your lesson will not be as powerful or as successful as you might have hoped. This, as you might imagine, will directly affect the establishment and maintenance of an invitational classroom.

A Word of Advice

"Students want, and need, to know the value of the various skills they are learning, and activities they are doing; thus explanation related to their real life is necessary before instruction begins."

—George Severns, former secondary teacher

Community

Human beings have basic needs. Things like water, air, and food are some survival needs. But we also need a feeling of belongingness—a knowledge that we are part of a group and are recognized by that group. Psychologists tell us that children are no different. Take a look at the following chart, which outlines some of the needs of students at various levels.

Grades/Ages	Needs
Elementary (5-11)	Warmth, support, assurance, participation, acceptance
Middle School (11-14)	Group membership, peer acceptance, admiration
High School (14-18)	Acceptance, respect, peer group confirmation

As you review the chart above, you'll note that at all ages and at all levels, students want and need to be respected members of a group ("Acceptance"). Effective group membership is essential to establishing positive learning environments where collaboration, meaningful student interaction, class cohesion, and individual motivation are valued. Creating a sense of "community" and placing students at the center of all decision-making (yes, even for Kindergarten students) are necessary for effective group process to evolve. This creates an invitational classroom—one where students are at the vortex of all that goes on in that room.

A Word of Advice

"Community building is essential to a successful classroom. A true community of learners is built upon strong peer relationships, cooperative learning, and group decision making."

—Anonymous

But social acceptance and cohesiveness does not come about overnight. It is a continual and ongoing process. And, for many students, it is a struggle. For example, many students might not feel welcome in a group simply because they don't know or are not familiar with their classmates. Another barrier to establishing a functional community in a classroom would be students who come from many different neighborhoods. In many cases, students may not have been taught how to behave courteously or even how to resolve conflicts peaceably. Most often, however, students frequently perceive that they have little in common with other members of the class simply because they don't know them. It seems reasonable, then, that one of your primary tasks - particularly at the beginning of a new school year - is to help students become familiar with each other. That task, in lieu of formal instruction, may be one of the most significant tasks you can do on the first days of school.

In order to establish (and maintain) a community of learners in your classroom, please consider the four principles below:

1. **A community of learners celebrates student events and accomplishments**. Many teachers advocate having students discuss their personal lives at the start of each day. In this format, students readily share events, personal likes and dislikes, or difficulties they may have faced. Community begins to actively happen as students empathize with others or celebrate their accomplishments.

2. **A community of learners provides success for all**. A community-centered classroom considers individual strengths, weaknesses, and student learning styles. In these classrooms a great deal of time is devoted to team learning and peer tutoring.

Teachers have discovered that the level of learning is higher when students of similar learning styles assist one another. Community building is a natural result of students being responsible to each other.

3. **A community of learners celebrates humor.** A sense of humor walks hand-in-hand with community. Students often are not sure how to react to a humorous response when a more business-like interaction is what they have experienced in previous classrooms. Students are soon able to understand that they can have fun and laugh while they learn. They are also able to experience a sense of personal appreciation for their own well-being when a teacher values humor as a daily occurrence.

4. **A community of learners has a fair, purposeful classroom structure.** Students respond to a classroom structure that is fair and understanding. Classroom management plays a major role in how students perceive their classroom structure. Unfortunately, teachers often rely on discipline as the central component of the learning process. As we will learn in Chapter 9, procedures are much more effective than discipline in fostering a fair and understanding classroom.

Teacher Roles in Creating Community

In the chart below you will notice several comments and reactions you can share with students, feedback that will help establish a coordinated community of learners in your classroom. I would urge you to practice these and make them a natural and normal part of your everyday conversations with students. In so doing, you will be establishing yourself as an appropriate model of behavior and response. Over time, students will begin to emulate these statements in their daily interactions with others in the room.

Praiser	"Thanks for sharing that with us." "That was a helpful suggestion." "A great idea!"
Questioner	"What do you think about this one...?" "Let's discuss that idea..." "Does anyone have an idea?"
Organizer	"What material do we need?" "What would be some appropriate web sites?" "I'll get that." "I'll make sure we're ready."
Summarizer	"You said...." "What I heard you say is...." "I heard you say something different than...." "Your idea goes along with _____ 's."
Participation Expert	"We'd like to hear from...." "Let's have a show of hands." "_____ , what do you think?" "Take a minute to think about what you want to say."
Observer	"This is what I saw...." "One of the things I noticed was...." "So, what you are saying is...." "Let me get this right. You are saying that...."
Manager	"What is the problem we are facing?" "How can we solve this?" "What do you think would be a better way to...?" "What is stopping us from making progress here?"

What a Great Idea!

A friend of mine who teaches fifth grade in a school district just outside Philadelphia does something every year that I simply love. At the end of each year he invites each student to write a letter to the person who will be occupying her or his desk the following year. The letters contain information about some of the subjects the student will study, some behavioral rules and regulations, field trips to be taken and guest speakers who may visit, typical homework assignments, and even some of the bad jokes and funny things they can expect from the teacher. Each of these letters is placed on a desk and the student who occupies that desk in the forthcoming year is "greeted" by the previous occupant of the desk on the first day of school. Cool!

As a first year teacher, you might want to consider the following modifications of this idea:

- Use your class list and write a short letter (from you) to the new "occupant" of a desk. Personalize each letter with a student's name (include a few extras for any last-minute arrivals).

- Write a letter for each student as though it was being sent by the desk itself ("Hi, I'm your new desk for this year and, boy, do I have a lot of stuff to tell you. You and I are going to do some great things together.")

- As each student arrives on the first day, make sure there is a thank you card on her or his desk ("Thank you for being in our class this year. I look forward to your participation. We have many exciting things to learn and I welcome you to our classroom community.").

- Type and print out an e-mail message for each student welcoming them to the class. Invite students to type their own e-mails on the classroom computer welcoming fellow classmates to the new year.

Here are some additional ideas to help you establish a community of learners in your classroom:

1. Don't assume students know how to work in groups. Some instruction and modeling may be necessary so that students understand their roles and the responsibilities of all group members.

2. Make sure most of your lessons incorporate group work. Provide multiple opportunities for students to get together and work on a common project. I have discovered over the years that group work has had the most positive benefit on student achievement than almost any other strategy.

3. Have fun with your students. Learning doesn't always have to be serious to be effective. Inject a sense of frivolity, playfulness, merriment, laughing and joking into your lessons and you will discover the "universal cement" that bonds a group together. I'm not saying you have to be a comedian or tell lots of jokes, but be aware of those moments and situations when some levity and good humor can loosen things up.

4. Try to eliminate the following statements from your conversations with students. These comments will do more to "disinvite" students from becoming members of an accepting and welcoming classroom than anything else:

    *   "Because I said so."
    *   "You're not smart enough for that, yet."
    *   "You can't do that."
    *   "It's simple; it won't work."
    *   "You've got to be kidding me (sarcastically)!"
    *   "I really don't care what you do."
    *   "OK, go ahead. But don't say I didn't warn you."

5. Hold periodic classroom meetings. Many primary teachers use something called "Morning Meetings" —a regularly scheduled event every morning in which the members of the class come together in a central location to talk about the lessons for the day, what's happening in their families, "Show and Tell," events or celebrations they've attended, weekend happenings, or

current events. It's also a time used for slightly more academic matters such as a counting drill, spelling word of the day, a phonetic review, a song to sing, a weather report, or simply a read-aloud session. These meetings are essential to building the invitational classroom that engages students in a cooperative spirit of group harmony.

6. Use inclusive pronouns whenever you can. Use "we" instead of "me." Use "you" (plural) instead of "you" (singular). Use "us" instead of "I." The simple injection of inclusive pronouns into your daily conversations with the class can create some very positive feelings of "group-ness" that can go a long way in bringing everyone together.

What a Great Idea!

I'm a fan of self-deprecating humor, simply put, laughing at myself. I might reference the ever-growing bald spot on my head, the few extra pounds around my middle (OK, the more than a few extra pounds around my middle), my tendency to mispronounce names (most recently, "Yup, I did it again. I know your name isn't Turtle, it's Tuttle. My sincere apologies. I'm apparently having another 'Bad Hair Day.'"), or my increasing episodes of absent-mindedness ("Oh, look, today I'm wearing one blue sock and one brown sock. Well, not to worry - at least I know I have another pair just like them at home.").

Letting students know that I'm human and subject to making mistakes or slight embarrassments invites them into my world. It also lets them know that we all have idiosyncrasies, foibles, and quirks that sometimes influence what we do and say. Let's accept it and (as appropriate) laugh about it.

Positive Expectations

In conversations with thousands of teachers across the country-both novice and experienced teachers intent on creating invitational classrooms that value group dynamics and personal interactions, I have found that there is one consistent theme that surfaces time and time again in all those conversations. That is, invitational classroom are built upon a strong foundation of positive expectations. That is to say, if we sincerely believe all our students can and will achieve to the best of their abilities AND that we are committed to making that a reality, then the invitational classroom becomes not a wish, but a reality.

Consider the following statements:

- "I believe that every student in my classroom can achieve."
- "I believe that success is possible for each child in this room."
- "I believe that when we work together we can succeed together."
- "I believe that part of my job is to help each student realize her or his potential."
- "I believe that I am a good teacher and that I will be able to use my training and skills to help each student become a good student."
- "I believe we are going to have a great year together."

I think you can easily see a theme here—a belief in success will form the foundation upon which actual success will happen. Notice that none of the statements above say anything like, "Some of these kids will succeed, and for others there's just no hope." Nope. All of those statements are inclusive; all of those statements are embedded with the conviction that academic progress is possible for everyone. And when there is the possibility of success for all, then there is also the possibility for an invitational classroom—one that embraces a common purpose and a common goal.

By definition, a positive expectation is an optimistic belief that whatever you teach, whatever you do, and whatever you say will result in academic success or personal achievement. This positive attitude is reflected in the activities you share with students, the lessons you design, and the procedures and expectations you set for your classroom. It is, in so many ways, what separates the "average" classroom from the exceptional classroom. So too, is it what separates the "typical" classroom from the invitational classroom.

QUOTABLE QUOTE

"Teacher expectations and student achievement research has been known for more than 50 years. It states that teacher expectations play a significant role in determining how well and how much students learn."

—Jerry Bamburg

Here are a few tips:

- Let every student know—from Day One—that she or he will succeed.

- Exude confidence to each and every student that growth and achievement are possible.

- Don't be afraid to say to every student, "I believe in you."

- Believe in the phrase (from *The Three Musketeers*), "All for one and one for all!"

- Create a classroom climate in which students support each other with frequent offers of help.

- As my mother used to say, "You attract more flies with honey than you do with vinegar." Allow me to modify her words in terms of your classroom: "You'll help more students succeed with positive expectations than you will with negativity, criticism, and complaints."

The invitational classroom is one built on positive expectations. It is a classroom structured on the principles of inclusion, support, encouragement, reciprocity, and mutual cooperation. Believing in your new students will help ensure a learning environment that "invites" success in everything you do.

Chapter 5

The First Day; The First Week

Do you remember your first kiss? Do you recall the anticipation, the fear, the anxiety, the trepidation? Do you remember all the various thoughts that were bouncing around in your head? What if he doesn't like me? What if she doesn't do it right? What if I miss? That was certainly a scary time, right?

Well, your first day of teaching can be a lot like your first kiss. You might have seen expert teachers create magic in a classroom and read all the latest books and resource materials. And still you're scared! Guess what—you're not alone. Of all the questions new teachers ask, "What do I do on the first day of school?" is probably the most common. Each year, more than 150,000 beginning teachers ask that same question.

And, here's why your first day is so critical: What you do on that first day and on that first week will ultimately determine the success or failure you experience for the remainder of the school year. That may seem harsh at first blush, but it is a truism that has stood the test of time with hundreds of thousands of teachers in hundreds of thousands of classrooms.

That first day is an open opportunity for you to offer students a safe, predictable, and nurturing environment that is well-managed and dedicated to their academic success. Unfortunately, many new teachers make a fatal mistake that first day or week—they do a series of fun activities, or "light" lessons, or gaming situations. "Start them off easy and then later we'll get into the real meat of the curriculum," seems to be a prevailing philosophy. What frequently happens is these same teachers spend the remainder of the year patching up "holes" in their program, and in the end, losing valuable instructional time. But, it doesn't have to be that way. Let's take a look.

The First Steps

In conversations with hundreds of teachers across the country, I always got one consistent piece of advice—new teachers need to concentrate on a systematic, well-planned, and organized opening to the school year. This fact alone will be instrumental in ensuring an effective opening to this new learning experience (for both you and your students).

Those conversations with experienced teachers also indicated that a sequential set of procedures was essential to first day success. What follows are six principles to follow in designing a most successful first day. Plan your activities around these basic concepts and you can ensure a year that gets off to a most positive beginning:

    A. Plan Ahead—Advance Work

    1. Making a Connection

    2. Sharing Yourself

    3. Building a Community

    4. Classroom Routines

    5. Teach a Lesson

A. Plan Ahead - Advance Work

The first day of school is an exciting one for everybody—teachers and students alike. True, it's also a day filled with some stress, some uncertainty, and some apprehension. It's no wonder new teachers lose a little sleep in advance of that all-important first day. That's normal. But, just as a CEO prepares in advance of a major speech to her company or a long-distance runner plans his strategy in advance of an Olympic marathon, so too will you be engaged in some planning activities in preparation of that critical event in your professional life.

Undoubtedly, you will be making several visits to your school and to your future classroom over the summer months. While you will be spending time getting your room in order you should also devote some time towards getting some basic information about the typical expectations for all teachers. Much of this information may be handed to you in the form of a new teacher packet, some may be on the district web site, and some may need to be obtained from colleagues or the school's administrative assistant:

- The Common Core, State Standards, and District Curriculum
- School Calendar (holidays, test periods, professional development days, faculty meetings, athletic events, special events)
- Daily Schedule (school delays/closings, opening and closing hours, bell schedule, specials)
- Attendance Procedures (reporting attendance, reporting absences, forms and paperwork)
- Student Cumulative Records (location, security)
- Special education forms (location, completion, security, communication with parents)
- Free and reduced lunch lists
- Student Safety Issues (fire drills, lockdowns, suspension/ expulsion, student injuries, student medication, substance abuse, safety patrols, playground supervision)
- Grading and Reporting Student Achievement (progress reports, report cards, parent conferences, grade books, students with IEPs, promotion/retention, graduation requirements)
- "Specials" (specific forms and procedures for the library, gym, music room)
- Health forms (vaccinations, procedures for visiting school nurse, injury reports)
- Technology (computer use, internet access rules, social media policies, tech lab, use of personal technology)
- Permission slips (field trips, excuse from P.E.)
- Support Staff (volunteers, instructional assistants, paraprofessionals, classroom mothers, aides)
- Miscellaneous (dress code, field trips, assemblies, fund raising, school visitors, exchange students)

One of the essential documents you will receive during the summer is your class list(s). A week or so before that all-important first day it would be important to put together a preliminary seating chart (subject to certain modifications later in the year). It is always advisable to have students assigned to a desk as they enter the room, rather than to have them arbitrarily select a seat on their own. This quickly establishes a business-like atmosphere during those first few moments of that first day.

One very effective way of assigning seats is to write each student's name on an index card and have that card placed on the top of a specific desk. As students enter the room, ask for their name, greet them warmly, check your seating chart, and direct them to their desk. Another option would be to randomly assign numbers to each of the desks throughout the classroom. Each student is given a corresponding number in your grade book according to their alphabetical listing. As a student enters, you check her or his number, and point them to the appropriate desk. It's important that each student have a pre-assigned desk before they enter the room - but keep the assignment of desks random. This will reduce the possibility of last year's cliques re-forming again this year. The randomization ensures that students have the opportunity of forming new friendships with their new classmates.

What a Great Idea!

As a new teacher you may be inclined to check the records and/or talk with last year's teachers to discover who the "bad kids" are and who the "good kids" are. You may want to use that information as a way of determining a classroom seating chart. That is, by placing the "bad kids" near the teacher's desk. The thinking is that that proximity will allow you to have many heart-to-heart talks with the "troublemakers" in an attempt to nip bad behavior early before it has a chance to fester. By having the "bad kids" close by it will be easier for you to keep an eye on them throughout the period or class day.

<u>Please don't do that!</u>

If you do, you will be sending a very powerful and irrevocable message to those students: "I know you are a bad person, other teachers know you are a bad person, and, this year, I'm going to treat you like the bad person you are from the very first day of school." That message is loud and clear—a message that is now permanently attached to their personality and to everything they might possibly do in the classroom for the rest of the year. And, what do you think will happen as a result? Yup, they will behave exactly as you expected them to. In other words, their behavior will prove that you were right about their "badness" and your need to have them close by. They are permanently labeled. Their destiny is sealed from Day One. They were a troublemaker last year and they will, most certainly, be a troublemaker this year.

The key is to treat all students equally, Don't come into your first year with lots of preconceptions about how students will behave this year based on how they might have behaved last year. Give them a break! Give them an opportunity to "turn over a new leaf," give them the same opportunities to shine as you would any other student in your class—that is, give them the same level of support, encouragement, and opportunity as is deserving of any other student. No lectures, no "pep talks," no "I'm keeping my eye on you" speeches. Treat them the same as everyone else, not differently from everyone else. Give them a seat in the group, not a seat away from the group! Help them belong to your "invitational classroom."

Calming Your Fears

Will you be nervous your first day? Yes! Will you be a little stressed your first day? Yes! Will you be jittery your first day? Yes, yes, yes to all of the above. I certainly was and so were millions of other teachers. It's a natural and normal process of the first time you do something. You were probably nervous the first time you got behind the wheel of a car or went out on your first date. Know that it is inevitable, but also know that there are a few things you can do to ease your nervousness and make this all-important day run smoothly.

1. In the days before school begins be sure to thoroughly plan— no, over-plan—for that first day. It is far better to have way too much material or overextended lesson plans than it is to run short and have to scramble for something to do. Follow the outline in this chapter and be sure you have more than is necessary. It would also be a good idea to check—and check again—to be sure there are sufficient supplies to complete all that you have planned.

2. The night before your first day pack your briefcase or book bag with all of the tools and supplies you'll need. Don't try this on the morning of your first day, you'll undoubtedly leave something behind (for me, it was the classroom seating chart.) Take your time and be methodical. Having a prepared checklist is always helpful.

3. Get up a little earlier than normal (your nervousness may wake you up earlier anyway). Take your time getting dressed. In fact, you may want to put on an extra nice outfit in celebration of this momentous event.

4. Have a heathy and hearty breakfast. Take your time. Don't wolf down a granola bar and think that your nutritional needs have been met for the day. You're going to need a little extra energy today.

5. Pack a wholesome lunch. The food served in the cafeteria on the first day may be "iffy" —you want something that is both satisfying and healthy.

6. Leave for school a little earlier than you might normally do. Arriving at school an hour before classes start will give you some extra time to make sure all "your ducks are in a row" before students enter the room. Oh, and please don't exceed the speed limit—a ticket on your first day will definitely not put you in a good frame of mind (Not that I would know anything about that!).

A Word of Advice

"Be sure to have restful night in order to rise early in the morning to clear your mind and prepare your day. Rushing and running out your front door sets you and your children up for a disruptive day."

—Morgan Lanzalotti, current elementary teacher

7. One of the things you want to do before the students arrive is to review your class list and seating chart two or three more times. Practice the pronunciation of names. Know where each student will be seated and begin to associate each student with a specific desk.

8. If time allows, take a few moments to chat with a colleague. A brief conversation reminds you that you are both in this together and that there is a support system already in place to assist you with any "bumps" or "hiccups" along the way.

And, now, it's time to "rock and roll!"

1. Making a Connection

Students come to any new class or classroom with lots of anticipation (and perhaps some apprehension) about their teacher. They are most interested in who you are as a person (Are you nice, friendly, or kind... or are you mean, commanding, or dull?). You can get your year off to a great start with your initial contact with students.

QUOTABLE QUOTE

"A smile is the shortest distance between two people."

—Victor Borge

a. Put on your best smile and smile, smile, smile.

b. Meet and greet every student at the door. This sets the tone for the day and establishes a positive atmosphere. Sitting behind your desk or standing behind a podium to welcome your students sends a negative message. Getting out of that "comfort zone" and meeting your students at the classroom door as they arrive demonstrates an extra effort on your part. It does make a difference.

c. In elementary schools, parents will often come along with their child to make sure they get to the proper classroom (and to make sure that their child has a really nice teacher). Take a few moments to welcome and greet each parent.

d. I prefer to shake the hand of every student, ask them their name, and personally welcome them to the class. This is just something we do in any other social encounter. Not only is it good manners, but it shows a willingness to make a personal connection with each individual.

e. If you know ahead of time that you'll have second-language learners (those whose native language is something other than English) in your classroom, try to learn a greeting or welcome in her or his native language. A simple *"Buenos dias, Carlos."* or *"Wie geht es dir, Angela?"* can mean a lot to a new student.

f. Have a welcoming note or letter on each student's desk. This sends another positive message in the first few moments of a student's arrival. It also gives them something to read and reflect on as they are getting settled in to their new environment. You may wish to invite students to discuss the note with a fellow classmate.

2. Sharing Yourself

Be sure your students see you as a human being first, rather than an authority figure in the classroom. Take time early during the first day to introduce yourself. Tell students something about yourself, particularly about your life outside the classroom. This can include some or all of the following:

- How to spell your last name
- Where you grew up
- Some of the things you did or places you visited as a child
- Where you went to college

- Why you wanted to be a teacher
- Your hobbies and interests
- Your favorite subject when you were in school
- Your family
- Places you've traveled
- Books you've read
- Why you are looking forward to working with them.

It's important for students to know that you have experiences and interests not unlike those of other adults. In fact, I've often found it helpful to share a funny incident from my past, an embarrassing moment I had in school, or some self-deprecating humor. These humanizing touches cue students that their teacher does human things and is not always perfect.

What a Great Idea!

Before the start of the school year put together a PowerPoint presentation about yourself. Present students with photos of your life from your early years to the present. I've always gotten a very positive reaction from students when I've showed them some of my baby pictures as well as photos of me when I was their age (there's one of me standing in a crib, with a low-hanging diaper that always produces gales of laughter). Often, children are delighted to learn that their teacher was once a child just like they are.

A very effective tool, even before school begins, is to send your students a brief newsletter to introduce yourself. As soon as you get your class list, compose a communique (*Miss Smith's Chronicle,* for example), blog, e-mail blast, YouTube video or web page that provides some inside information about who you are: hobbies, books you read during the summer, how excited you are to meet everyone, your family life, etc. This will help students and their parents get to know you even before they set foot in your classroom.

3. Building a Community

Besides knowing who you are as a person, students also need to know that the place in which they will spend much of their time (the classroom) will be safe, inviting, and comfortable. As we discussed in the previous chapter, establishing an invitational classroom is critical to the academic success you want students to enjoy this year.

A Word of Advice

"When it comes to the first day of school, teachers are often just as nervous as the students. Tackle those anxious feelings by dedicating your first days to getting to know those students for who they are. A survey is a great way to get to know your students' learning styles, personalities, and interests. By collecting this information, you can prepare yourself to connect to the students on a personal level.

—Darian Kiger, current secondary teacher

What follows is a selection of "icebreakers" you may wish to use on the first day—an opportunity for students to get to know each other and an opportunity for you to begin building that invitational classroom. Feel free to modify these according to the grade or age levels of the students with whom you work. I'm certainly not suggesting that you use all of these on the first day. Rather, select one and share it with the class. Save the others for successive days (one a day for each of the next six days, for example). Give students a chance to get to know each other, but also tell them there's something even more important coming up.

1. Have a scavenger hunt. Have students search for others in the class who have special experiences or features and have them sign off on a special card. For example, have students search for the following:

    • Someone who has lived in another state
    • Someone who has a red-headed relative
    • Someone who has a skateboard
    • Someone who has a three-syllable name

- Someone who has a birthday in February
- Someone who speaks another language

2. Invite students to assemble into various groups. Invite each group to discuss and agree on one favorite for each of the following: a musical group, a vacation spot, a favorite movie, a favorite movie/TV star, the best fast-food place in town, etc.

3. Schedule a class meeting or roundtable early in the day. This can be a circle of chairs or everyone sitting cross-legged on the floor—you, too! Take time to talk about some of your expectations as well as some of the exciting projects you've planned. Invite students to share some of their fears or anxieties, too.

4. Pair students and invite them to work together to complete information forms on each other. Prepare those forms ahead of time so that the emphasis in on the face-to-face communication, rather than the generation of items for discussion (e.g. favorite singer, best movie, coolest celebrity, favorite dessert, best summer activity, number of siblings, "If I had a million dollars, I would….")

5. Invite students to create a "First Day Time Capsule." What artifacts (from the first day of school) should be placed in a sealed time capsule (e.g. opening day photo, teacher name tag, sharpened pencils, first class assignment, etc.). Actually assemble a "time capsule" and "bury" it in the principal's office to be opened on the last day of school.

6. Use Discovery Education (www.puzzlemaker.com) to create a puzzle from your students' names.

7. Invite students to organize themselves into various groups according to some of their "likes." For example: favorite sports team, favorite singer, favorite song, favorite movie, favorite Nintendo game, favorite web site.

8. Check out Ice Breakers Web (www.icebreakers.us). Here you'll discover lots of icebreaker ideas, most of which are geared for adults. With a little imagination and creativity you can make these appropriate for students as well.

9. Design a classroom blog. Invite students, either individually or in small groups, to contribute regular posts to the blog. Check out www.kidblog.org.

10. Place students in random groups of three. Invite each of the groups to discover ten things they have in common.

11. I like to have younger students do a name poem on the first day. Provide each student with a sheet of colored construction paper. Ask students (or assist them) to write their name vertically down the left side of the paper using large letters. Then invite them to write a self-descriptive adjective or phrase for each letter in their name. Here's an example:

    - J - Jumps rope
    - U - Understands Spanish
    - L - Loves cats
    - I - Irish
    - E - Energetic

These name poems can then be posted throughout the classroom. Take time during the first 2–3 weeks to refer to the name poems regularly.

12. Engage students in a get-acquainted game such as a Human Scavenger Hunt. Make up a set of index cards, one for each student, and then ask the students to find someone in the class who:

    - Has been in an airplane.
    - Has a baby sister.
    - Has a summer birthday.
    - Is wearing something blue.
    - Has visited a foreign country.
    - Is in an after-school sport.

13. For older students, post a philosophical statement on the wall and use it to initiate some discussion with students on the first day. Select one that has personal meaning for you (you might want to use different statements with different classes or different periods). Here are a few I've used:

    - "You can't earn if you don't learn."
    - "Imagination is more important than knowledge." —Albert Einstein

- "There is nothing more dangerous than a closed mind."
- "Education is a process, never a product."
- "Education is never about achieving perfection, but rather about meeting challenges."

Be sure to provide students with first-day activities and assignments you're confident they'll complete successfully. It's vital for students achieve a measure of success on the first day, whether that success is being able to hang their coat on the proper hook in the kindergarten classroom or discover the solution to a brain puzzler in the advanced algebra class.

QUOTABLE QUOTE

"I realized if you can change a classroom, you can change a community, and if you change enough communities you can change the world."

—Erin Gruwell

4. Classroom Routines

This section may well be the most important section in the entire book. It will determine, in large measure, how successful you will be as a classroom manager. It will also have considerable influence on the behavior of your students in the beginning as well as throughout the year. What you are about to read will have a profound influence on whether your classroom runs smoothly or whether you spend the next nine months admonishing students for all sorts of misbehavior.

This will make a difference!

One of the first things you must address from "Day One" are the routines of the classroom. Indeed, an enormous body of educational research suggests that when classroom routines are firmly established, clearly explained, systematically taught, and consistently reinforced **FROM THE FIRST DAY** the class runs more smoothly and behavior problems are minimized.

Take a moment and ask yourself the following questions:
- How will students enter the classroom?
- What will be the first thing they must do after entering?
- How will they move to their desks?
- How will they get ready for the day/lesson?
- How will students respond in class? (raising hands, a signal or sign)
- How will tardiness and absences be handled?
- How will students interact with each other?
- How will papers be turned in?
- How will students exit the classroom (at the end of the day or end of a period)?

A Word of Advice

"The first days of school should be about routines. Teach explicit behaviors/routines rather than content; this will save you in the long run."

—Amy Glusco, former elementary teacher

As you can quickly see, there are a lot of things that must be addressed in order to ensure a fully functional and equally efficient classroom. In short, you need routines—established and expected practices that are a fundamental part of everyday life in the classroom.

Here are some typical classroom routines to consider in advance of your first day:

Start of the Day	During the Day
Attendance Handing in homework Entering classroom Greeting teacher	Attention signals Maintaining a quiet work environment Transitions between activities Working in groups Lining up/walking in line Arriving and departing from specialists Handing out materials Going to lunch, recess Emergency drills (fire, earthquake, tornado) Using the bathroom Sharpening pencils Feeling sick or getting hurt What to do when finished early Using classroom supplies Turning in assignments Students' personal desk space Turning in papers (name, date, etc.)
Out of the Classroom	**End of the Day**
Recess/indoor recess Assembly behavior To and from the school office	Getting ready Cleaning/straightening up Dismissal (bus, walkers, carpools) Gathering materials, lining up

QUOTABLE QUOTE

"Student achievement at the end of the year is directly related to the degree to which the teacher establishes good control of the classroom procedures in the very first week of the school year."

—Harry K. Wong

Equally important is the need to share with students a daily schedule of activities. Post this schedule in the front of the room, and use it to let students know a daily plan of action (for elementary students) or a sequence of procedures for an instructional period (for secondary students). This schedule offers students an expectation for each day. There's comfort in knowing how a lesson or day will be conducted. Students, just like adults, are creatures of habit, and enjoy having the security of a planned sequence of expectations.

Suggested Routines

ELEMENTARY	SECONDARY
Enter classroom	Enter classroom
Greeting from teacher	Greeting from teacher
Hang up coats	Go to seats
Go to seats	Quick motivational activity
Independent activity	Take attendance
Class welcome	Review lesson format
Salute flag; pledge	Go over lesson objectives
Take attendance	Begin the lesson
Sing a song	Incorporate group work
Discuss calendar, weather	Independent work
Lunch count	Collect assignments
Collect homework	Dismissal procedures
Discuss daily schedule	
Begin first lesson	

Students should have some expectations of how their day or a certain period will be framed. These predictable routines assure a well-managed and well-disciplined classroom.

The KEY to Success

There's one thing you must do on that very first day that will determine any success you envision for your class the remainder of the year. This is so critical and so essential that if it is not accomplished then you will be setting yourself up for all sorts of behavioral issues later in the year. But, the sad reality is that tens of thousands of new teachers will fail to enact this one action—and tens of thousands of new teachers will be constantly scrambling to maintain order in their classroom. Tens of thousands of new teachers will be tearing their hair out, beating their heads against the wall, and enduring all sorts of physical or mental agonies. They will be frustrated, angry, and upset. And their classrooms will slowly—ever so slowly—devolve into behavioral chaos and confusion. Instructional time will be diminished and scholastic achievement will be compromised. They and their students will forever be in "The Land of the Lost."

Please, oh please, don't be one of those teachers!

Here's the key: teach each of your pre-determined classroom procedures ("Wait a minute, Doc, that sounds just a little too easy; just a little too simple!"). But, here's the rub: it works. Allow me to elaborate.

On "Day One" you are going to teach your students a specific procedure you have put in place in your classroom. In fact, you are going to teach that procedure to an excess such that it becomes second nature for all your students. You are going to teach and practice, teach and practice, in such a way that your students will perform this procedure in a specified manner each and every time they are in the room. No excuses. No exceptions. No deviations.

For example, let's say you have a specified procedure about how you want students to enter the classroom. For illustrative purposes, I'm going to select an established procedure as illustrated in one of the PowerPoint programs at the end of this section

- Enter the classroom quietly
- Greet the teacher and your classmates
- Take your green homework folder out
- Hang your book bag on the wall
- Place your green folder on your desk
- Sit down

Here's **exactly** what you'll do:

1. Borrow a student's book bag and pretend to be one of the students in the class. Go outside the classroom and go through the procedure exactly as it has been written and exactly as you want students to perform it: a) enter the classroom quietly, b) greet the teacher (a student sitting at your desk), c) greet other

students in the class, d) take a green homework folder out of the book bag, e) hang the book bag on the wall, f) place the green folder on a desk, and g) sit down.

2. Go through the procedure again. Describe each of the actions you are performing and reference each of those actions on a chart or poster you have prepared ahead of time.

3. Do the procedure a third time. As you perform each of the separate actions, invite students to tell you exactly what you are doing.

4. Now, ask a single student to go through all the actions of the designated procedure. If something is left out, ask the student to start from the beginning and go through the entire procedure from beginning to end. Be sure to compliment the student for performing the procedure correctly.

5. Invite another student to go through each step in the procedure from start to finish. Ask the class to describe each step as it is performed. Try to make these simulations as authentic as possible by using materials or props normally available in the classroom.

6. Ask another student to perform the procedure step by step and exactly as it has been demonstrated. No variations and no deviations are allowed. There is only one way to do a specified procedure.

7. When you feel confident that students are "comfortable" in knowing all the specific steps of a designated procedure, then it's time to get the entire class involved. In this case, you'll want to send everyone out into the hall and ask each and every student to enter the room in exactly the same way as they have been taught and in exactly the same way as you and their classmates have demonstrated. If someone makes a mistake or leaves something out she or he goes back to the starting position and goes through the entire procedure again. Your ultimate goal is to have everyone in the class do it in exactly the same way every single time.

8. Congratulate them. Let them know that they did something to perfection. They did it right, they did it perfectly! Let them know that there is only one way to come into the room and they did it that one way. They're the best!

Guess what? You have just initiated the first step…the critical first step in a positive and effective classroom management plan. You've taught your students a procedure that leaves no room for interpretation, it allows for no compromise or variation - it is a standard of behavior for every single individual in that classroom. No exceptions, no modifications, and no alterations. Everybody—EVERYBODY—knows what to do and how to behave when they enter the classroom.

When your students come into the classroom the following day they should each be following the procedure as it was taught (and practiced) the previous day. If someone, even if it is just one student, violates the expected behaviors, then a new practice session is in order. Start with Step 1 above. The objective, as you might gather, is for each of your established procedures to be fully ingrained in the mindset of every student. Anything less and you open yourself up to any number of behavioral issues throughout the remainder of the school year.

Now, once students have executed a procedure perfectly, it's time to teach a second established procedure (NOTE: Don't attempt to teach more than one procedure a day. But, do attempt to teach all your established procedures during the first 2–3 weeks of school.).

Remember those tens of thousands of OTHER new teachers I talked about at the beginning of this section? For those teachers, classroom management is a most haphazard event. Most often students are told what to do (a set of rules posted on the wall of the classroom serves as a daily reminder), but <u>they are never given systematic practice in how to carry out those directives</u>. It would be like me making up a list of all the things you should do in order to become an accomplished long-distance runner, but never giving you the time to practice all those training routines. In other words, it would be similar to "talking the talk, but never walking the walk." And, yet, it's the way classroom teachers start off their year time and time again.

If, as so many new teachers tell me, classroom management is a major concern and major issue in their classroom, then it stands to reason that our approach to classroom management should be precise, exact, and definitive. There needs to be precise expectations of behavior, students must be taught the accompanying procedures, they must have multiple opportunities to practice those procedures, and, most important, they must be consistently held to those expectations—not every once in a while, not every other Tuesday, not just when they feel like it—but EVERY SINGLE TIME! In so doing you focus on one of the most significant words in good classroom management: <u>consistency</u>. It's "consistency" that will ultimately decide your instructional effectiveness.

Dear readers, you now have the ultimate key to success on your first day—the ultimate key to your success all year long. Please use it to unlock all kinds of incredible potential for your students.

<u>Possible Classroom Procedures</u>

Following are two examples of classroom procedures (elementary and secondary) for your consideration. These are offered as PowerPoint presentations to be shared with students on the first day of classes. They also serve as templates for the kinds of procedures you may wish to establish in your classroom along with a presentation vehicle that can be used year after year. You are certainly welcome to adjust or modify these examples in terms of the unique characteristics of your classroom or teaching situation. Also, consider some of the suggestions earlier in this section as you begin to develop the specific procedures for your classroom.

<u>Elementary Procedures (a suggested PowerPoint presentation)</u>

Welcome to our Class
PROCEDURES

- Enter the classroom quietly
- Greet the teacher and your classmates
- Take your green homework folder out
- Hang your book bag on the wall
- Place your green folder on your desk
- Sit down

- Raise your hand when you need help
- When I need your attention I will ring my bell. Stop what you are doing and make eye contact with me.
- Keep voices low at all times.
- There is no talking in the hallways

- Show respect to all individuals
- Always use good manners
- Show courtesy at all times
- Share
- Help other students when asked

- Speak in complete sentences
- Always put items back after you use them
- Keep your hands and feet to yourself
- Respect the property of others
- We are a team - always be willing to do your fair share

- Pencils are to be sharpened at the end of the day
- Always have three (3) pencils ready in your pencil box
- Keep your pencil box inside your desk

- At the end of the day clean up around your desk
- Obtain your book bag/backpack
- Place all necessary materials in your book bag/backpack
- Place your chair upside down on your desk
- Wait until the teacher asks you to line up

REMEMBER:

We are a team!

We are a community!

We support each other!

WE ARE GOING TO HAVE A FANTASTIC YEAR!!

Thank You!

Muchas Gracias!

cảm ơn bạn

Secondary Procedures (a suggested PowerPoint presentation)

WELCOME to Miss Alwine's class

PROCEDURES

- A procedure is the way things are done in a classroom
- When things are done correctly - learning happens
- To be a successful student please follow these procedures

Start of Day

- Enter the classroom quietly
- Go to your assigned seat
- Place all necessary materials on your desk
- Get ready for work

After the Bell

- Start working on the assignment posted on the whiteboard
- Do the work in your red journal
- When finished, wait for further instructions

During Class

- Always listen to the teacher
- No talking when teacher is speaking
- Raise your hand if you want to say something
- Ask questions

While Working

- Make sure you understand all directions
- If you don't, ask for help
- Treat everyone with respect
- Use your time wisely
- Always do your best

Your History Journal

- Use a pen or pencil to write your notes
- Always date and sign your daily entries
- Keep your journal organized
- Your journal will be collected from time to time
- Maintain your journal at all times

When the teacher raises her hand
- Stop what you are doing
- Face the teacher and wait quietly
- No talking or whispering
- Pay close attention

When your work is done
- Check over all work to ensure it was done correctly
- If the assignment is to be turned in, place it in a brown folder
- Someone will collect all the brown folders
- Start your reading assignment

Dismissal
- Clean up your work area
- Wait for the teacher (not the bell) to dismiss you
- Push in your chair
- Depart quietly

If You are Tardy...
- Stand by the teacher's desk
- Present her with your Tardy Pass
- Go to your seat
- Get the current assignment from a fellow student
- Begin work

If You were Absent...
- Get the assignments from your classmates
- Do the necessary work at home
- Check with the teacher for a revised "due date"
- If a test is missed, arrange with the teacher for a make-up date
- If you have an unexcused absence you will not be allowed to make up any assigned work

Expectations
- Bring all necessary materials to class
- Always demonstrate respect to everyone in the room
- No food items will be allowed
- Cell phones are "OFF" and stored away

Consequences
- Warning
- Conference with student
- Detention point
- Parent contact
- Referral to Administration

Here's to an INCREDIBLE Year!

5. Teach a Lesson

Using the guidelines in Chapter 13, put together a mind-bending, eye-opening, and incredibly creative lesson that actively engages your students in one of the major concepts or subjects of the coming school year. Consider the following;

- Put together a lesson that will tap into students' background knowledge. What do they know? What are some of their misconceptions about a topic? How extensive is their prior knowledge?

- Make the lesson a fast-paced one - one that will mentally engage them in some very positive learning experiences. This should not, necessarily, be a "fun" lesson, but rather a lesson that is full of energy and passion. Let them see you at your best as a classroom teacher. Give them an inside look into joy and enthusiasm you have about teaching (and that you hope they will have about learning).

- Make sure the lesson addresses the variety of learning styles evident in every classroom. In other words, make sure there is something for everyone.

- So, too, will it be important to ensure that every student in the class is able to demonstrate some level of success within this lesson. The important thing is to have a lesson that guarantees academic recognition for every student.

- NO: "Read the first chapter in the textbook and then answer all the odd-numbered questions at the end." YES: "Listen to this story and then we're going to construct a model of the giant's castle." Make sure the lesson is "hands-on, minds-on" —that is, there should be some information delivered to students as well as the opportunity to do something with that information. In most cases, when students can produce some tangible product on the first day, they achieve a sense of self-satisfaction and accomplishment.

- Provide a very short, but motivational, homework assignment. Here are some possibilities:

  o History: Interview your parents or grandparents about a recent historical event.

  o Science: Locate a discovery or invention that was not around 20 years ago.

  o English: Write your own epitaph.

  o Math: Find three mathematical equations used in popular media (billboards, magazine advertisements, TV commercials, etc.).

  o PE: Discover what the world record for the hammer throw is or what is the hammer throw? For men? For women?

  o Art: Find a Salvador Dali painting and tell what it means to you.

There's your first day. It's complete, it's thorough, and it addresses the major elements that precede a most successful school year. Follow this plan and, you too, will enjoy a fantastic and dynamic beginning—a beginning full of incredible possibilities!

What a Great Idea!

Invite each student to write an "Exit Slip" at the end of the first day indicating:

- One new person they met
- Two new things they learned
- Three things they are looking forward to this year

The First Day; The First Week

Using our six-stage model (**A** + #**1-5**) above here's what your first day of teaching might look like (for the purpose of these charts, and others in the book, I am arbitrarily placing those of you who are middle school teachers in the "Secondary" category).

Day 1

ELEMENTARY	SECONDARY
Assumption: Students remain with a single teacher for the entire day.	Assumption: Students attend a class period of approximately 60 minutes in length.
A. Plan Ahead - Advance Work 1. Making a Connection 2. Sharing Yourself 3. Building a Community 4. Classroom Routines 5. Teach a Lesson 6. Lunch 7. Specials 8. Teach Lesson #2 9. Paperwork Chores[5] 10. Homework Assignment 11. Dismissal	A. Plan Ahead - Advance Work 1. Making a Connection 2. Sharing Yourself 3. Building a Community 4. Classroom Routines 5. Teach a Lesson 6. Paperwork Chores 7. Homework Assignment 8. Dismissal

Days 2 - 10

ELEMENTARY	SECONDARY

Assumption: Students remain with a single teacher for the entire day.	Assumption: Students attend a class period of approximately 60 minutes in length.[6]
1. Making a Connection 2. Building a Community 3. Classroom Routines 4. Teach a Lesson #1 5. Teach a Lesson #2 6. Lunch 7. Specials 8. Teach Lesson #3 9. Paperwork Chores 10. Homework Assignment 11. Dismissal	1. Making a Connection 2. Building a Community 3. Classroom Routines 4. Teach a Lesson 5. Paperwork Chores 6. Homework Assignment 7. Dismissal

The first day—the first week—is a critical time for the success of your classroom and the success of your first year teaching. Attend to the steps outlined above and you can be assured of a most memorable year for all the right reasons!

---

5 These might include any or all of the following: permission slips, health or medical information, optional insurance forms, family information sheets, letter from principal, or anything that requires a parent or guardian signature.

6. There's a lot of variation here. I've seen high school class periods as short as 38 minutes and as long as 95 minutes (and everything in between). Please adjust the time frames for the suggested activities in keeping with the schedule of your specific school.

Chapter 6

<u>The Community of School</u>

Your job as a classroom teacher is not to simply be an instructional leader for your students. You will also be asked to contribute to the greater good of the school community in which you live and work. The degree to which you are willing to do that will often determine the success you enjoy in your classroom. In this chapter, we take a look at the people you need to know to make that happen.

<u>You Are Not Alone!</u>

As a teacher, it is quite easy to walk into a school, enter your classroom, close the door, and not see any person over the age of twenty-one for the entire day—or even an entire week! The very nature of teaching often isolates us from the rest of our peer group, associates, co-workers, and colleagues. Contact with large intelligent beings may be minimal or nonexistent.

Teaching can be a very isolating profession. Most of your time will be spent alone in the classroom with students. It's important to know that your success as a classroom teacher is often determined not just by how well you are teaching a group of youngsters, but also by how well you are connecting with the larger community.

Although you may enjoy the many opportunities you have to interact with students, it is important to interact with adults, too. Unstructured and informal situations with colleagues are particularly important. Sometimes we are so busy trying to foster a sense of community in our classrooms that we forget to maintain our membership in the community outside the classroom. But teachers need to share ideas, debate, laugh, and commiserate with other staff members. Our commitment to this interaction is necessary to both our professional and personal growth.

To be a well-rounded first-year teacher, allow yourself time to interact informally with adults in your school community. Start a book club, converse over a cup of morning coffee, or meet for dinner once in a while.

Get together with colleagues to see a movie, volunteer at a local charity, or just talk about things other than school. Participate in the community choir, a theater group, a bowling league, a service organization, or a fund-raising walk. You'll be better for it!

A Word of Advice

"A lot of new teachers fall into the trap of working in isolation. Don't be afraid of bothering your co-workers. They've been there, done that, and want to help as much as they can. Reach out for help, ask them questions, and collaborate with others in your content area whenever possible. It's a great opportunity to help distribute the workload and share ideas.

—Darian Kiger, current secondary teacher

It is equally important to take time to recognize that the community we call "school" would not exist or survive without the work and dedication of many individuals. Shouldn't we celebrate the work of all the members of our community? I think so.

Make Friends with School Staff (Two in Particular)

What if I told you I have a piece of inside information that will virtually guarantee your success as a classroom teacher. Would you be interested? Of course, you would! Then here it is: the two best friends you could ever have in a school are the school secretary (administrative assistant) and the custodian(s). These two people, more than anyone else, run a school. It doesn't matter whether you are teaching in a rural, suburban, or inner city school or whether you're teaching elementary school or high school; your friendship with the secretary and custodian(s) will virtually guarantee your success as a teacher!

Why is that? Just think about all the tasks and duties these people provide. How would the school be able to function, how would it exist from day to day, without the work and efforts of these individuals? The number of times the school secretary saved my neck or the number of times the custodian got me something I really needed are more than the number of pages in this book. They were my lifesavers when I needed materials ordered, a lightbulb fixed, a report sent in on time, a bucket and mop for a classroom "accident," a call made to an irate parent, or a bunch of tables in my classroom for a special science experiment.

My friendship with the custodian and secretary paid more dividends than I could ever imagine. Notice that I used the word friendship. I depended on these people so I could do my job. I valued their support, I valued their input, but most important, I valued their camaraderie and amity. Establishing, fostering, and maintaining positive relationships with the secretary and custodian(s) is important both professionally and personally. Here are some guidelines:

- Don't assume that less education means less intelligence. One of my custodian friends can tear down and rebuild a computer hard drive faster (and better) than any technician at the local computer store.

- Learn the names of the secretary and custodian early on. Take the time to find out about their families, hobbies, and pastimes. Talk with them about their lives away from the school.

- Always treat the secretary and custodian with respect and courtesy. Greet them every morning with a smile and a pleasant comment.

- Here's a neat idea. Make it a point to stop and converse with the secretary and custodian every day. Move beyond the simple "Hi, how are you?" greetings we often exchange with people as we rush through the day. Take two or three minutes for a brief conversation or a friendly talk ("Say, those Broncos are really looking good this year!"). You may discover something interesting. You may discover a kindred spirit.

- As appropriate, send them a birthday card or note thanking them for their work.

- Talk positively about the secretary and custodian in your conversations with colleagues. Acknowledge and celebrate their contributions to the school community.

Obviously, the friendships you establish with the secretary and custodian are not simply for the purpose of getting something done later on. These people are valuable and critical elements in the overall functioning of the school and of the community in which you work.

A Word of Advice

"Make friends with the administrative assistant! They often get you materials you need or put in a good word with the powers that be. Saying 'Hello' and asking about their day/family can go a long way."

—Nicole Hesson, former middle school teacher

The Principal Is Principle!

By definition, the school principal is the school's instructional leader. This individual makes almost every decision that affects the welfare and functioning of the school as a whole as well as of individuals within the school. The nature of your relationship with your building principal will have a major impact on your classroom performance as well as your mental state.

Here's one tip that will almost guarantee a positive relationship with your building principal: always keep her or him informed! The last thing any administrator needs or wants is a surprise. If you are inviting a guest speaker into your classroom, inform your principal. If you are setting up a terrarium with a collection of snakes, inform your principal. If you are assigning a controversial book for your students to read, inform your principal!

Keeping your principal in the loop, information-wise, is always a good idea. If you have a challenging student or are anticipating the storming of the office by an irate parent, be sure to let your principal know early on. A well-informed principal can assist you in working through a problem, particularly if she or he has information early in the process.

If you are planning to send any letters, messages, newsletters, or other types of communication home, it's always a good idea to run those by your principal first. That way, if a parent or community member has an issue or concern with one of those documents or the information in it, your principal will know how to respond in an appropriate manner.

Often, teachers make the mistake of seeing the principal only when problems or crises crop up. However, it's vitally important that you share the positive events and celebrations that take place in your classroom, too. Here are some ideas:

- Invite your principal to be a guest reader in your classroom.

- Talk with your principal and share the academic accomplishments of the class as well as of individual students.

- Invite your principal to observe a particularly exciting lesson, guest speaker presentation, or science experiment.

- When sending out holiday greetings, don't forget your principal, too. As appropriate, send a birthday card or a vacation postcard.

- Send your principal outstanding examples of student work. Attach a brief note acknowledging and celebrating the progress of selected individuals or the entire class.

Invite your principal to be part of classroom celebrations, birthday parties, or other special events. Occasionally send those homemade cupcakes, store-bought cookies, birthday cake slices, and other food items down to the principal's office. They may not get eaten, but they will let the principal know you are thinking about her or him, too. That's good public relations!

One of the mistakes new teachers make is to send students to the office for every infraction or every misbehavior. But keep in mind that whenever you send a student to the office, you are also sending a message - a message that you are not in control. As a result, your principal may get the impression that you cannot control your classroom or the behavior of your students and may form negative impressions about you.

That's not to say that a little office time might not be appropriate for some students. However, it's best to inform your principal early on about any potential challenges or any potential situations. Constant and continual information is very important. Then, if it is necessary to send a student to the office, the principal will be well versed about the situation and can handle it appropriately. Be sure you know the school's policy about sending students to the office. Have a conversation with your principal early in the school year to clarify any policies or expectations.

Principals have a plethora of administrative tasks—all with due dates. She or he has reports to file with the district and the state, attendance forms to compile, financial matters to attend to, and various and sundry other tasks and assignments. Each and all of them must be reported according to a set schedule. You can assist in this process enormously by getting in all your reports and paperwork in a timely fashion. Consider the following timely tips:

- Know when your lessons plans are due, and get them in on time.
- Send daily attendance lists to the office in a timely manner.
- Get any requisitions in on time.
- Order supplies and materials according to the established schedule.

I hope you will discover, as I did, that an open and honest relationship with your building principal can make all the difference in the world. Principals sometimes make decisions that are unpopular or irritating to you. Because they have many people to answer to: parents, teachers, superintendents, school board members, staff, and so on; it's not easy keeping everyone happy. Be sensitive to the pressures everyone heaps on the principal, and show some empathy. You may not get everything you want, but you may get a lot more if you try to look at your principal's position from all angles.

Lean on Me: Paraprofessionals and Paid Aides

If you are fortunate, you may have paraprofessionals or paid aides to assist you in the classroom. These individuals can increase your effectiveness by taking over a wide variety of tasks and assignments that consume valuable teaching time or need extra attention.

Paraprofessional and paid aides are a conduit from the school to the community at large. Whatever takes place in your classroom—your behavior and that of your students, as well as the goings-on of classroom life—will undoubtedly be reported to the general population at large. Use this fact to your advantage. Aides can be advocates for special programs or events. In addition, they can serve as valuable public relations spokespersons in their conversations with neighbors and friends.

Aides and paraprofessionals can assist in a wide variety of endeavors. Instead of assigning them to complete clerical and managerial tasks, take advantage of their involvement and expertise by inviting them to contribute to the following:

- Monitoring computer work
- Tutoring individual students
- Reading to small groups of students
- Demonstrating an experiment
- Conversing or counseling with individual students
- Reviewing math skills
- Monitoring classroom learning centers
- Setting up displays and/or bulletin boards
- Correcting papers and exams
- Working with bilingual students
- Preparing and gathering materials for a lesson
- Helping returning students with makeup work
- Gathering, grading, and returning worksheets
- Assisting with club meetings
- Helping with seatwork
- Assisting special needs students
- Providing enrichment activities

The most effective use of aides and paraprofessionals hinges on several criteria. You must properly and thoroughly train both aides and paraprofessionals. Take several days or weeks to orient these individuals to the practices and procedures of your classroom. Be sure they are aware of their role(s) and responsibilities.

- Take the time necessary to get to know your classroom assistants personally. Interview them about their families, their education, their background, and their lives away from school. The most effective teacher/aide relationship is one based on mutual trust, interests, and concerns.

- Always keep the lines of communication open.

- Provide a special place for an aide in your classroom, such as a desk, a file cabinet or drawer, or his or her own set of teacher manuals or other classroom materials. Remember that an aide is not a visitor to your classroom, but rather a colleague who can help you teach more efficiently and effectively.

- Be sure to regularly recognize and celebrate the contributions of your paraprofessionals and aides. A card, note, or special comment can go a long way to cementing this very important relationship. An aide is not your servant but someone who is also interested in the academic and social welfare of the students in your classroom. Be sure to reward her or his contributions appropriately.

A Word of Advice

"If you are working with paraprofessionals keep them in the loop! They are your eyes and ears when you aren't around."

—Kim Dunlap, current elementary teacher

Your Lifeline: Substitute Teachers

It's inevitable. You'll get sick, need to attend a conference, or have some kind of family obligation. Either you or the school will need to call in a substitute teacher to cover your class. Imagine the fear and trepidation of that person who walks into an unfamiliar classroom to teach an unfamiliar group of students with an unfamiliar lesson plan. It's pretty scary! You can greatly assist any potential substitute teacher with a little preplanning. The preparations you do early in the school year will save you, your students, and especially the substitute teacher any unnecessary aggravation or concerns.

When students know a substitute teacher is in for the day, their potential for mischief increases dramatically. The feeling is that because their regular teacher is away, they can "have a little fun" with the new person. I've always believed that an ounce of prevention is worth a pound of cure, so here are some suggestions:

- Early in the school year, state your expectations for behavior when a substitute teacher is in the room. Post these expectations, include them in student notebooks, and put a copy in a substitute teacher's file.

- Create a YouTube video directed at your students. In it, inform them of proper behavior and remind them of class procedures. Ask any substitute to play this at the beginning of the day so she or he and your students know what is expected.

- If you know you will be absent (attendance at a conference, for example), consider sending a letter home to parents several days in advance. Inform them about expected classroom behavior, and invite them to discuss those expectations with their children.

- Set up a buddy system with a nearby teacher. Whenever either of you is absent, the other will make frequent checks into the partner's classroom. Let students and any substitute teacher know about this arrangement.

- Let your principal or supervisor know about the rules of conduct or expected classroom behavior when a substitute is in. Invite them to visit the classroom when you are absent, and let students know that there might be visitors whenever you're absent.

Most teachers have a special file folder or desk drawer in which they place materials that are useful for a substitute teacher. A substitute teacher will probably be unfamiliar with your class or your routines, so it's vitally important that you share information that is both practical and timely. Include the following items in a folder, a notebook, or a file drawer for the substitute:

- A map of the school building.
- Daily schedule of activities.
- Class list.
- Attendance forms and procedures for filing them.
- Seating chart(s).

- A schedule of "pull-outs." Students will come and go for music lessons, guidance office appointments, remedial reading classes, library time, and other responsibilities. Be sure these are clearly spelled out.

- Procedures for bathroom breaks, hall passes, early dismissals, lunch, and recess

- Emergency procedures for natural disasters, terroristic threats, and unwanted school visitors

- Student handbook.

- Administrative or school duties, including playground duty, bus duty, recess duty, or lunchroom duty. Be sure these are current.

- Classroom rules and procedures.

- Names and location of special teachers.

- Information about special needs students.

- Bus information.

- Location of textbook manuals.

- Location of supplies, materials, and equipment.

- Teacher handbook.

What a Great Idea!

Instead of trying to cram all the information a substitute teacher needs into a single file folder, try using a plastic file crate (available at any office supply store). Put dividers into the crate, and use colored file folders for each of several categories (red: rules and procedures; green: schedules and routines; yellow: lesson plans; blue: school maps and handbooks). A substitute teacher will be able to quickly and easily locate the information she or he needs.

Whether you will know ahead of time you'll be absent or have to be out for an emergency for which you could not plan, you can still provide lessons for any potential substitute. Some teachers write generic lesson plans that are included in any materials left for a substitute teacher. These open-ended lesson plans can cover basic concepts of a subject, an extension of a previously learned concept, or a series of cross-curricular extensions for any topic.

Whenever you write your regular daily or weekly lesson plans, photocopy them. Place the extra copy in an active file folder on your desk (bright orange or bright yellow) before you leave for the day. That way, if you suddenly get ill or need to attend to a family emergency and cannot make it to school the next day, your most current lesson plans will be right on your desk and ready for any incoming or last-minute substitute teacher.

Include with one or more generic lessons some of the following for use by a substitute:

- A collection of puzzles, brain teasers, or creative-thinking activities
- A collection of joke books or poetry
- One or two YouTube videos related to a general topic
- Children's or adolescent literature to be read aloud to students
- Directions for a scavenger hunt, listening activity, or mini-mystery
- A list of suggested art activities or creative hands-on projects

As part of the information you provide for a substitute teacher, invite anybody covering your class to leave you a note detailing the day's activities, the behavior of the students, and any unusual or strange occurrences that may have taken place. Plan some time immediately after your return to review this note and discuss it with your students. Be sure they know that you are intimately aware of everything and anything that took place while you were away.

Here's another tip: if you have had a particularly good substitute teacher in your classroom, let your principal know. You may be able to get that same substitute the next time you are out. Also, consider sending the substitute teacher a card or note thanking her or him for their coverage of your classroom. That's good public relations; and good human relations, too.

A Word of Advice

"Get to know your support staff including aides, secretaries, custodians and food service personnel. By getting to know the personal side of these people, and allowing them to get to know you, you will nurture some very powerful allies in your quest to help students."

—Jane Piepmeier, former elementary teacher

As a teacher, your primary responsibility is to educate students. But beyond that, you are also part of a community—the school community. Remember these tips:

- Many people are necessary to keep a school functioning. Get to know them!

- It's important to communicate and interact with adults as much as with students.

- Work on team-building, with support staff as well as with fellow teachers.

- Celebrate the work of the people behind the scenes - those who often don't get the recognition they deserve.

The community of school is just as important as the community you and your students establish inside the four walls of a classroom. Those two communities embrace each other and support each other, thus ensuring a most positive educational experience for all your students.

Chapter 7

<u>Your Hidden Ally – Parents</u>

In 1944, the nuclear physicist Isidor Isaac Rabi won the Nobel Prize for his work on atomic nuclei. After his acceptance speech, he was asked about some of the major influences in his life. He told the story about how he grew up in Brooklyn. When his friends all came home from school, their parents always asked them, "What did you learn in school today?"

However, when Isidor came home from school each day, his mother always asked him, "Izzy, did you ask a good question today?" He told how that single question from his mother every day helped him develop the inquisitive mind necessary for academic success and his eventual scientific discoveries.

What a Great Idea!

Here's a nifty idea I always share with parents: invite parents to change the typical question they ask their children every day. Instead of asking their children, "What did you learn in school today?" they should inquire, "What questions did you ask in school today?" By making this slight change, parents will be able to have more stimulating conversations with their youngsters instead of a series of painfully brief responses ("Nothing!"; "I dunno!").

It has often been said that parents are a child's first and best teachers. Without question, parents provide children with the basic foundation on which successful learning experiences can be built. The support, encouragement, patience, and understanding of parents have a profound effect on both the academic and social development of children. Indeed, when parents are involved in the academic affairs of their youngsters, students' scholastic achievement mushrooms significantly. This is equally true for elementary students, middle school students, *and* high school students.

A Word of Advice

"Get to know parents early and with a positive start. Take time to call each parent within the first week of starting - introduce yourself and say one nice thing about their child."

—Amy Glusco, former elementary teacher

Developing a successful outreach effort to solicit parent involvement is not always an easy proposition. It demands some planning and an attention to specific factors that can ensure the success of those efforts. Following are some principles for your consideration:

- Regular Daily Time. It is important that parents be provided with activities and designs which will help them take an active role in the learning process on a regular and consistent basis.

- Purpose and Motive. Parents and children must understand the relevance of any home-based activities. That is, how does a particular assignment relate to the day-to-day lives of youngsters? Completing workbook pages has little relevance to children's lives—collecting water samples from a nearby stream or interviewing one's older relatives can!

- Support and Encouragement. Parents should understand that the activities and ideas you suggest to them are backed by a system of support. Parents like to know that should they have any concerns or questions, they are free to contact you to resolve any problems.

- Informality. Parents should realize that learning happens in any number of informal situations as well as formal ones. For example, when parents and children talk about the eating habits of a family pet they are involved in an informal science activity. So too, when parents and children discuss their ethnic heritage they are involved in a valuable learning activity.

- Interaction. Whatever activities or projects you suggest to parents as extensions of your classroom program keep in mind that there should be a maximum of parent-child interaction built into those activities. Parents should always be encouraged to interact with their children in meaningful discussions and conversations.

Success tips for Parent Involvement

Following is a compilation of ideas which can be made part of any classroom activity—strategies which ensure sustained family involvement.

- Outreach efforts need to offer life-like activities that capitalize on the natural and normal relationships between parents and kids. In other words, don't offer suggestions that are a repetition of school-like activities, but rather provide opportunities for families to interact in mutually supportive pursuits.

- Encourage parents to participate continuously throughout the length of an instructional unit.

- Be patient with parents. Some may be reluctant to get involved with your efforts due to any number of extenuating circumstances. Keep trying and never give up on ANY parent.

- Encourage parents to participate in the affairs of the classroom through volunteering, observing, or sharing their hobbies, vocations, or vacations. Keep this process as non-stressful as possible and provide a host of sharing opportunities throughout the year.

- Make a regular effort to communicate with parents through a brief phone call, short note, or e-mail (this is particularly appropriate for those parents who do not participate regularly).

- Parents must know that your outreach efforts are a natural and normal part of classroom instruction.

- Invite students to act as "recruiters" for their own parents. Solicit their ideas as much as possible.

- You must be a good role model for parents—that is, be enthusiastic and committed to the idea of parent engagement.

That desire will rub off on families and stimulate greater participation.

- Communicate to parents the fact that their involvement is ultimately for the benefit of their children.

- Coordinate your outreach efforts with some local community agencies (churches, temples, social service organizations, fraternal groups, etc.).

- When sending any written information to parents be careful that you do not use educational jargon. Keep your tone informal and to the point; don't talk down to parents and don't insult their intelligence.

- It is vitally important that you be friendly, down to earth, and truly interested in parents and their children. A sincere interest to work together will provide the fuel for any type of outreach effort.

A Word of Advice

"You better be in touch with parents, or you are missing a tremendous public relations opportunity. When middle school and high school teachers start a conversation with parents, then positive opinions about teachers in the community escalate."

—Phil Monteith, former secondary teacher

Open House

Open houses, back-to-school night, and meet-the-teacher night are one of the annual rites of passage for every classroom teacher. Whether you are teaching elementary school, middle school or high school, you will undoubtedly be part of this event every year. Open houses occur sometime during the first few weeks of the school year and are an opportunity for parents to get to know you and their child's academic program.

These special events provide parents with an "inside look" into the daily activities and occurrences of your classroom. It's also a wonderful opportunity for you to actively recruit parents as partners in the education of their children. Here are some tips and ideas that can help you make this annual event successful and purposeful:

1. Send out personal invitations beforehand. Instead of asking students to take them home (where they may wind up in the washing machine), consider mailing or e-mailing the invitations. On the invitation, include the following information: name and address of the school, date and time of the event, your room number (and how to find the room), your name, and a brief outline of the evening's schedule.

2. Plan your presentation and what you will be saying to parents beforehand. Be sure you share something about yourself (where you grew up, your education, your family, your educational philosophy) as well as some of your goals for the year. Your presentation should be no longer than ten to eleven minutes tops! If your presentation is longer than eleven minutes, it will definitely fall on deaf ears (take it from me—this is an inviolable rule!). Here are some topics you might want to cover:

Elementary School	**Middle School/High School**
Daily schedule	Classroom behavior
Homework	Homework
Grading	Grading
Classroom rules	Field trips
Remedial help	Report cards
Special programs	Fund-raisers
Reading curriculum	Extracurricular activities

3. Dress professionally—remember, first impressions are often lasting impressions. Men should wear a coat and tie or at least a dress shirt and tie along with pressed slacks. Women should wear a pantsuit, blouse and skirt, or dress. Incidentally, go "light" on the perfume and aftershave.

4. Prepare your room appropriately. Hang a "Welcome" sign outside the door, and be sure your name and the room number are prominently displayed. Have a sign-in sheet for parents as well as a handout listing the activities and presentations for

the evening. Freshen up your bulletin boards, and print a daily schedule on the white board. Set out sample textbooks, and be sure all desks and tables are clean. Be sure each child's desk has a folder with samples of the student's work. Keep in mind that some parents may not have fond memories about *their* school experiences, so here's a great opportunity for you to win them over!

What a Great Idea!

A friend of mine shares this very important piece of advice: When setting up your room for back-to-school night or open house, be sure to have plenty of adult chairs available. During my first year of teaching first grade, I forgot this rule. As a result, I had many very large adults trying to sit in many very small chairs. It was quite embarrassing to watch people trying to stand up at the end of my presentation (fortunately, there are no YouTube videos of that event!).

5. Greet each and every parent at the door with a handshake and a smile. This is a wonderful opportunity for you to put your best foot forward. Be sure every parent has a name tag (remember that the last name of a student and the last name of her or his parents may be different—always, *always* check beforehand). Provide a tray of refreshments (ask for contributions, particularly if different cultures are represented in your classroom) and appropriate beverages.

6. As parents arrive, direct them to a table on which you have a stack of index cards, pencils/pens, and an empty shoebox. Invite parents to write a question or two on a card and place it in the box. At the end of your presentation, quickly shuffle through the cards and respond to general questions or those most frequently asked ("How much homework do you give?" "How is reading taught?"). Inform parents that you will contact them personally to respond to more specific questions or ones

that focus exclusively on their child's work or progress ("Why did Angela miss recess the other day?" "When will Peter be able to see the reading specialist?").

7. After your presentation invite parents to stay and look at their child's work. Circulate around the room, try to meet all the parents again with another handshake and smile, and offer at least one positive remark about their child. This is not the time for personal conferences ("I'd really like to talk with you, Mrs. Smith. May I call you to set up a personal meeting at another time?").

8. For open houses at the middle school and high school levels, parents typically follow a much-abbreviated schedule of classes that their child participates in each day. It's important that you keep your presentation short and snappy because parents will need to move to several additional rooms throughout the evening.

Here are some additional tips and ideas that will add some pizzazz to your open houses or back-to-school and meet-the-teacher nights:

- Create a PowerPoint presentation of daily activities to show parents.

- Produce a brief three- to four-minute video of one or two specific academic activities. Upload it to YouTube and make it available to parents throughout the evening. It can also be e-mailed to parents unable to attend the evening's events.

- "Employ" your students to act as guides, tour directors, and maître d's.

- Consider a very brief demonstration lesson.

- Stay away from "educationalese." Don't use jargon or technical terminology. You may use the word *curriculum* quite frequently; however, parents may have no idea what that word means.

- Provide handouts on how parents can become active supporters of your classroom program (read to their child, provide an appropriate study area at home, etc.). Include community resources such as the public library, too.

> # A Word of Advice
>
> "Think of your students and parents as your clients. After all, in paying taxes, parents are paying your salary. Once you win them over with your dedication and expertise, they will be on your side, no matter what challenges come your way."
>
> —Suzanne Barchers, former classroom teacher

Face to Face: Parent-Teacher Conferences

If there's one part of the school year that strikes fear into the heart of any teacher—it's *parent-teacher conference* time. Teachers who have been around a while will be more than willing to share some memorable stories about strange parents and even stranger conversations with those parents. Nevertheless, parent-teacher conferences are a wonderful opportunity to extend lines of communication between home and school, keep parents informed about their children's progress—both academic and social—and for developing cooperative strategies that can ultimately benefit every student.

You may be nervous about the thought of parent-teacher conferences. However, here's something important to remember: most parents are just as nervous as you are. Your first and primary goal should be to help make them feel comfortable. A friend of mine once said, "It's important to remember that children are ego extensions of their parents." If you tell a mother that her son is failing three subjects, you are, in effect, telling the parent that she, too, is a failure. On the other hand, if you tell Mr. Velasquez that his daughter is the most outstanding science student in the school, Mr. Velasquez will be mentally patting himself on the back all evening long.

Productive and successful conferences take careful planning. You should think about three stages: before, during, and after.

1. Before the Conference

Send a personal letter or e-mail to each parent to confirm the day, time, and place of the conference. Inform parents ahead of time about the purpose of the conference. Gather file folders or portfolios of each student's work. Be sure your schedule is coordinated with other teachers in the school. Many parents will have more than one child in school and need sufficient time with each teacher.

If necessary, make arrangements for an interpreter for non-English-speaking parents. Review notes on each student's behavior, academic progress, and interactions with peers. Establish no more than two or three concerns or issues. More than that will discourage most parents. Clarify ahead of time who, exactly, will be attending each conference. Is it the child's biological parents, a relative, a guardian, a grandparent, a foster parent, or who? Check and double-check names.

Invite parents to bring a list of questions, issues, or concerns. Have sample textbooks readily available. Establish a waiting area outside your classroom. For reasons of confidentiality, you only want to meet with one set of parents at a time.

Don't conduct a parent-teacher conference from behind your desk. A teacher's desk is sometimes referred to as "power furniture," and it tends to inhibit conversation and makes many parents uncomfortable (perhaps a throwback to their days as a student). Instead, conduct your conferences at a table. Don't sit across from parents; instead, sit on the same side of the table as your guests. You will discover heightened levels of conversation and "comfortableness" on the part of parents this way.

2. <u>During the Conference</u>

Greet parents in a positive manner with a smile and a handshake. Keep in mind that a well-run parent-teacher conference focuses in on the following "must do's" every time:

- Provide parents with specific academic information.

- Invite and obtain additional information from parents.

- Listen carefully to parents. If you're nervous, you will tend to "take over" the conversation by as much as 90 percent. Try for a 50-50 balance.

- Combine your perceptions and their observations into a workable plan of action. Ask for parent ideas, and use those ideas in addressing challenging situations. Let parents know that you are always available for follow-up (phone calls, personal meetings, etc.).

When talking to parents, always remember: show, don't tell. Provide specific examples of a student's work or behavior rather than labels or adjectives. Instead of saying, "Frankie is poor in math," paint a clear picture for Frankie's parents: "Last week Frankie struggled when we were learning to add two-digit numbers, and he didn't finish his assignment." Always provide parents with concrete examples (sample papers, for example) rather than very broad generalities.

If you are sharing some negative information with parents, be sure you "sandwich" it. Begin with some positive information, then share the negative information, and conclude with another piece of positive information.

Always look for common solutions ("I understand your concern with Carmelita. Let's see if we can work on this together"). Have some duplicated resource sheets available for parents. These may include (but aren't limited to) the following: a list of community social service agencies, a homework help line, a list of private tutors in the community, websites for homework help, etc.

Always use "active listening" skills. If a parent says something about the child, try to use some of the parent's words in your response. For example, if Mr. Brown says, "Yeah, Tommie always seems to be shy whenever he's around other people." You say, "I understand that Tommie is hesitant to talk with other people; that sometimes happens in class. Perhaps I could put him in a smaller group so he will be less inhibited." By using active listening, you help build positive bridges of communication essential in any good conference.

What a Great Idea!

Be careful of conversational traps. Experienced teachers will tell you that some topics should never be part of parent-teacher conferences, including the following:

- Comparing one child with another
- Psychoanalyzing a child
- Psychoanalyzing a parent
- Arguing with a parent
- Focusing on family problems
- Blaming the parent for the child's problems
- Talking about other teachers

Don't be afraid to ask for parent input or feedback ("By the way, Mr. Wilson, how have you handled Bobbie's silliness at home?"). By the same token, never give parents commands ("You should...." "You must...."). Rather, offer some concrete and specific suggestions in the form of an invitation ("Mrs. Harper, based on our conversation this evening, I'm wondering if you and Michelle could spend an additional ten minutes a night on her spelling words?"). It is far better to "invite" parents to become part of the solution, instead of "telling" them what they should do or should not do.

Summarize some of the major points, and clarify any action that will be taken. Most important, always end a conference on a positive note! Don't just dismiss parents from the table. Stand up with them and personally escort them to the door with a smile, a handshake, and a "Thank you for coming."

3. After the Conference

Save a few minutes after each conference to jot down a couple notes. Don't take notes during the conference; it tends to inhibit many parents and makes eye-to-eye conversation difficult. Record your observations, perceptions, and suggestions on a 3 X 5 index card with the student's name at the top. File these in a recipe box for later reference. Also, consider creating a spreadsheet on your laptop to quickly record important notes.

Plan for some "decompression time" between conferences. You need time to gather your thoughts, regroup, and get ready for the next conference. A long string of back-to-back conferences will only add to your stress and increase your anxiety.

Most important, be sure to follow up (as necessary) with phone calls, notes, or e-mails to every parent, including those who didn't attend ("I'm sorry I missed you at the parent-teacher conferences last week. May I call you for a personal meeting?"). Immediate feedback is necessary to ensure parent cooperation and participation in any shared solutions.

A Few More Ideas

You can use a wide range of projects and activities to get—and keep—parents involved in the affairs of the classroom. Consider some of the following.

- Develop and design a series of orientation programs for parents new to the school or district. It would be valuable to develop a PowerPoint program, a series of brochures, a classroom blog, family guides, or other appropriate orientation materials to assist new families in learning as much as they can about your academic program.

- Work with a group of parents to prepare a notebook of home/community activities for use during vacations. Include games, reading activities, places to visit, and sites to see in the community. Distribute these notebooks to all families prior to a vacation period, especially summer. Provide parents with a periodic newsletter (an attachment to a group e-mail) updating them on classroom activities and projects.

- Provide parents with a calendar of upcoming events in the classroom. Many teachers send/post a periodic newsletter, a blog, or a web page specifically for their classroom. Include information on books you will read in the coming weeks, field trips, science projects, videos you will see, guest speakers, etc. Publish/post this on a frequent basis, and distribute it to all families.

- Offer parents a series of informal workshops throughout the year that focus on various aspects of the classroom program. The workshops can address specific topics (forms of poetry, history of selected countries, math facts, reading strategies, etc.) as well as ways and methods parents can help support teachers' instructional efforts.

- Establish regularly scheduled informal meetings with parents. You can set these up as brown-bag lunches, a meeting over tea and coffee, or a bring-your-own-dessert gathering in the evening. The intent of these meetings should not be to provide instruction but rather to give you an opportunity to meet informally with parents and discuss common goals and objectives. If you can hold these meetings in a neutral location, such as a local church, YMCA, or community room, parents might be more inclined to come.

What a Great Idea!

Use the telephone as an instrument of good news. Often parents associate the telephone as something used to convey bad news (missed homework, tardiness, behavior problem). Call parents frequently to convey good news about a youngster's academic progress or to thank them for their help on a project or homework assignment. Call one parent each week to relay some good news about what his or her child is doing. (NOTE: While e-mailing or texting parents is often easier and more efficient, a personal phone call sends a very powerful message to parents about your desire to reach out and contact them in a more personal manner.)

QUOTABLE QUOTE

"A child educated only at school is an uneducated child."

— George Santayana

Getting Nonparticipating Parents Involved

It's a sobering fact that given the best of intentions and variety of offerings, some parents will still not want to participate in the affairs of the school. We often say that lack of interest or desire are the reasons why some parents choose not to work with the school. Unfortunately, such an attitude becomes self-defeating in the long run. That is, if you believe there will always be a group of parents who will not contribute to the welfare of their youngsters, you will have established a self-fulfilling prophecy that is difficult to undo.

Given the fact that the modern family has a host of appointments, meetings, after-school sporting events, visits, shopping trips, errands, and doctor visits to deal with on a day-to-day basis, it's important that we explore every option for families to participate in the scholastic achievement of their children. Here's how I like to look at it: as teachers, we shouldn't spend a great deal of time worrying why some families are not involved in our classroom activities; rather, we should devote time to methods and procedures on how we can help them be informed, stay informed, and become functioning members of the school community. Here's a list of ideas many teachers have successfully used to enlist the participation and cooperation of parents—particularly those who have not been part of the classroom "game plan":

- Keep parents informed throughout the entire school year. Use available technology to your advantage in reaching out to the families of all your students.

- Be sure students are involved wholeheartedly in recruiting parents. Have kids write invitations or draft newsletters to their parents.

- As appropriate, be prepared to meet parents in their homes, at the shopping mall, or in a community location. Some parents have a fear of schools and would be more comfortable in a neutral site.

- Don't punish nonparticipants for not getting involved. Take time to find out why they are not engaged. You may be surprised to discover that most of the reasons parents do not become involved have nothing to do with lack of time but rather center around lack of sufficient information.

- Consider scheduling meetings with parents at times convenient to their schedule (not necessarily your schedule). Mornings, afternoons, evenings, weekends, weekdays, and the like are all possible.

The key to effective outreach efforts with parents is the fact that *all* parents—those who always participate *and* those who typically don't participate—are solicited and encouraged to become part of the academic team. The bonds established between home and school can be powerful ones in terms of the effectiveness of any classroom program. When parents are employed as partners in the classroom, students are afforded a wealth of exciting educational possibilities.

A Word of Advice

"Parents are your partners in this journey. Reach out to them even before the school year begins. Let them know who you are and your goals for their children. Find out who they are: their interests, hobbies, and talents."

—Anita Meinbach, former classroom teacher

Part III

◆

Successful
Classroom Management

Chapter 8

<u>Creating a Positive Learning Environment</u>

Have you ever been in a cheap motel room? You know, the kind that has a single bed in the middle of the room, a lack of wall decorations (other than one dusty print of a colorless bowl of flowers), ancient and well-worn furniture, a tattered rug, and a closet with a single hanger in it. The bathroom is often small, cramped, and musty. You're just there for one night, but you can't wait to get out.

Unfortunately, many classrooms are the same way.

Effective teaching is dependent upon environmental factors just as much as it is dependent on psychological, social, and personal factors. The way you lay out your classroom and the ways your students perceive your classroom will have a major impact on their level of comfort, their willingness to participate in learning activities, and most important, their behavior. Your classroom design will send one of two messages to your students:

- This is a comfortable place that supports my needs, both physical and psychological, and one in which I feel secure and respected. I enjoy being here.

- This is an environment devoid of feeling, social opportunities, and intellectual stimulation. It is a place I have to be in, not a place I want to be in.

As teachers, we need to keep in mind that learning does not take place in a vacuum. We might be excellent teachers and have exciting lesson plans filled with valuable resources. We might even have motivated, excited and involved students. Still, the environment or classroom in which all that is to take place will determine, to a large extent, how successful we will be as teachers.

Classrooms devoid of interest, lacking in intellectual stimulation, or absent in social engagement are classrooms that often have a negative impact on students' ability to learn. How you set up your classroom will be a major influence on how your students will succeed both academically and personally.

<u>Making a Good First Impression</u>

When you visit someone's home for the first time, what's one of the first things you do? You probably look around at the furniture, its arrangement, the decor, the interior decorating, and a dozen other things. You try to get a sense of this new environment. Often, when you visit someone's home for the first time, you can get an idea of what type of people they are, whether they have a sense of color and balance, and whether their style is compatible with yours. In short, even before you sit down in the living room or wander out to the deck, you have a pretty good idea of the personality of your hosts as well as their decoration philosophy.

The same is true for students. As soon as they enter your classroom, they'll get an initial impression of you and the classroom in which they will be spending the next nine months of their lives. It's been said that first impressions are often lasting impressions, and nowhere is that more true than on the first day of class. Students, from kindergarten to twelfth grade, will be able to determine:

- Your organization skills (orderly/sequential; random/haphazard).

- Your personality (fun/exciting; dull/drab).

- Your creative skills (prepackaged posters, banners, bulletin boards; original art work, decorations, displays).

- Your classroom management plan (detailed/specific; loose/ unstructured).

- Your instructional preferences (multitasking; singular activities).

If you've ever been in a classroom in which all the desks were in straight rows and straight lines, you might have gotten the impression that it was an orderly classroom run by an orderly teacher and a place not subject to change, modification, or variation. Such classrooms can be sterile and predictable…and not much fun!

A Word of Advice

"Would I want to be a student in my class? This is the question I ask myself every day. It helps me to stay focused on the reason I am a teacher...the kids! I want to build memories my students can take with them."

—Donna Albertson, current elementary teacher

Let's Make a Plan

Arranging the furniture may be the most important thing you can do before students arrive on that all-important first day. Use a piece of graph paper and draw your current classroom arrangement, including all the tables, desks, windows, doors, bookcases, cabinets, electrical outlets, bulletin boards, and even the wastepaper basket and pencil sharpener. I like to cut out small pieces of paper in the shape and scaled dimensions of all these items so I can move them around on the graph paper. Use this model to make decisions on the preferred placement of furniture in your room.

When designing your classroom, remember that furniture directs the flow of traffic within the classroom environment and defines the instructional activities that can take place within that classroom. The arrangement of furniture in a classroom is an important decision to make before students arrive on the first day. However, you should feel comfortable changing the arrangement several times throughout the year. Modifying and adjusting the configuration of students' desks (and yours) is just as natural as changing the location of the sofa, love seat, TV, coffee table, and lamps in your living room at home.

Here are some possible room arrangements.

1. Horseshoe Configuration: One of the most versatile designs for any classroom is the horseshoe pattern. You can set up two or three large semicircles of student desks facing the smart board or front of the room. Or scatter mini-horseshoe patterns of a few desks each about the classroom. This pattern opens up the center front of the room for oral presentations, skits, or small group work on the floor. A variation of the horseshoe pattern

is the "U" or three-sided arrangement of desks. Several desks form each of the two sides, and additional desks form the bottom of the pattern.

2. Clusters: Another popular way of arranging student desks is in clusters or small groupings of four or five student desks together. In a classroom of twenty-five students, you might have five clusters of five desks each. Separate each cluster with sufficient space for student movement. Clusters enhance social interactions among students and provide for easy access by the teacher.

3. Pairs or Triads: A variation on the cluster approach is the arrangement of student desks into small groups of two or three. Students create mini-groups of "study buddies" and can work together for extended periods of time on selected projects and activities.

4. Rows and Lines: You might want to consider rows or lines as an initial arrangement at the beginning of the year. By assigning students to specific desks, you can learn their names and get a sense of the different personalities and instructional needs quicker. Later, you can arrange the classroom in other configurations based on the needs and abilities of students.

5. Combination Approach: You might want to use a combination of several arrangements. A combination approach allows you several instructional options and signals to students that both you and your classroom are flexible. You might invite students to suggest a variety of flexible options according to planned units of study or personal preferences. By allowing students to make some choices in the physical design of the classroom, you're providing them with an important sense of ownership in the classroom.

The most important consideration in any arrangement of desks and other furniture in your classroom is that students must always have a clear and unobstructed view of all instruction. Whether you lecture, show a video, conduct a scientific experiment, invite a guest speaker, or use the Promethean Board, it's important that every student, no matter their physical placement, be able to see and hear what is going on.

What a Great Idea!

After you arrange the furniture in your classroom, take time to sit at each student's desk. Determine if you have a clear line of sight to the whiteboard, smartboard, or any important bulletin boards. Are things easy to read?

Soften It Up!

Remember that motel room I talked about earlier in the chapter? If you picture that room in your mind, one of the distinctive things you might notice is all the straight lines and sharp angles. All the furniture is square or rectangular, and all the features are equally square and rectangular. All that "squareness" is psychologically inhibiting.

Students need to know that your classroom is a psychologically safe environment. Many youngsters come from homes that are not psychologically secure or safe. Your classroom might be the only comfortable environment in their lives. Rounded edges, lines, and corners suggest psychological safety and comfort; more so than straight lines and angles. Here are some ideas for you to consider:

- Use throw rugs or carpets squares throughout the room.
- Include pillows, bean bag chairs, old sofas, and other soft furniture.
- Use a variety of fabrics (wool, burlap, cotton) in the room decorations.
- Include items students might find at home, such as photographs, aquariums, standing lamps, padded chairs, posters, and personal artifacts.
- Add a variety of plants—real or artificial; they are one of the most important "softening" elements in any classroom.
- Be creative! A friend of mine brought an old bathtub into his

classroom, tossed in some pillows, and turned it into a reading center for his third graders. What a great idea!

- Use cardboard or large appliance boxes to create private spaces or student study areas.

- Elementary teachers and secondary science teachers should consider the addition of classroom pets such as small mammals (hamsters, guinea pigs, mice), reptiles (snakes, lizards, turtle), birds (canaries, parakeets), and fish (guppies, goldfish).

But, don't make your room too busy. A room filled with too many stations, bulletin boards, artifacts, and displays can lead to visual overload. For some students, this can be disruptive and visually confusing. In fact, *The Journal of Neuroscience* published a study in 2011 that concluded that too many varied objects in a child's field of vision negatively affects their ability to concentrate. It slows learning, limits their ability to process information, and increases nervousness and irritability. The key is to create interest and calm.

My Space, My Place

Students of any age need to know that a classroom is their place; that it's not just the teacher's place into which they have been temporarily invited. If students have the impression that a classroom is "owned" by the teacher, they will be less likely to make an investment in learning. Classrooms that invite student engagement and celebrate the work of students are classrooms in which the best instruction takes place.

What is usually any child's favorite room in the house? For most kids it's her or his bedroom. Why? Because their bedroom is usually the one room in the house they get to decorate, arrange, or design. It's their room! A classroom should be no different. Students will feel most comfortable when they can personalize the classroom and when their contributions are valued.

Here are some suggested strategies:

- Provide plenty of spaces for students to post their work. This can include bulletin boards, walls, the classroom door, cabinet doors, wires down from the ceiling, or other special locations.

- As appropriate, invite students to bring in personal items from home to use in the classroom.

- Celebrate your students' different cultures and countries of origin by decorating with artifacts from those countries or cultures. These can include masks, posters, costumes, pictures, photos, murals, quilts, maps, trinkets, souvenirs, etc.

- It has long been known that classrooms with natural light and outside views have a relaxing effect on students, not a distracting one. By the same token, access to natural light improves learning and test scores.

- If possible, consider changing the lighting from glaring florescent bulbs to table and floor lamps. Some kids react adversely to florescent lights. Keep in mind that there is considerable evidence to support the correlation between lighting and academic performance. For example, students with autism and attention deficit hyperactivity disorder (ADHD) are particularly sensitive to environmental stimuli in the classroom. One study found that students diagnosed as hyperactive appeared to show improved attention under full spectrum (vs. florescent) lights. In another study conducted in 2010, it was reported that the bright light, flickering and buzz of worn fluorescent bulbs increases repetitive motions and agitation in autistic children.

- Color choices have been shown to affect attitudes, behavior, and learning, attention span, and sense of time. Older kids respond better to blue and green since those colors are less stimulating; younger kids can be overly stimulated by lots of bright, vibrant colors

- The use of music can positively affect the learning atmosphere. Use quiet background music to get the creative juices flowing. Upbeat tempos are appropriate for engaged activities. Classical music playing at the start of school tends to calm kids. Several research studies have demonstrated a clear connection between music and the ability of students to focus on a task at hand; in addition to elevating their attitudes for learning.

- Word walls are great, but keep them organized and not too busy. Too much visual information can overstimulate some kids and cause visual confusion in others. Remember less is more.

Talk to Me

When you begin to arrange your classroom space, consider how you want students to interact with each other and how you want to interact with your students. The answers to those questions will play a major role in the design of your classroom.

By now, you know that the best kind of teaching and the best kind of learning take place in a social environment. Students must have opportunities to discuss, share, and converse with each other in productive conversations. You need to consider how you might arrange desks and other furniture to facilitate that process. Obviously, the traditional rows and lines of desks do not stimulate group interaction. Also as you consider how you want to work with and interact with your students, keep these considerations in mind:

- In classrooms where desks are arranged in rows, teachers tend to call on students in the front desks as well as the center row (an upside-down "T" configuration) of the room more than students in other areas.

- Passageways and desk arrangements should be constructed in order to allow you to reach every student with a minimum of steps. Design your classroom so you can get to every student quickly.

- You need to physically move around the room at regular intervals. Students see teachers who "post" themselves in the front of the room for an entire period as dictatorial and disconnected. You need to have a close presence with students regularly throughout a lesson.

Your Space, Your Desk

The first object you see when you walk into any classroom is probably the teacher's desk. In many classrooms, the teacher's desk is a focal point: a place where students deposit homework; a place for student-teacher conferences; a place from which a teacher lectures; and a place where papers are read, graded, and filed.

But a teacher's desk can also be a psychological deterrent to learning. A desk, whether in a classroom, office, or executive suite, is a symbol of power. Its placement within a room says a lot about the person who occupies it. If it's placed in the front of the room, it says that the occupant wants others to know she or he is in charge, that she or he is the authority figure. That often causes discomfort and anxiety for many students. Rather than place your desk front and center in the classroom (the traditional way), try turning your desk around so it faces a wall, preferably in a corner and preferably in the back of the room. Then you'll send your students the message that your desk is just another piece of furniture, not a place of power.

Don't conduct your lessons from your desk. Move away from your desk, and use a small table, a lectern, or some other minor piece of furniture to hold your notes and other instructional materials. I know some of you might be saying that you worked long and hard to earn that teacher's desk. You're right, but it's far more important how students perceive you as an instructor than it is for you to exert some artificial power over them by parking yourself behind a large piece of furniture.

It's a Material World

With everything you need to teach and with the limited amount of space you might have in your classroom, it might seem as though there's never enough room to keep all the equipment, supplies, and materials at the ready for any and all parts of your instructional program. In deciding how and where to store your instructional materials, keep some things in mind.

- Materials must be readily accessible by you and your students. Students need to know exactly where all materials are kept and that they will be able to obtain those materials on their own. You might want to use a special check-out system so students can obtain materials on their own without your intervention.

- Materials and equipment that require safety precautions (hot plates and other electrical devises, crockery, etc.) must be kept in a location out of the reach of youngsters. Provide any necessary instructions and precautions to students early in the school year.

- Materials and equipment kept in containers, storage cabinets, or lockers must be labeled on the outside for easy and quick identification. For younger students or those lacking adequate reading abilities, have an illustration or photograph of the object(s) on the outside of the container.

- Supplies and materials should be kept in a variety of locations in the classroom so they're readily accessible at all times and are evenly distributed throughout the room. Some supplies will be in constant use and need to be obtained quickly and easily. Paper towels, scissors, pens, chalk, pens and pencils, and string are items used fairly often and should be supplied in several locations throughout the room.

How you store your supplies and materials and what you keep your equipment in will be limited only by your imagination and the design of your classroom. My experience is that there is no limit to the ways and methods teachers have used to store materials.

Designing Your Classroom

After reading this chapter, you might be wondering how you'll ever be able to design your instructional environment - your classroom. Remember that a well-designed classroom is in a state of constant evolution; it is always subject to change and modification depending on the students who occupy it as well as the instructional activities you have planned for those students. As you think about how to create the best possible learning environment for your grade or subject area, you might want to keep these things in mind.

1. Traffic Patterns: Is there room to move around the room? Take a look at how students will move into the room, to their desks, and between activities or locations within the room. You need to be sure students with physical challenges can safely negotiate the room. Traffic routes to and from frequently used places also need to be clear, unobstructed, and easy. Consider the following routes for each student in the room:

   o From a desk to the pencil sharpener

   o From a desk to the wastebasket

   o From a desk to the water fountain or sink

   o From a desk to you

○ From a desk to the bathroom (in the classroom or outside the classroom)

○ From a desk to the door and vice versa

○ From a desk to a center activity or small group location

Not only must you consider the traffic patterns for individual students but also for larger groups as well. The class will need to exit the classroom *en mass* at the end of a period, for recess, lunch, their specials (art, music, PE, library), and end-of-day dismissal. Plan for an efficient flow of lots of bodies through your room.

Keep large objects and furniture away from your classroom door. Students will need space to enter the classroom (often in small groups) as well as exit (often in large groups). Consider this: an average student, standing, takes up approximately eighteen square inches of floor space. Allowing for an additional foot of empty space between each student, a group of five students waiting to exit the classroom would need a minimum of 12.5 square feet of open space near the door. Plan the entranceway to your classroom accordingly.

2. Different Activity Areas: In most classrooms, there will be a variety of activities and activity areas for students. You need to carefully plan these so they don't interfere with each other or with other instructional tasks that take place during the course of the day. You don't want a messy area near the computer(s). You don't want a noisy area near a quiet reading area. And you don't want a small group area near the front of the classroom where most instruction takes place. Consider the placement of the following:

○ Neat/messy areas

○ Quiet/noisy areas

○ Individual/small group areas

○ Stationary/movable areas

○ Permanent/changing areas

3. Monitoring: To conduct a well-run classroom, you need to be able to monitor students regularly and consistently throughout the period or throughout the day. That means you need to be able to see what students are doing from any location in the classroom. It also means you can get to students quickly and easily when they need your assistance or some type of intervention (for classroom management, for example).

   ○ Be sure no large furniture blocks your line of sight from any location in the room. Also, be sure students can see you easily, no matter from what activity or spot in the room they might be.

   ○ Frequent eye contact between you and your students is both necessary and essential.

The organization of your classroom plays a pivotal role in the success you will enjoy as a teacher as well as the success your students will enjoy in your room. The environment does have a positive and significant impact. You and I certainly feel much more comfortable in our respective living rooms than we do in a $29.95-per-night motel room. The same is true with your students. If you can make your classroom a comfortable and inviting place to be, your students will be much more comfortable in all their learning tasks. Students will expect to be successful when the environment supports those expectations of success. Create a positive environment, and you create positive learning opportunities.

QUOTABLE QUOTE

"We are now at a point where we must educate our children in what no one knew yesterday, and prepare our schools for what no one knows yet."

—Margaret Mead

Chapter 9

<u>Setting and Maintaining</u>
<u>Behavioral Standards</u>

Take a few moments and imagine the following: You wake up one morning and realize your alarm clock never went off. You're going to be late for your first morning class. You throw on your cleanest dirty clothes, swipe a brush through your hair, grab some books and head for your car. You dash out of your apartment complex and onto the highway where the speed limit is sixty-five miles per hour. But you're late. So, you put the "pedal to the metal" and inch the speedometer up to 90 MPH. It's not too long before you see those flashing red and blue lights in your rearview mirror. You pull over and before long a police officer approaches your car. You explain to him your (very good) reason for speeding and instead of giving you a ticket, he lets you off with a warning. Whew! Before long you're on campus, find the last parking space in the student lot, and are in your seat just before the professor walks in the door. Boy that was close.

The next morning the same thing happens. Your alarm clock fails to wake you. You dash out of the apartment and speed on down the highway. In no time a cop pulls you over and you tell your sorry tale once again. Guess what? He lets you off with a warning and you make it to campus just on time.

The next morning—the same thing. You are speeding down the highway at 95 MPH, get pulled over, and, once again get a warning about safe driving. "Hey," you say to yourself, "this is working out pretty good. All I'm getting is a bunch of warnings—not one ticket."

The next morning your alarm clock goes off at the right time. You get up, put on some clean clothes, have a nice relaxing breakfast, casually grab your backpack and get into your car. You're not late, not even close. You've got plenty of time to make it to campus before that early morning methods course. But, still, you decide to speed on down the highway at close to 100 MPH. Once again, the flashing lights appear, you get pulled over, a cop approaches your car and—Yup, you guessed it—all you get is another warning. This is just too good to be true. You can speed all you want and you know that the worst that can happen is another warning—no consequences, no fines, no points on your license, no penalties, no sweat!

You certainly realize that the scenario described above is a work of fiction. It could never happen in real life. But, guess what, it happens almost every single day and every single year in a plethora of classrooms across the country. It happens with new teachers as well as with experienced teachers. It happens with young teachers, old teachers, elementary teachers, middle school teachers, secondary teachers, teachers in public school and teachers in private schools. It is so deeply ingrained in the American educational system that it is virtually impossible to eradicate. It is the single most decisive element in effective classroom management—the single most critical factor in good classroom management. The single biggest mistake anyone could make as a teacher.

And, believe it or not, many teachers continue to make that mistake year after year!

Let's take another look at the scenario above. There was a legally posted speed limit (65 MPH). You drove considerably faster than the posted speed limit (faster than the law allows). In other words, you broke the law. You were pulled over by a police officer. The police officer knew you broke the law. Yet, he only gave you a warning, not a ticket as the law stipulates. A warning! Again and again you broke the law and again and again all you got was a warning.

Guess what? You have no incentive to adhere to the law simply because you know that every time you break that law, the worst that will happen is a warning. How are you going to travel down that highway in the future (whether you are late or not is immaterial)? Of course, you're going to drive down that highway as fast as you can regardless of the law. What's the worst that can happen? A warning! No big deal.

Now, let's reconfigure the scenario above in terms of a typical classroom. Let's see if this sounds familiar. You have a posted expectation in your classroom—something like "Raise your hand and be recognized before speaking." You've told your students that anytime they want to respond to a question or pose a question of their own they should raise their hands. You've also informed them that when they don't raise their hand before speaking there will be a consequence. You should quickly realize that there is now a procedure (a "speed limit") in place in the classroom and that when that "law" is broken there is a consequence—a "ticket."

Now, you're in the middle of an incredible second grade science lesson about "Living and Non-living Things." You're listing some of the features of living things on the whiteboard when Tommy blurts out, "I have an aquarium with lots of big fish in it." You turn to Tommy and say, "Tommy, that's fine, but you know you should raise your hand before speaking."

You've just issued a "warning." You continue recording items on the whiteboard when Tommy, without raising his hand, asks, "Are plants living things?" You turn to Tommy and ask him, "Tommy, what did we say about raising your hand?" "I have to raise my hand?" he replies. "That's right, Tommy, you have to raise your hand." You've just issued another warning. A few moments later Tommy tells you he's going to the bathroom. You gently ask Tommy what he should have done before asking his question. He tells you, "I should always raise my hand." "Yes, you're right, Tommy. Let's make sure you do it next time. Now, you may go to the bathroom." Another warning.

Do you see what's happening? It's subtle, it's sublime, and it's beginning to grow. It's like a 1950's radioactive movie monster from another planet that slowly, very slowly, begins to get larger and larger. It grows, it expands, and it begins to take over your classroom square inch by square inch. Simply put—rules are broken and there are no consequences, only warnings.

But, it gets worse!

Because now your students are beginning to get a very subtle message. It's OK to break a rule, because the worst that can happen is a warning. We are not responsible for our behavior, our teacher is. Most of the time our teacher will let things slide. Most of the time we'll just get a warning. No big deal.

Now, there is a crack in the classroom management dam and water is slowly beginning to leak out. The flow is small at first, but in time it will become a torrent:

- One or two students will come running into the classroom.
- A few students will jostle each other as they line up for recess.
- A single student will sing as he gets a pencil from your desk.
- Two girls will pass notes back and forth.
- Someone will leave the room without asking first.
- A student will put his homework on the corner of your desk instead of in the "Homework Basket."

Yup, there it is. It's growing. It grows and grows and grows. And each time it pops up you find yourself repeating a rule, handing out reminders, talking louder, becoming impatient, issuing threats—and giving lots of warnings! You've lost them and now you have a gigantic problem on your hands—a problem that has grown into a very large, very persuasive, and very ugly monster!

Stop!

Your Classroom Management Plan

I'm going to offer you a classroom management plan that is guaranteed to work every time, every day, and all through the year. (Did you notice the word "guaranteed" in the preceding sentence?). But, this plan comes with a caveat: you must follow it exactly—no deviations, no exceptions, no changes. Any modifications or adjustments and all bets are off. The plan isn't complicated; in fact, there's just four steps to follow. But, focus your attention on these four steps and you will see something very magical happening in your classroom: students behaving and students learning.

Ready? Here are the four steps:

1. Establish a set of inviolable classroom procedures.
2. Practice those procedures.
3. Establish a set of consequences if any procedures are broken.
4. Enact any necessary consequences.

Simple, right? Well, not exactly. That's because this plan will be in opposition to what you experienced as a student in various elementary and secondary classrooms or it may be in opposition to what you learned in your teacher education program. Most of what you have probably experienced has been <u>reactive</u> in nature. That is, something happens and the teacher reacts in a certain way. You have undoubtedly observed and you have certainly learned some of the techniques and strategies teachers often use on how to "properly" react to any misbehavior in a classroom. Unfortunately, what you have read or have been taught is "management after the fact."

In contrast, this plan is <u>pro-active</u>. It sets up expectations for behavior before the fact, before any possible misbehavior can occur, and before any possible disruptions might arise. It teaches appropriate behavior in advance, not after inappropriate behavior has been demonstrated. It is "management before the fact."

A Word of Advice

"Find something you like about ALL your students— especially the most difficult ones. It might be hard, but it's an important part of building a positive classroom culture (and it can help with classroom management)."

—Nicole Hesson, former middle school teacher

Let's take a closer look at the four components:

1. Establish a set of inviolable classroom rules.

Most classroom teachers have a set of rules for their students to follow. Often, these rules inform students about what they can or can't do in a classroom. The intent is to create a sense of order and comfort so teaching and learning can take place. But for classroom rules to be effective, you should create or base them on a few simple principles.

- Students should have a sense of ownership of the rules. Invite students to contribute a set of expectations about behavior. Take time at the beginning of the school year to solicit their input.

Most often, you'll discover that the classroom rules students suggest fall into several specific categories. In a classroom meeting, for example, second-graders might say that there should be no kicking, no hitting, no pinching, no poking, etc. All those behaviors fall into the category of "personal space." As you brainstorm, continue to look for groupings or clusters of ideas. Take time to talk with students about how they can combine their ideas and suggestions into the following categories:

○ Honoring personal space (using cell phones, keeping one's desk clean, lining up, sharing supplies)

○ Respecting property (using the classroom library, using a computer, moving through the classroom)

○ Considering the feelings of others (sharing supplies, listening to intercom announcements, being a classroom helper)

○ Paying attention (listening, talking, answering questions, coming to attention, taking tests, handling emergencies, pledging allegiance, taking attendance, taking lunch counts)

○ Academic matters (handing in work, making up work when absent, formatting written work, finishing work early, asking questions, making up missing or late work, homework assignments)

○ Using appropriate movement (entering the classroom, exiting the classroom, being tardy to class, managing restroom breaks, sharpening pencils, fire and emergency drills, going to the nurse)

What a Great Idea!

Students have a tendency to create classroom rules beginning with "No" or "Don't." Such rules tend to breed and perpetuate negativity. Instead, frame rules in positive terms. Instead of "Don't hit people," say "Respect other people." Instead of "No talking when someone else is talking," say "Take turns talking." This little grammatical modification will result in major benefits for you and your students throughout the year. The final list you create will be a personal one for students because they helped create it. They will have that all-important sense of ownership and will be more inclined to follow the rules they helped create.

- The best set of classroom rules is one students can remember and use every day. When a list of rules becomes long and exhaustive, students will never be able to remember, much less conform to, those rules. The "Rule of Five" says there should be no more than five basic rules in any classroom. The clustering activity mentioned in the preceding section will help you cluster student suggestions into a manageable list of rules.

- The rules should be appropriate to the grade level. "Absolutely no talking" would be a very difficult rule to enforce in a kindergarten class where students are very verbal and very social. Making sure the rules are appropriate for your grade level also means you need to be sensitive to potential exceptions. Creating a rule for your high school social studies class such as, "All homework must be turned in on time—no exceptions" does not allow for the inevitable unplanned events that often impact an adolescent's life (sports, jobs, social life). And while we're on the topic, when crafting rules for secondary students, try not to create rules with absolutes. Words like "never" and "always" don't give you or your students any latitude when unexpected events happen. Allow yourself some flexibility within the context of any rule. This also humanizes any rules you create.

- Be sure all students understand the classroom rules. You might have a rule posted in the classroom such as "Respect other people." It's important that you clearly spell out examples of that rule in practice for students. For example, you might say, "Always listen when someone else is talking," or "Be sure to share any games with your classmates." It's valuable for students to know the specific types of behaviors expected of them. It's equally important that you describe those behaviors in terms and examples that are concrete and specific for the grade level you're teaching. For every rule, you must communicate in clearly defined terms and language students will understand, give the specific rationale or reason for a rule, and offer concrete examples of the rule as you want it to be practiced.

- Do the classroom rules enhance or hinder learning? Hindering rules are often too specific: "All homework must be turned in to the blue box on my desk by 2:55 each day." Compare that rule with "All homework should be turned in on time." The latter rule allows some flexibility and doesn't cause unnecessary stress for students. The first rule places more emphasis on the time of delivery than it does on the actual homework assignment.

- Be sure your classroom rules are consistent with school rules. Although you might think it would be nice to have your students take responsibility for using the restroom on their own and want to establish that as one of your classroom rules, the school might have a policy that every student must have a bathroom or hall pass to leave the classroom. Be sure any rule in your classroom doesn't contradict a school rule.

- Keep parents informed. Good classroom rules do not exist in isolation from the rules of behavior practiced at home or in the local community. Inform parents of your expectations for students though newsletters, phone calls, blogs, parent-teacher conferences, classroom web sites, group e-mails, or other means of communication. When parents know what you expect (rather than trying to guess) they will be much more supportive of your actions.

Teaching your students specific rules also eliminates a frequent communication problem. Both new and experienced teachers (myself included) often have a tendency to say things like, "Stop that," "Cut it out," "You shouldn't do that," and "Stop it." Go back and look at those commands again. What is "it"? What is "that"? Those words have no meaning—they are imprecise, vague, and ambiguous. They do not define a specific action or behavior—especially for students.

The commands listed above also put an emphasis on the negative ("Don't," "Stop," "shouldn't") essentially telling kids what they shouldn't do, rather than telling them what they should do. As a result students often get the notion that rules are always bad, they're always negative. In essence, there's no negativity or positivity with any good rule, they're simply statements of behavioral expectations. They are dispassionate and without emotion. As they should be.

A Word of Advice

"Everyone wants to know the reason for the various laws, rules, etc. Have students help suggest and describe a respectful atmosphere that will help them have an atmosphere in which they can learn best."

—George Severns, former secondary teacher

2. Practice appropriate procedures.

This is a critical element in any classroom management plan. Yet, sadly, it is the one element new teachers frequently neglect. It is quite one thing to establish a set of rules on how students should behave, it is quite another thing to ensure that students know exactly what each rule means in terms of its importance in the efficient running of a classroom. For example, you may have a rule that states, "Respect your classmates." That's a good rule for any classroom, but what does it mean? You and I probably know exactly what it means only because we have had years of experience in both giving and receiving respect. With youngsters, that's not always true.

In other words, we should not assume that students know how to demonstrate respect, for example. How do they demonstrate respect on the school bus? How do they demonstrate respect when they are out on the playground? How do they demonstrate respect with a classmate? Unfortunately, we often assume, or take it for granted, that kids come to school with some basic skills and behaviors. In many instances, that's not the case. They need to be taught.

Now here's a rule for every person reading this book: If you have a rule, teach the rule. In short, don't arbitrarily assume that kids know what that rule means.

I'd like to invite you to go back to Chapter 5 and review the entire section on how to teach a procedure. For the purpose of illustration, I'm going to replicate the basics of that section and use them to illustrate a proven method for teaching a specific classroom rule:

Rule: Practice courtesy with everyone in the room.

1. Grab a few books from your desk and pretend to be one of the students in the class. Slowly walk through the classroom and "accidentally" bump into another student. Immediately say something like, "I'm sorry. Please excuse me for bumping into you."

2. Go through the sequence again. Describe each of the actions you are performing and reference the rule on a chart or poster you have prepared ahead of time.

3. Do the sequence a third time. As you are performing, invite students to tell you exactly what you are doing.

4. Now, ask a single student to go through the sequence. If something is left out, ask the student to start from the beginning and go through the entire sequence from beginning to end. Be sure to compliment the student for performing the procedure correctly.

5. Invite another student to go through each step in the sequence from start to finish. Ask the class to describe each step as it is performed. Try to make this simulation as authentic as possible by using materials or props normally available in the classroom. Ask another student to perform the procedure step by step and exactly as it has been demonstrated. No variations and

no deviations are allowed. There is only one way to do a specified sequence.

... feel confident that students are "comfortable" in
... steps of a designated sequence, then it's
... se, pair up students in the
sequence of steps exactly
makes a mistake or leaves
to the starting position and
again. Your ultimate goal is
in exactly the same way...

now that they did something
they did it perfectly! They're

much time should I devote to
Here's my suggestion:

ol year devote about 30–45
oom rules (one rule per day).

de about 20 minutes a day for

devote 20–30 minutes a week to
revisit selected class... es

Some teachers think that this is wasted time—time taken away from the more important instructional tasks. But nothing can be more important than a well-crafted and well-articulated classroom management plan. If it's true that "an ounce of prevention is worth a pound of cure," it stands to reason that the time you take at the start of the school year to teach those rules will pay enormous dividends throughout the rest of the school year.

3. Establish a set of consequences if any procedures are broken.

Remember all those "warnings" you got when you were speeding down the highway? You could drive as fast as you wanted, for as many times as you wanted, and you would never, ever get a ticket. Life was good.

You knew, just knew, that the only thing that would happen would be a warning. Not a bad deal. There was absolutely nothing to stop you from speeding again and again. Sure there was a rule—a speed limit—but, so what? There was absolutely no penalty if and when that rule—that speed limit—was ever broken. Yup, you were "in like Flynn."

But, as you also read, that same scenario is played out in thousands of classrooms every year. Teachers have rules, students break the rules, teachers give out lots and lots of warnings. Sure, these teachers want to be "The Good Guy"; they want to be seen as nice and friendly people; they think that they can get student respect by easing up now and again and letting a few things slide in the process. "Students always behave when you are nice to them," they say. Well, guess what? It doesn't work!

Here's the simple truth of classroom management: If you have a rule, there must be consequences if the rule is broken. Break a rule, suffer the consequences! Simple. Students must know what will happen if a rule is broken AND teachers must enact the appropriate consequence when that rule is broken. Not some of the time. Not most of the time. ALL THE TIME.

Here's another truth: students want and need consistency in their lives. They need to know what to expect; a classroom life full of uncertainties and insecurities does little to enhance their developing personalities or self-concept. Knowing that you, as their teacher, will <u>always</u> follow through is essential in adding structure and form to their lives. Once again, the key word here is <u>consistency</u>.

Here's a sample set of rules AND consequences established by one classroom teacher. She had the rules (in large letters) on a poster in the front of the classroom. Right under that poster was another poster with the consequences (again, clearly spelled out) also highlighted.

"RULES of the Road"

1. Listen and follow directions.
2. Raise your hand before speaking or leaving your seat.
3. Keep your hands and feet to yourself.
4. Respect your classmates and your teacher.

Consequences

1st time a rule is broken: Warning

2nd time a rule is broken: Time-Out

3rd time a rule is broken: Letter home

You will quickly notice that the word "Warning" is included on the poster above. But, you will also note that it is there just one time. Unlike all those warnings you got when you went speeding down the highway, in this classroom a student gets one warning and one warning only. Instead of an endless series of constant nonconsequential warnings, in this classroom it's "once and done." And, that's the way it should be!

So, here's your new rule: each student can get one warning, but one warning only—no more. And, while we're on the topic of warnings, here's some good advice: when giving a warning always use the least invasive form of intervention. Here are some examples:

- Nonverbal warning (Teddy is poking his neighbor. You walk over to Teddy and gently place your hand on his shoulder.)
- Quick group warning ("Oops—we need everyone standing still.")
- Anonymous individual warning ("Hmmm, someone's not focused on me.")
- Private individual warning ("Sandra, you didn't follow Rule #2.")
- Rapid fire warning ("Joseph, eyes front. Great!")

A good warning is issued immediately after the infraction and quickly, with the least disruption to the class. It doesn't have to be loud, it shouldn't be long, and it should be directed at a specific individual. Saying something like, "Rocco, I'm going to need to see you after lunch today" is ineffective and inefficient. If a rule is broken the warning should be immediate or it loses all its power.

New teachers often make a critical mistake when it comes to warnings: they will often ignore misbehavior. They'll let it slide, they'll say something like, "Well it's the first time, I'll have a talk with him next time," or they'll totally ignore it for the sake of getting a lesson done.

No, no, no. Don't ignore any misbehavior. You set up a set of rules for the classroom for a reason. You and your students must abide by those rules. If you don't, chaos ensues. If you ignore an infraction, you are essentially saying to students, "The rules really don't matter. I just wasted our time by putting them up there on the wall. They really aren't all that important. Do whatever you want." What ultimately happens, as you might expect, is that the misbehavior persists and, in most cases, becomes more pronounced. Alas, you've created a monster.

Oh, one last piece of advice here: a good classroom management plan is for everyone in the class—and that means EVERYONE. Every single student in the room is expected to follow the rules, comply with the rules, and adhere to the rules. Absolutely no exceptions! If you make exceptions you're chipping away at the intent of your rules. If you let Tommy, Billy, and Ned get away with something because—well, because they're—you know, they're boys, then you've just shot yourself in the foot. You've lost an ounce of credibility and you've lost an inch of respect. And, it will, over time, add up! By spring you'll be spending a major portion of your instructional time slapping Band-Aids all over your classroom management plan—if, indeed, there's anything left. Bottom line: 100 percent of your students must follow the rules. Period.

4. Enact any necessary consequences.

Short story: If there's a rule and someone breaks that rule, then there must be consequences. If you run your car into the side of my house you've just broken a rule (you shall not destroy someone's private property.). Because you've broken that rule you are, therefore, subject to any necessary consequences (pay a fine, pay for repair work to my house, get points on your driver's license, etc.). Quite obviously, if there were no consequences for a broken rule, rules would be broken all the time.

And, so it is in your classroom. If a rule is broken you must follow through. **Every. Single. Time.** Once again, it all comes down to one word: consequency. The strength of your classroom management plan is ultimately structured on its consistency. If there are exceptions, if there are special circumstances, if there is any "wiggle room," your plan is essentially "dead in the water." Maintaining consistency is the essential ingredient in any successfully managed classroom. Students expect it and students want it. Without it, behavior erodes.

If a consequence is in order, here are some tips on how to deliver "the news":

- Do not go into any long and drawn out explanations. You'll quickly defuse the power of the consequence. One or two brief sentences are usually sufficient.

- Attach the consequence directly to the rule so there is absolutely no misunderstanding ("Jennifer, that's the second time today you haven't raised your hand before talking. Please escort yourself to Time Out.").

- Please keep all your personal opinions to yourself (NO: "You know, guys, Mrs. Fracking really gets upset when some of her students are talking when she's talking. I can't teach my lesson very well and that makes me very, very angry. And, you know, I just don't like getting angry with my students."). By injecting your personal opinions into the conversation you're shifting the focus away from the infraction and the inevitable consequence. In other words, this isn't about you.

- Be dispassionate and unemotional. A rule was broken, a consequence results. Don't offer a sad face, slumped shoulders, or a frown. State the broken rule and state the resulting consequence without passion, emotion, or attitude. In that way, everybody gets the same identical response. You've maintained consistency.

- Don't physically escort them to Time Out. By doing so, you're taking over some of their responsibility. If someone breaks a rule for the second time, then they are responsible for getting themselves over to Time Out. If you intervene by leading them over by the arm or holding their hand, then you will be shouldering some of their responsibility.

- Very important: Keep it short, keep it brief. If you're spending more than ten seconds handing out a consequence, you're spending way too much time. Nothing disrupts a classroom more than a teacher giving a long lecture on why so-and-so is being sent to the Time Out corner. Get it over and done with and get right back to teaching that lesson!

- Most important: Every day everyone starts out with a "clean slate." Nothing is carried over from the day before. Just because Jason didn't walk quietly in the hallway on two occasions on Tuesday doesn't mean that he has two strikes against him when school begins again on Wednesday. He starts new, he starts fresh—just like everyone else.

Punishment

A quick word here about punishment—a term I've not used up to this point. Punishment, by its very nature, is something that occurs after the fact. It occurs after a deed. If you've embraced the philosophy in Chapter 5 and this chapter, then you would agree that if punishment is handed out frequently, then it, most likely, means that something wasn't taught very well in the beginning. Students didn't learn the rules; students weren't systematically taught the expectations for behavior. It was assumed that they knew how to behave ("Hey, you, stop that! You know better than that.").

In reality, punishment is a short-term solution that often creates some long-term problems. Chief among those problems is the fact that it seldom creates any kind of change in your students. Oh, sure, there might be a temporary modification of behavior, but it won't be long-lasting or sustaining. What we often discover is that students who are punished frequently lack a sense of self-discipline ("Someone else will control my behavior from the outside."), self-control ("Why should I behave, someone else is going to tell me what to do anyway."), and self-respect ("I really don't like myself very much because I'm always being yelled at."). In short, punishment seldom prevents problems as it puts the emphasis on negative reactions rather than positive behavior.

Setting and maintaining behavioral standards may well be the most important thing you do as a new teacher. To be sure, the process is challenging simply because you will, for the first time, be the person in charge. You will make the decisions and you will carry out the actions. But, ultimately, you will discover, as so many teachers before you have, that a solid and well-structured classroom management plan will make

all the difference in the world in terms of your personal teaching success
and your students' ultimate learning success.

Chapter 10

The Do's and Don'ts
of Classroom Management

It's important to remember that classroom management does not come about overnight—no matter how many hours you devote to it in the summer before you begin your first year. Classroom management is an evolutionary process—one filled with typical ups and down, mistakes and errors, and lots of on-the-job training. Classroom management does not come from a textbook, it comes from the day to day interaction with students. It is, in so many ways, a "trial by fire" —a rite of passage every classroom teacher must experience.

It's like learning to drive. Remember those days? When you first got behind the wheel of a car you were scared, frightened, nervous, anxious, and about as "up-tight" as you could possibly be. You listened to what your mother or father was telling you in one ear and what you had read in your state's driving manual in the other. You were thinking back to all the times you were a passenger in a car and how the driver reacted in certain driving situations. You were trying to remember all the rules and regulations. You were, quite literally, awash in information—in fact, you were swamped by information! And, then you had to drive. You had to do it by yourself. You may have bumped into something, cut a corner a little too closely, went a little too fast, or (like me) ran the car completely through the garage door (Ouch!). Truth be told, you made a lot of mistakes.

But, now you're an accomplished driver. You feel a lot more comfortable behind the wheel of a car—any car. You know the rules and regulations, you know the parts of the vehicle, and you know how to keep yourself and your passengers safe. So it is with classroom management. The first time you try it, you'll make some mistakes. And the second time, and the third time, and so on. But, in time you'll develop some perspectives and some routines that work. You'll learn about the inner workings of kids and your own approaches to those workings. Your classroom management plan will begin to emerge from those experiences. It will be a combination of what you have learned from this book, what you have gathered from your colleagues and other professional resources, and what you have experienced each and every day in the classroom.

Malcolm Gladwell, in his classic book *Outliers* (2011), presented convincing evidence and compelling research that to become an accomplished professional in any field you need to log about ten thousand hours of practice before you are an expert. If you do the math, you'll discover that for classroom teachers that will take about five years— five challenging years of your career. That may seem as though a tough responsibility just got tougher. But, it doesn't have to be—here's why:

- Take it slow. You're not going to learn everything in one year. Just like you didn't learn everything about teaching from a single college course, so too will you need extended time to integrate, process, and execute all the strategies and techniques necessary for good classroom management.

- Good classroom managers don't come about overnight. No one is born an exceptional classroom manager. It takes times and patience. It takes practice and persistence. It takes experience and contemplation. Great cathedrals don't rise up overnight; don't expect your classroom management skills will be perfected in your first year.

- Classroom management is an evolutionary process; it changes, adapts, and is constantly modified, particularly in its early stages. What you will be doing in your classroom five years from now will be considerably different than what you might set up this year. There's nothing wrong with that. Change is good.

- Good classroom management doesn't come from a course or a book, this one included. It comes from experience. To become a good classroom manager you need lots and lots of hands-on time managing a classroom, not reading a book or attending a course.

Now, that said, let's take a look at some of the dos and don'ts of good classroom management. Some of these may be self-obvious, but that doesn't make them any less important. It's just that every now and again we need a friendly reminder about things we often take for granted. So too, will you discover some reinforcing concepts originally presented in the previous chapter. This is not my attempt to "beat a dead horse," but rather an emphasis on some critical and necessary concepts that can ensure your classroom as a model of excellent classroom management. And a few of these tips will be new, fresh takes and new eyes on situations and conditions that frequently surface in many classroom environments. I sincerely hope you discover more than a few nuggets here for your classroom.

QUOTABLE QUOTE

"We cannot solve our problems with the same thinking we used when we created them."

—Albert Einstein

Do's

1. Most important: <u>teach</u> essential classroom routines from "Day One." This is the most critical element in good classroom management. The time spent on teaching those routines (rather than teaching an academic topic or subject area) will pay off handsomely later in the year. If necessary, please re-read Chapter 9.

2. Second most important item: teach students the consequences when they fail to adhere to the routines. Let students know that THEY, not you, are responsible for their behavior. You are not a behavior manager; you are merely the one who monitors the classroom to ensure that appropriate behaviors are expressed in standardized ways.

3. Model the behaviors you expect from your students. Comments such as "You know how to walk in a straight line, now do it" are inappropriate. Students need to actually see how YOU WALK in a straight line in order to get a mental conception of what that looks like. "Here, watch how I walk in a straight line from the library to our classroom" is what they need, not vague suggestions about what is expected.

4. Practice, practice, practice: don't neglect frequent and contact practice sessions during the first few weeks of school. Some things take time to learn. We don't learn to run a mile in under four minutes without lots of practice. We don't learn how to serve a tennis ball without lots of practice. We don't learn how to do an inward pike dive into a swimming pool without lots of practice. Students need lots of practice, too, before they become accomplished "behaviorists."

5. Use precise language. Saying something like, "You should always be courteous to other people" doesn't always mean a great deal to youngsters. They need specific vocabulary and exact terminology. For example, "When you come in the door in the morning please say 'Good morning' and shake my hand." Often, the precision of your words will determine how well students will be able to follow established routines.

6. The same thing holds true when commenting on students' work. As teachers, we have a tendency to say things like, "Good job!" or "Way to go!" or "Terrific work." Those types of comments often fall on deaf ears because they don't identify the specific item being recognized. For example, which of the following would you rather receive from one of your teachers: "You did a good job, Sarah." or "Sarah, your systematic analysis of the author's major argument in the book was focused, detailed, and exceptional. One of the best I've ever read."

7. Be sure to recognize the behavior of all students, not just the good students. We all like to know we're doing a good job and we all like to be recognized for our efforts. That recognition needs to be frequent, regular, and sustained, irrespective of whether we are the top student in the class or the one struggling at the bottom of the academic ladder.

What a Great Idea!

Here's something I have been doing for many years. Feel free to use this in your own classroom, too—you'll see some magic taking place.

Each week during a course, I select one or two students and write each of them a "Thank You" note. I have a stack of several different thank you cards on my desk (obtained from the nearby Hallmark store). I take about 4—5 minutes and write a personal note to an individual student and thank that student for something she or he did in the course or shared in an assignment. For example, I might celebrate a series of comments the student made during an in-class discussion, I might recognize a particularly good assignment the student submitted, I might thank a student for helping another student understand a concept, or I might simply thank a student for her or his commitment to teaching. I address each card to the student's campus mailing address and drop them in the mail. I don't do any follow up ("Hey, did you get the card I sent you last week?"), rather I allow the student to decide if he or she would like to comment on the card. If they do, that's fine; if they don't, that's OK, too.

The sending of these cards is never announced in class—I don't tell students I'll be sending them thank you cards sometime during the length of the course. It's just something that's done "behind the scenes" —something unexpected and something out of the ordinary. [NOTE: I don't send these as e-mails or text messages. Students get far too many e-mails and texts, but seldom receive a personal letter—especially from one of their instructors. In short, e-mails and texts don't carry as much "weight."].

What I've discovered over the years is a magical transformation. Students come to class with improved attitudes, an increased willingness to face the challenges of a classroom discussion, a heightened spirit of "bonding" with the instructor, and more camaraderie with their classmates. Sure, it takes some time out of my day and it is extra work, but the benefits to both individual students and the entire class are simply incredible.

Example:

Dear Colleen:

   I just wanted to take this opportunity to thank you for your insight and contributions during our discussion about effective classrooms in Tuesday's class. You displayed a marvelous ability to ask the right questions and pursue lines of reasoning that were both perceptive as well as insightful. You contributed much to our overall understanding of what a well-run classroom is all about. I am certain your future classroom will be one overflowing with equal measures of energy, compassion, and communal sharing. Thanks so much.

Best,

Dr. Fredericks

I used the same technique as a classroom teacher, too. There, I referred to the strategy as "Two-minute Notes." Each morning I would come to school a few minutes early. I'd sit down at my desk, take out my gradebook, and identify two students (I simply went down the list of names recorded in my gradebook). Then, I'd write each of those two students a brief note complementing them on their progress on a particular assignment, a contribution they made in class, a task they did without being asked, or simply their pleasant personality. I'd then place each of those two notes in each student's mailbox in the back of the room where they would be waiting when the students arrived in the morning. Once again, I never asked students if they got the notes or what they thought of them. I'd let them decide if they wanted to respond. Not surprisingly, I saw the same kind of magic taking place in those classrooms as I currently do in my college classes.

Example:

Dear Sonya:

WOW! All that hard work you did on your science project really paid off. Your contributions helped the class achieve high honors at last week's science fair. Thank you so much for your effort and for your energy. It made a real difference.

Sincerely,

Dr. Fredericks

Try it! You'll be amazed at what happens.

8. As highlighted in Chapter 9, routines need to be taught. Posting a sign in the front of the classroom is not enough. It is vitally important that students go through the physical actions of a designated behavior.

9. Make yourself comfortable in using affective words such as *kindness, compassion, sympathy, gentleness, thoughtfulness, consideration, helpfulness, charity, understanding, empathy, support, care, and carefulness* in your conversations with youngsters ("Jeremy, t thank you for your thoughtfulness in helping Ramón [a new student] learn about our classroom procedures."). Such an emphasis stresses classroom values that are worthwhile and necessary in any classroom management plan.

10. Keep your classroom clean and tidy. Educational research, along with anecdotal records, confirm the fact that students are more calm and focused in an organized classroom than in unorganized one. So too, is a tidy classroom more inviting, less stressful, more purposeful, and less confusing. All those are clear factors in a well-managed instructional environment.

11. Offer opportunities for students to self-evaluate their personal behavior plans. You might want to engage the class in a group discussion: "Tell me some of the challenges you're having with this routine." or "How could we make this routine more memorable?"

12. Use modeling as much as possible. Establish yourself as a model for behavior. Take a few minutes at regular intervals throughout the week to model what it is you expect students to do (show them explicitly). By the same token, encourage children to model the procedures for their classmates at regular intervals, too.

Remember that classroom management is not an "add-on" to the classroom curriculum. It is an intrinsically essential component of every classroom curriculum. It is the jelly to your peanut butter, the cheese to your macaroni, the Hansel to your Gretel, the soap to your water, the salt to your pepper, the spaghetti to your meatballs, and the eggs to your bacon. In other words, they are inseparable. You need to work as hard on your classroom management plan as you do on your everyday curriculum. Simply put, you can't have one without the other!

QUOTABLE QUOTE

"Almost all surveys of teacher effectiveness report that classroom management skills are of primary importance in determining teaching success, whether it is measured by student learning or by ratings. A teacher who is grossly inadequate in classroom management skills is probably not going to accomplish much."

—Jere Brophy and Carolyn M. Evertson

Don'ts

1. Avoid manipulative language. This includes statements such as the following, "I like the way Stewart is sitting quietly at his desk." or "I like the way Jessica's group is working together." Comments such as those shift the responsibility for appropriate behavior from the child back to the teacher. If students are doing things because they are things the teacher likes, then they are practicing those behaviors for the wrong person. Even though this practice is commonly taught in many schools of education, there are several issues with these comments:

   - Although advised otherwise, there is a tendency to concentrate on a few "good" students. Teachers tend to use the same students over and over again as their "good examples." It's very challenging to ensure that every student is similarly recognized.

   - The students recognized as "good" are sometimes ostracized later by classmates. During recess or lunch they may become the focus of unwanted attention ("Oh, goody, goody. Here comes Miss Blankenship's favorite student. I guess we'll be sitting with 'The Queen' today.").

   - The recognition of one student at the expense of many indirectly punishes the others. Often, it's the tone of voice that signals a displeasure from the teacher about the behavior of many. In reality, it's a focus on their "misbehavior" rather than on what is correct about their behavior.

   - What is often ignored with these comments is the established procedures for classroom behavior—those expected routines that you want students to follow every time. By saying that you "like the way someone is sitting" at a certain point in time doesn't always reinforce what the actual behavior is. Specific words that define the behavior are infrequently used. It's like saying, "I like ice cream" —a statement that presumably incudes all possible flavors of ice cream. On the other hand, saying something like "I like mint chocolate chip ice cream on a sugar cone," is more specific and detailed. It's those details that are often missing from the 'I like" statements.

2. Don't use long explanations and extended rationales when talking with a student. The more you talk, the more you take control of the conversation as well as the student's behavior. You want the student to be responsible for her or his behavior; not you. Besides, long extended harangues about what's right and what's wrong quite often fall on "deaf ears."

3. By the same token, don't invite misbehaving students to explain their misbehavior ("Why did you throw your notebook at Jeremy?"). This is always a big mistake! The reasons are many: explanations are stressful for the student, they're often difficult to put into words, they foster resentment, they undermines your authority, and they will damage any relationship you might want to effect with a student. Student explanations are always uncomfortable and unproductive.

4. Don't reward students for good behavior ("If everyone completes their geography worksheet on time I'll pass around extra snacks."). Rewards promote extrinsic behavior and they turn that behavior into work. Students get the message that if they are "paid" for something, then that something is a form of work. As a result, students frequently develop a sense of entitlement ("The only time I'm going to do anything is when there is a reward at the end."). Rewards also foster a competitive atmosphere in the classroom, rather than a cooperative one.

5. Always remember: You are not their friend. Friends don't set up procedures and detail consequences. Teachers do. This is a difficult concept to wrestle with during your first year of teaching simply because you want to be a fun and friendly individual rather than a mean and dictatorial instructor. But, keep in mind that this is not an "either/or" situation. It's not black and white. You are establishing a code of conduct, a paradigm of expectations, and a blueprint for good behavior. That's what good teachers do. It has nothing to do with building friendships with your students and everything to do with what they are expected to do and the consequences of not doing it.

6. Don't hand out lots of reminders about how students should behave. Allow me to rephrase that: Don't hand out ANY reminders about how students should behave. When you remind students about proper behavior you are undercutting your classroom management plan. A reminder is simply a <u>suggestion</u> on how students should behave, it does not identify a procedure and its consequence. A litany of reminders sends the message that there are no consequences to inappropriate behavior, only suggestions. When you give lots of reminders you are assuming responsibility for classroom behavior—students can behave in whatever way they want since the teacher will only remind us on how to behave. Your classroom management plan is weakened significantly.

7. Don't use extrinsic control ("I like the way you are behaving today, Jason."); increase the amount of internal control ("Jason, how are you doing with our classroom procedure about lining up for specials?"). Classrooms in which intrinsic rewards are emphasized over extrinsic praise are classrooms in which students accept more responsibility for their own behavior. They become less teacher-dependent and more self-independent.

8. Sorry, but here's a string of "Don'ts" you want to eliminate or significantly reduce. These will do more to interfere with a positive classroom management plan than anything else.

   • Don't be a pessimistic teacher ("Well, Eric is always going to be a troublemaker."). Every student—EVERY STUDENT—deserves a "fair shake."

   • Don't let anger get in the way of your classroom management. When we're angry we don't think clearly, we often act irrationally, and we often damage personal relationships. None of those are appropriate for the classroom.

   • Don't be impatient. Good classroom management takes time; it doesn't happen overnight. Stick with it, stay the course, keep the pedal to the metal (please select your own idiom). Patience is a virtue—particularly in changing student behaviors.

- Don't get frustrated. Remember, you're starting something new and there may be a few "bumps" in the road.

- Don't be overly sensitive. Kids will say things they don't mean and kids will do things they're not ready to do. Kids will be uninformed, immature, and juvenile. Kids will be kids. Don't take it personally.

- Don't be easily irritated. Yes, some things students do will tick you off. But, if you let every little thing get under your skin, then you'll set yourself up for an early retirement.

Classroom management will always be a challenge. But, addressing it "head-on" (as opposed to dealing with it as it arises) will ultimately determine the behavior of your classroom. In short, good classroom management is a proactive enterprise.

Chapter 11

Preventing Classroom Problems

I am certain that, sometime in your educational career, you experienced one or more of the following classroom teachers. At the very least, you undoubtedly heard about these teachers in the hallways or cafeteria of your school.

- **Mr. Sarcastic:** "Hey, Luke, did you really pick out the colors in that shirt or did you just throw up all over yourself this morning?"

- **Miss Embarrass:** "Jennifer, if you're still having trouble with those big ugly pimples all over your face, I can recommend a good doctor for you."

- **Mrs. Overreaction:** "OK, you guys. Since you still don't know the rules about talking in class you're all going to have to write an extra five-page paper about good manners."

- **Mr. Bargainmaker:** "Listen, if you guys turn your essays in tomorrow on time I'll give everyone an extra twenty minutes of free time."

- **Mrs. Putdown:** "Hey, Krista, why don't you haul your big butt over here."

- **Miss Nag:** "How many times have I told you? How many times have I told you? If I've told you once, I've told you a million times, get your feet off the desk. Get your stupid feet off the desk! How many times do I have to tell you? How many times?"

- **Mr. Makefunofyou:** "Billy, it's clear to me that you are certainly not the sharpest knife in the drawer!"

- **Miss Confrontational:** "You'd better wipe that smirk off your face or I'm going to wipe it off for you."

- **Mrs. Screamer:** "Are you kidding me? ARE YOU KIDDING ME? **ARE YOU SERIOUSLY KIDDING ME?** ARE YOU TOTALLY KIDDING ME?"

- **Miss Pushover:** "Having a new cat in the house <u>is</u> pretty special. Why don't you take a couple more days to do your science project?"
- **Mr. Commander:** "In this room, it's <u>my</u> <u>way</u> or the <u>highway</u>!"

As evidenced in Chapters 5 and 9, classroom management is a major concern and a major issue with most classroom teachers. Maintaining open lines of communication, good behavior, adherence to established protocols, and respect for each other consumes a lot of thought and also a lot of time on the part of teachers—particularly new teachers, like you, who wish to establish a class climate that is both supportive and functional.

Those same teachers work hard to establish procedures and practices that ensure a smooth-running classroom—a classroom where learning is a high priority for each and every student and where every student has the opportunity to succeed. But, here's something to think about—something that often derails those good intensions.

Sometimes, it's the teacher who's the problem!

As you read through the list of personalities above, you probably recognized several of those individuals. Each of them, too, probably wanted a well-managed and well-run classroom with a minimum of disruptions and a maximum of academic achievement. But, their comments and communications with students often got in the way. In a sense, they were their own worst enemy. They shot down all their good intensions with flippant asides, a cavalier attitude, and off-the-cuff remarks. Everything they had established previously was being clearly eroded through their own misbehavior.

Sometimes, it's the teacher who's the problem.

Let's take a look at some of the biggest mistakes new teachers make. Many of these might be inadvertent or casual; others might occur in the heat of an emotional moment, or without clearly thinking through all the implications and consequences. I think it would be safe to say that these are behaviors you want to eliminate from your repertoire. In short, please don't be the problem!

- Sometimes, in an effort to be funny or "cool" we use sarcasm to make a point or to illustrate an issue. My personal experience has been that students, of any age, react negatively to sarcasm. It does nothing to promote a mutual respect between teacher and students.

- Embarrassing students never works—never ("Hey, Donna, can you speak up. I can't hear you through your lisp.")! Think about the last time you were embarrassed. You probably felt pretty bad. Double or triple that feeling and that's how your students, whose emotions are still developing, will feel, too.

- You give the concept of "work" a bad name when you use it as a form of punishment. Work should be its own reward. In other words, students need to understand that to make any progress work is involved. If work is a form of punishment, then they will never embrace it as a way to move forward. They will reject it every time.

- Never be confrontational ("Hey, wise guy, how 'bout you and me out in the hallway?"). That's simply a "power play" between two individuals. When you confront a student usually the message is, "I'm the one with all the power and you're the one without the power. I'm going to win every time." Confrontations never result in good relationships.

A Word of Advice

"Don't engage in a power struggle with any student. Ever. Most of us have had at least one teacher who used his/her power to force performance/conformity. Remember what that felt like? Exactly. Always create an environment of mutual respect."

—Steph Crumbling, current elementary teacher

- Sure you get angry, sure you get upset, and sure you get ticked off! But never take it out on kids. When students experience constant anger they also experience low self-esteem and low levels of confidence. Anger frequently destructs, it never constructs.

Always avoid mass punishment. The intent is that peer pressure will result in a change of behavior for a few select students. ("It's obvious that Robert and Edwardo can't behave, so we just won't celebrate Linda's birthday today."). Guess what? It never works.

- Nag, nag, nag. Oh, please, don't be a nagger! If you resort to nagging you're essentially saying to students that you are the one who is taking the responsibility for their behavior - simply because you will be the one to remind them over and over and over again. Nag, nag, nag…no, no, no!

- Don't make fun of kids ("Well, you know what they say about kids from the trailer park!"). Always build them up, never tear them down. Constantly making your students the object of your jokes will always backfire on you. Whatever respect you may have engendered will quickly disappear.

- Always be a positive role model. That means don't dress like your students, don't try to talk like your students, and certainly don't try to be "cool" by acting like your students. You should be a positive role model: acting professionally, talking professionally, and behaving professionally.

- Don't make bargains with students in order to get them to do something. Bargains send the message that everything in a classroom is negotiable—behavior is negotiable, homework is negotiable, assignments are negotiable, and expectations are negotiable. If you can't stick to your word, your students will take advantage of you every time.

- To gain control in the classroom, new teachers sometimes direct students to follow all their orders or directives ("It's my way or the highway!"). Being a commander works well in a military situation, but it seldom works well in a classroom. You are not a commander; rather you are a facilitator. Please make sure you know the difference.

- New teachers, in order to get on "the good side" of their students, often become a pushover ("Sure, we can extend that deadline for a few more days."). You want your students to be happy and cheerful, and to do that you might bend the rules a little, stretch the consequences somewhat, or overlook a few minor infractions. As soon as you open that door, however, you open up your classroom to all manner of potential infractions.

- Never allow students to harass, ridicule, or demean each other. You want to build a "community of learners," not an "asylum of misfits." When students tear each other down the chances for community quickly dissolve.

- Watch out for extreme negativity. This is when your comments to the class are couched in negative and/or highly authoritative terms. ("It's obvious that nobody knows what a theorem is. It looks like many of you will fail the test on Friday.")

- Avoid constant blaming. This is when one or two students are singled out and consistently blamed for every little infraction that may occur. ("Alright, who made that noise? Was it you again, LaToya?")

- A lack of instructional goals is always dangerous. Often teachers will engage students without a clearly defined or clearly understood (by students) goal for the lesson. ("Okay, is there anything anyone wants to talk about before we begin?")

- Short message: Yelling at your students never works. It always builds an impenetrable wall lined with bad feelings.

- Never ignore serious misbehavior. The reason you established the procedures and consequences of your classroom (see Chapter 9 again) is to curb that behavior in the first place. Ignoring it will certainly not make it go away. It will always be there festering.

- Sometimes new teachers, in order to make a point, deal with a single student at length. These teachers often disrupts their instructional rhythm by spending an inordinate amount of time on one student. ("I can't believe you are still talking, Sierra. I've told you over and over and over again about talking in class." Five minutes of lecture ensue.)

Be aware that the "problems" listed above may seem like simple violations of common sense. And, indeed, they are. But the truth of the matter is that these are some of the major "boo-boo's" new teachers often make in their first year of teaching. As you might imagine, these miscues will have a significant effect on your effectiveness as a teacher and your students' ultimate success in your classroom.

A Word of Advice

"Behavior management is the key to all of your success during your first year teaching. You may not always know what to do or what the best choice is to make, but when you have mutual respect, communication, rules and boundaries in your classroom, your children have the best possible chance to really learn and grow."

—Amanda Cuff, current elementary teacher

A Few Words on Discipline

You may have noticed that in this chapter, as well as the two preceding chapters (9 & 10), I have not used the word "discipline." That has been intentional. That's simply because a well-managed classroom does not have to resort to discipline. In fact, there is considerable research to support the notion that outstanding teachers are those who manage their classrooms; while ineffective teachers are those who discipline their students. Let's look at this concept in more detail.

As you will recall from Chapter 5, the establishment of classroom procedures should be one of the first things you need to do at the start of a new school year. Those procedures are at the heart of a well-established and well-maintained classroom management plan. They clearly delineate expectations of behavior as well as the consequences for anything that would violate those expectations.

Discipline, on the other hand, is an "after-the-fact" event: something that occurs AFTER a rule or standard has been violated. It does not establish good behavior up front, rather it punishes bad behavior as a concluding event. In other words, discipline temporarily stops misbehavior; it does not reinforce the good behavior every classroom needs. Or, as one colleague put it, "No learning takes place when you discipline, only a large interruption in that learning!"

Let's take a closer look at the differences between "Procedures" (as emphasized throughout this book) and "Discipline" (as emphasized in those "Brand X" books):

Procedures	Discipline
Established before the fact	Occurs after the fact
How things are done	How students behave
No penalties or rewards	Penalties and rewards
Intrinsic	Extrinsic
Student self-responsibility	Teacher directed
Sets standards for appropriate behavior	Temporarily stops misbehavior
Control from inside	Control from outside
Statements of student expectation	Statements of condemnation
Productive learning time	Wasted learning time
Increases time-on-task time	Decreases time-on-task time
How the classroom is organized	How students should comply

In your review of the chart above you will undoubtedly see that discipline is reactionary—that is, it is a reaction to something (usually negative) that a student has done. Procedures, on the other hand, provide everyone in a classroom with standards of expected behavior long before any possible disruption of that behavior. With procedures, there are no assumptions that students intuitively "know how to behave." The guidelines and standards are clearly spelled out and clearly delineated. Everybody knows what is to be done from <u>Day One</u>.

Students who have been in school for any length of time come into a new classroom with certain expectations and certain assumptions. Here are some common ones:

- The teacher makes the rules.
- Kids follow the rules.
- Kids will break the rules.
- The teacher will discipline the kids.

Look again at those statements and you'll notice they are all teacher-centered. If the kids do things right, everything's OK with the teacher. If the kids do things wrong, the teacher punishes those kids. The simple expectation is that since that's the way it has always been done, then that's the way it will continue to be done. As in their past experiences, it is the teacher who is doing all the "heavy lifting." Thus, according to many students, teacher discipline (as opposed to self-discipline) is how a classroom is run.

What a Great Idea!

Here's a most impressive intervention that will help you deal with difficult students. Known as the *Two-by-Ten* strategy, it was developed by former teacher and researcher Raymond Wlodkowski and has proven to be extremely successful by a plethora of teachers. With this strategy, a teacher focuses on her or his most difficult student. For two minutes each day, ten days in a row, the teacher and the student have a personal conversation about anything in which the student is interested (G-rated, of course). What Wlodkowski discovered was an 85% improvement in that student's behavior. In addition, he also discovered that the behavior of all the other students in the class improves as well.

The method gets rave reviews from classroom teachers from coast to coast. That's simply because students who act out are usually calling out for attention. Typically, we give them the attention they seek, but it's usually negative (e.g. discipline, punishment, etc.). On the other hand, the positive and personal attention of the Two-by-Ten strategy helps them build a strong supportive connection with an adult authority figure. What often results, according to many teachers, is that that student now becomes an ally in the class—a promoter of the invitational classroom so necessary to academic success.

It's simple:

- One student
- Two minutes a day.
- Ten days in a row.

<u>Flight Information</u>

If you have flown commercial airlines, you know that just before a plane takes off one of the flight attendants comes on the intercom system and gives a speech similar to the following:

We'll be taking off momentarily, so please make sure your carryon baggage is stowed securely, either in an overhead compartment or under the seat in front of you. Mobile phones and other electronic devices should be turned off. There are six exits on this plane: three doors, on each side. All exits are clearly marked with an exit sign. Please t a k e the time to find the exit nearest you.

If you're seated in an exit row, please review the responsibilities for emergency exit seating, on the back of the safety information card which is in your seat pocket. If you are unable, or prefer not to do this, please let us know, and we will be happy to find you another seat. If there is a loss of cabin pressure, the panels above your seat will open, and oxygen masks will drop down. If this happens, place the mask over your nose and mouth, and adjust it as necessary. Be sure to adjust your own mask before helping others.

In the event of a water landing, life vests are under your seat. Whenever the seat belt sign is on, please make sure your seat belt is fastened. Smoking is not allowed on our flights, and federal law prohibits tampering with, disabling, or destroying a smoke detector. Thank you for your attention. We hope you enjoy your flight.

People often wonder why that speech is given time and time again on each and every flight. People who fly a lot (e.g. business people) frequently complain that they hear that speech over and over again. They know what the rules are, why do they have to listen to that stupid speech every time they get on an airplane.

The reason is simple. Practice. Most people don't fly every single day. They may fly a couple of times during the year or just once or twice in their lifetimes. But the procedures for flying never vary; they are always the same. By going over the "expectations for behavior" prior to each flight the flight attendants ensure that everyone is getting consistent information and consistent practice. Everyone on the plane knows what is expected of them and they are given practice in knowing those expectations. Those review sessions ensure that everyone knows what to do in the event of a loss of cabin pressure, how to fasten their seat belt[1]

Sound familiar?

I know it's been said before, but it's so critical to the success of your classroom management plan: establish basic procedures and practice those procedures frequently. An effective classroom management plan is not based on what teachers do to stop misbehavior, but rather on how problems are prevented ahead of time. If there was an airplane emergency, you certainly wouldn't hear the flight attendants yelling at passengers, "If we told you once, we've told you a thousand times, you're supposed to LIFT UP on the buckle to get out of your damn seat. Weren't you listening to us when we told you earlier? Are you stupid or what? Now, let's go over this again." Quite obviously, that would be an absolute waste of time—a waste of precious seconds that might be critical to the safety of all the passengers. But, that's what often happens in many classrooms: a waste of precious instructional time to discipline students. According to research from several observers, teachers in a typical classroom lose about 50 percent of their teaching time because of students' disruptive behavior and the inevitable discipline that follows. In devoting 50 percent of our instructional time to matters of discipline, that means we only have about 50 percent of our instructional time to devote to instructional matters. In a way, we're only giving our students half of their education. That's simply unacceptable!

Suggested Procedures

Every classroom is different and the dynamics between classrooms vary tremendously. That said, here are a few suggested procedures you

---

1. People often complain that after years of buckling the seat belt in their car, they still have to endure instructions on how to fasten a seat belt in an airplane. "That's silly," they often say, "Everybody knows how a seat belt works!" But, the next time you get on an airplane take a closer look at the seat belt. You'll notice that it's designed completely different than the one in your car. On an airplane seat belt you must lift up the buckle to release it; in a car you must press a button or a catch device. In an airplane emergency, knowing how to get out of your seat quickly and safely (often in seconds) could be critical to your survival. That's why you're taught the procedures for fastening and releasing an airplane seat belt (as opposed to your car seat belt) every time you take a flight. By the way, flight attendants are trained on how to get everybody off a completely full airplane in 90 seconds or less. That's right—90 seconds!

might want to consider for your classroom. This is certainly not meant as an absolute list; don't feel pressured to include every one of these in your classroom management plan. Consider these as examples—as possibilities—for you to consider as you begin the process of building a positive classroom environment. Pick and choose from these examples and consider drafting your own procedures in light of your own philosophy and comfort level.

Classroom Procedures

1. Respect everyone and everything around you.
2. Speak kindly.
3. Be helpful and responsible
4. Take care of classroom and school property
5. Try your hardest each and every day

Classroom Procedures

1. Always do your best
2. Use kind words and actions
3. Always have homework and supplies
4. Follow dress code policy
5. Keep hands, feet, and objects to yourself

Classroom Procedures

1. Follow directions the first time given
2. Clean up after yourself
3. Keep your eyes and ears on the speaker
4. Be respectful to one another
5. Always do your best

Classroom Procedures

1. Be on time for class

2. Be prepared to work

3. Treat everyone and their property with respect

4. Keep your work neat and organized

5. Be a good listener

Classroom management is not about getting kids to do what you want them to do. That's what dictators do, and you're not a dictator. Classroom management is providing an environment in which positive teaching and positive learning can occur simultaneously. Classroom management is not control from the outside; it's order from within.

What a Great Idea!

Teachers often make the mistake of using "stop" messages rather than a "start" message. For example, "Stop talking. We need to get started." A better message is "Get out your math books, and turn to page 44." The effect is tremendous. It establishes a productive, businesslike tone for the lesson. The focus is not on the (negative) behavior, but the importance of the lesson.

Here's the final word: you have to teach, and have your students practice, your expectations for behavior. Perhaps the worst thing we can do as educators is to <u>expect</u> that our students will know how to behave in a classroom environment. Just because we post a set of rules on the wall of the classroom doesn't mean that students will follow them. By the same token, just because we put someone in an airplane seat doesn't mean she or he will know how to operate the seat belt buckle. They must be taught. And, they must practice. And, so it is with classroom management.

Chapter 12

<u>Time Management</u>

I always chuckle to myself when people tell me that teachers have it easy. Oh, if they only knew! Grading papers after school and on weekends, volunteering to coach various athletic or academic teams, coming in early to set up a special lesson, and spending holidays and vacations doing research or looking for new teaching ideas are all part and parcel of the life of a teacher. On top of that, you can add all the daily interruptions, distractions, unanticipated problems, or visitors and the myriad decisions that must be made. Moreover, there's convincing research that the average classroom teacher will make more than 1,500 educational decisions every school day. In an average six-hour school day, that's more than four decisions every minute.

It's no wonder many teachers feel stretched to their limit by the end of the day.

Have you ever said, "There just isn't enough time," or "I wish I had more time!" Often, it seems as though there aren't enough hours in the day to do all the tasks on our to-do lists. We often run out of time whenever we tackle a new chore or duty. Time, or the lack of time, seems to be the master of our lives. However, I've learned that I can take control of my time, instead of time taking control of me. In this chapter, I'll show you some ways you can take charge of your time. As a result, you'll get more done, the quality of your work will improve, and you'll have more time to attend sporting events and dinner parties.

Time Robbers

What steals your time? Or what consumes your time so you're out of time for other tasks and duties? In conversations with teachers at all levels and in all types of schools, I have found that they most often cited the following chores, duties, and assignments:

- Classroom discipline
- Taking attendance

- Managing student behavior
- Non-instructional activities
- Visitors
- Noises and distractions
- Distributing and collecting papers
- Telephone calls
- PA announcements
- Unplanned interruptions
- Talking
- Paperwork and clerical tasks
- Bus duty, hall duty, or cafeteria duty
- Grading and record keeping

What's interesting about this list is that fact that a significant number of educational research studies have confirmed that more than half of a typical school day is consumed by non-instructional matters.

Think about this: time is about control. When you allow time to control you, you never have enough of it. On the other hand, when you control your own time, you can allocate your time available to complete tasks and duties. For example, when your friendly author person (that's me) was asked to write this book, I was quite excited. Then, I realized I had to construct twenty-two exciting, dynamic, informative and very interesting chapters filled with wisdom and lots of friendly advice (in addition to holding down a full-time teaching position). Was I disheartened? No, because after writing more than 150 books, I've learned that the best way to write a multi-chapter book is to break it into chunks.

By dividing an assignment (such as a book project) into smaller pieces, it becomes more manageable. I didn't look at this book as a twenty-two-chapter project; rather I looked at it as a series of magazine articles. Each "article" would be between twelve to fourteen single-spaced manuscript pages long; would have about 4,300 words, and would go through approximately twelve to fourteen drafts. I pictured this project as a collection of short articles, rather than an overwhelming 95,000 word book.

"Chunking" a task or assignment into smaller pieces helps make the overall assignment more manageable. You can do as I do: after I finished each "article" for this book, I checked it off a master list. As I went along, I saw more and more check marks on my list. That was a positive stimulus and a positive incentive. Imagine how I would have felt if I just listed the entire book on my "To Do" list. It never would have been checked off until the end, and I might have become weighted down by the enormity of the project.

Here are some tips you can use for managing any major project:

- Divide the project into smaller, more manageable chunks (lessons instead of a whole unit; paragraphs instead of a whole report; columns instead of a whole spreadsheet).

- Record each individual chunk separately on a list.

- Focus on completing one chunk at a time.

- Check off each individual chunk as you complete it; then move on to the next chunk.

- Look at how rapidly your check marks accumulate on your list, and use that as motivation to keep going.

- Give yourself a reward for the completion of two, three, or five chunks (I reward myself with macadamia nut cookies for every three chapters, or "articles", I write).

A Word of Advice

"You need to go slow in order to go fast. Take your time setting and securing clear expectations, procedures and rotations. Once those are in place, then you're ready to dive into your standards. Take your time!"

—Dawn Ramos, current elementary teacher

<u>Just Say "No"!</u>

Teachers are special people. We love working with others - students, parents, colleagues, and maybe even our administrators. By our very nature, we are "people persons." We like to go out of our way to help others and especially to help our students succeed. But as teachers, we have a tendency to say "Yes" too many times. We volunteer for too many projects; we get on too many committees; we get involved in the lessons or units of our colleagues; or we willingly take on duties simply because somebody asked us to.

Saying "No" may be one of the most difficult things you do as a classroom teacher. You are in a helping profession, and saying "No" simply goes against your philosophy or the reasons why you decided to become a teacher. Even after considerably more than four decades of teaching, I still find it challenging and difficult to say "No" to another committee, volunteer group, or special request from a colleague ("It will only be for a few days—honest!"). You see, teachers tend to be workaholics—it's the nature of the job. As a result, you're likely to be confronted with lots of requests and lots of "invitations." Use these ideas for saying "No" with style and grace:

- "I'd really like to, but I'm overcommitted right now and don't think I'd be able to do it justice."
- "Thanks for asking, but I really need to spend some more quality time with my children , my spouse, my friends, myself."
- "I appreciate your confidence in me, but I have other tasks that demand a lot of my time."
- "I have a lot of assignments already on my calendar. Can I get back to you at a later time?"
- "I know how important it is to you, but I need to give myself some 'recoup' time now."
- "No thank you. I'm not ready to take on that additional responsibility just yet."

<u>Share the Load</u>

One of the best ways you can increase the amount of time available to you in your classroom is to share the responsibility of certain (often daily or repetitive) tasks with your students. Give your students classroom responsibilities and decision-making power, and you'll increase your available time. Numerous tasks, chores, and assignments must be accomplished every day. Most teachers do these out of habit or because they see them as "teacher jobs" or responsibilities. Here are just a few:

- Taking attendance
- Taking lunch count
- Handling homework
- Handling late-arriving students
- Handling classroom visitors (often unannounced)
- Beginning the day
- Obtaining instructional materials (textbooks)
- Handling comings and goings
- Assigning seating charts
- Transitions from one activity to another
- Responding to requests for assistance

Yes, you have a lot of things to do every day in your classroom. How can you get a grip on it all? The answer: turn some of those responsibilities over to your students. "But my students are too young, too old, too dependent, too…," you wail. Not to worry; any child can benefit from taking on classroom responsibilities. The ultimate benefit will be more time for teaching and more time for learning. The following suggestions are for saving time (and your sanity); feel free to modify and adapt them to other daily duties and chores in your classroom:

- When students arrive in the morning, have each student remove a clothespin with his name printed on it from a special coffee can. Then she/he clips his clothespin to one of two strings strung across a bulletin board. One string is labeled "Packers," the other string is labeled "Buyers." You quickly have a count of who brought their lunch and who is buying it in the cafeteria.
- Purchase small Styrofoam cubes from a local hobby store. Glue a 1 X 1-inch square of red paper to a toothpick, then stick the toothpick into a cube. Make enough for all your students, and

distribute them to the students. When a student needs assistance with an assignment or doesn't understand a task, she or he can pull the flag out of his or her desk and place it on the desktop. By glancing around the room frequently, you can determine who needs individual help. Students don't need to call out and disrupt the flow of instruction.

- Place all your materials and supplies in properly labeled drawers, cubbies, cabinets, compartments, and storage bins. Assign the task of "materials engineer" to two students each week on a rotating basis. Those students are responsible for obtaining the necessary materials for selected assignments, experiments, or other instructional tasks to be completed by a small group or the entire class.

- In some classrooms, there are many tasks to accomplish in the morning (hang up jackets, put notebook inside desk, use the attendance chart, put homework in a basket, get a book, etc.). I found it advantageous, particularly at the beginning of the school year, to make a list of all those duties. I duplicated the list onto sheets of card stock (65-pound paper) and laminated them. I taped one of these cards in the upper right corner of each student's desk. When a student came in, she or he would use a crayon or wax pencil to check off each item as it was completed. Later in the day, we wiped off the cards so they were ready for the next day.

- Glue a picture of a boy on one sheet of card stock and a picture of a girl on another sheet. Laminate both sheets, and hang them by a string on hooks in the back of the classroom. When a student needs to use the restroom, she or he goes to the back of the room, turns over the appropriate card, and leaves. Upon returning to the classroom, the student flips the card back to the picture side. You can continue teaching without any unnecessary interruptions.

- Instead of using paper passes for students to leave and use the restroom, make a large block of wood for the restroom pass. Make the block large enough so it won't fit inside a student's pocket. Paint it a special color, and print your name in large letters along the side. Hang it by a chain in the back of the classroom. Provide a single block rather than two separate blocks (only one student out of the room at a time).

• Pencil sharpeners can be a frequent interruption in any classroom. Rather than have students use the pencil sharpener during the day or during a lesson, assign one student each week as the "tool master." That student is responsible for sharpening a collection of pencils at the beginning of the day and placing them in a special container (an empty coffee can, a shoebox, etc.). Students who need a pencil can obtain them from the container on their own.

• Obtain colored baskets or trays from your local office supply store. Designate these as homework bins for your students by color:

  ○ Red: Place completed homework here.

  ○ Green: Get your homework assignment from here.

  ○ Blue: Obtain homework assignments that were given out when you were absent from this bin.

  ○ Yellow: Place uncompleted homework here. (This can alert you to students who did not understand the assignment, had difficulty completing it, or simply chose not to do it.)

Creating these routines and procedures will mean little unless you take the time to teach or train your students in how to use them. Clearly explain a routine to students and provide sufficient opportunities for students to practice it under your supervision (you might need to model some routines before encouraging students to practice them). This training time early in the school year will save you countless hours during the remainder of the year.

A Word of Advice

"The hardest part of managing time in the first year is all the 'stuff' they never told you in college. This includes, but is not limited to, assemblies, nurse pull outs, safety drills, student melt-downs and fights, technology failures, substitutes that need help, and many other types of emergencies."

—Donna Cherry, current secondary teacher

The Paperwork Conspiracy

What's the number-one time management problem for most teachers? You guessed it: dealing with paperwork. That includes all the reports, tests, attendance forms, graphs, letters, memos, mail, announcements, materials, and requests that consume not only our time but our desk space as well. One efficiency expert estimated that of all the pieces of paper that go into our filing cabinets every year, fully 95 percent of it will never come out again; or only come out to go into the trash can! It's obvious we're "paper packrats." We hate to throw away anything, and we hoard paper, save paper, move paper from one place (on our desks) to another and file, catalog, and store paper until the proverbial molehill becomes an actual mountain.

Are you, like me, constantly buried under mountains of forms? Do you spend most of your day shuffling, arranging, or filing endless sheets of paper? Well, welcome to the club! There are ways of gaining control over the "Mt. Everest" of paperwork you must deal with every day. Try these suggestions:

- Use colored file folders to file papers. Select a different color for each subject or for each period of the day.

- Business management experts coach you to handle a piece of paper only once. It's tough to follow, particularly for teachers, but try to keep it in mind the next time you stuff your briefcase with papers.

- Like most teachers, you probably have lots of books. These may be professional books, old textbooks, or resource books. If you haven't looked at a book in two years, donate it to your local library or community fund drive.

- Designate one day every month (for example, the third Tuesday of the month) as "filing day." Use it to file all the papers that have accumulated on your desk during the month.

- Designate one day every six months as "purging day." Use it to get rid of all the files and papers you haven't used in the last twelve months.

- Use your computer as a filing system. Use your word processing program to organize frequently used forms, exams, and records.

- Designate a special file drawer for each subject you teach. Organize it with colored files:

  o Red: lesson plans

  o Green: tests, quizzes, and exams

  o Blue: handouts and worksheets

  o Yellow: transparencies and PowerPoint disks

  o Black: unit plans

  o Gray: supplemental resources and websites

  o Purchase two file baskets from a local office supply store. Label one "To and from the School Office"; the other "To and from Home." Place them on your desk, and keep the papers you typically handle moving in and out of them daily.

Maximize Your Instructional Time

As a classroom teacher, you want to engage your students in productive learning time. This is time when your students are engaged in meaningful and appropriate work. The more productive learning time you have, the more your students will learn. The challenge, of course, is in creating a classroom that maximizes that time. Several teachers point to four strategies that increase students' productive learning time:

1. Keep things flowing.

2. Teach transitions.

3. Be clear; be close.

4.   Get a handle on "pull-outs."

Let's take a look at each.

1. Keep Things Flowing

Flow refers to the way in which learning activities move smoothly and briskly. There's no stop-and-start rhythm to the class, but rather one activity leads naturally into another activity. You can maintain that flow through an awareness of the following:

- Ignore minor behaviors that have nothing to do with the lesson. For example, a student is twisting a strand of her hair. It's not necessary to stop the lesson and point out that behavior to the student. Move over to the student, put a hand on her back, nod, and keep the lesson going.

- Some teachers jump back and forth between activities. They start one activity or lesson, go back and make a comment about a previous lesson or activity, and then return to the new activity. Keep your lessons flowing in a forward direction.

- Often teachers will continue to explain a point or concept until, as students would say, "It's been beaten into the ground." The trick is to know when students understand and then stop at that point.

2. Teach Transitions

Transitions are those times during the day when you move from one activity to the next. Because students work at different paces and different levels, some may be able to make the transitions faster than others. Thus, transition time often leaves openings for misbehavior and disruptions. To avoid this, consider the following:

- Let students know when (in two minutes, for example) an activity will end: "We'll have a whole-class review of triangles in two minutes."

- Let students know what they can expect in any subsequent or follow-up activity: "After lunch, we're going to continue looking at the structure of onion cells."

- Be sure your lessons have clear beginnings and endings. Review the lesson objectives before the lesson begins and again at the conclusion of the lesson. Verbal cues are also valuable: "It's time for science to begin. I hope you're ready for the adventure."

- Establish clearly outlined routines for transition times. Provide opportunities for students to practice those routines: "When you come in, be sure you complete your 'Fabulous Five' chores before you sit down."

3. Be Clear, Be Close

Students achieve when they know exactly what is expected of them. Incomplete assignments are often the result of incomplete directions. As a result, time is wasted. It's equally important that students know you are available at all times. The amount of learning that takes place in a classroom is often related to the distance you maintain with your students. Time is saved when you are readily available. Here are two considerations for you:

- Always provide clear, precise, and thorough directions to any assignment. If students are asking lots of questions about what they're supposed to do, the directions were not clear and precise.

- Closely monitor student progress by circulating throughout the room and maintaining a physical presence with the students. Your desk should just be a place to put papers, not a sanctuary from students.

4. Get a Handle on Pull-Outs

Pull-outs are those students who must leave the classroom and may include students who have appointments with the guidance counselor, lessons with the reading specialist or music teacher, or instruction for gifted students. With so many comings and goings, it's often difficult to keep track of everyone, much less teach a complete lesson to every student. Here are some suggestions:

- Laminate a personal schedule for each pull-out student and tape it to the corner of her or his desk. Teach the student how to exit the classroom with no disruption to the class. Make each student responsible for her or his own schedule. This is not something you have to monitor all the time.

- Work closely with the teachers your students are leaving class to see. Try to arrive at a schedule that will cause the least disruption to your classroom.

- Check with the administration or other teachers about any procedures for students needing to make up missed classroom work. Initiate a "study buddy" program in your classroom so that each time a student leaves, she or he has a buddy who is responsible for obtaining the necessary information and passing it along. If feasible, provide time in class for this exchange to take place.

Remember, time can be your ally or your enemy. It's all in how you look at it. Teach your students how to use it wisely, and master the ideas in this chapter. You'll be more in control of your classroom…and your life.

Part IV

◆

Effective
Classroom Instruction

Chapter 13

<u>Creating Successful Lessons</u>

If you were taking a cross-country drive you would, most likely, consult a map or the GPS on your cell phone before starting out. You'd want to know some of the routes you would be taking, some of the sites you might see, and some of the places you might want to spend the night during this long journey. In other words, you'd want to do some advance planning before setting out on the road (no sense getting lost half-way there).

Well, a lesson plan is like a roadmap (or a pedagogical Siri, if you will) for teachers. It is a way to carve out what you want your students to learn, how you'll help them learn the material, and how you'll know if they actually learned that material. In essence, lesson plans exist for several reasons:

- To ensure that students are taught what they need to know (as established by the school, the district, or the state)

- To prepare for and attend to individual differences between and among students

- To ensure effective and efficient teaching so classroom time is used appropriately

- To serve as a way for teachers to evaluate their teaching effectiveness

By the same token, a well-constructed lesson plan must answer three critical questions:

- What do you want students to learn?

- How will you teach it?

- How will you know if students learned what you taught?

So, let's take a look at what's involved!

A Plan of Action

First, let's examine the more traditional method of designing lesson plans. In the old days (like when I started teaching) we designed lessons around a bunch of activities, taught those activities, and prayed that students learned something along the way. It was like being out on a stormy sea in a small boat and hoping that, at some point, you would be able to eventually reach the shore safely.

Now we have a new way of thinking about lesson plan design. Known as "Backward Design" it reverses traditional thinking and begins at the opposite end of the planning process: the destination. In contrast to more traditional lesson plans, in "backward designed" lessons the teacher starts with goals, creates or plans out assessments, and finally constructs the lesson.

The idea in backward design is to teach toward the "end point" or learning goals. This ensures that the content taught is focused and organized. The teacher is able to focus on a) addressing what the students need to learn, b) what data can be collected to show that the students have learned the desired outcomes (or learning standards), and c) how to ensure the students will learn (through relevant activities and methodologies).

Here are the three main stages of backward design:

1. Identify desired results

   - What should students know, understand, and be able to do?

   - What standards should students master?

   - What are the "big ideas" (principles, theories, concepts, points of view, or themes)?

2. Determine acceptable evidence

   - What will you accept as evidence that student understanding took place?

   - What would be the most effective assessment methods?

3. Plan learning experiences and instruction

   - How can I link background knowledge with content knowledge?

- What are the types of questions I need to ask?
- What activities or exercises will equip students with the needed knowledge and skills?
- What methodologies should I employ?
- What materials and resources are best suited to accomplish these goals?
- How will I give students a sense of "ownership" in what they're learning?
- How will students become more responsible learners?
- How can I relate concepts to the "real world" of students' lives?

Notice that in backward design you will be addressing the specifics of instructional planning—choices about teaching methods, sequence of a lesson, and resource materials—*after* identifying the desired results and assessments. As a result, you will have a clear goal in front of you, which allows you to focus your planning and teaching in the direction of your ultimate destination.

What's the Plan, Stan?

OK, now we have the basics of lesson planning. Let's put all that into a workable and functional structure that keeps us organized and on target. What follows is an organizational format you can easily use to plan your lessons—any lessons. All you need do is to fill in each of the designated areas and when completed, you will have an easy-to-use lesson plan for any classroom. After this outline, I've provided you with the specifics of each of the plan's essential ingredients.

Lesson Plan Outline

Lesson Topic: _____

Date: _____

1. Identify Desired Results

   Standards:

Ultimate Goal(s):

Specific Lesson Objectives:

2. <u>Determine Acceptable Evidence</u>

   Assessment of Prior Knowledge:

   Assessments (throughout the lesson):

3. <u>Plan Learning Experiences and Instruction</u>

   Motivational Opening:

   Direct Instruction + Methods:

   Student Activities + Strategies:

   Alternative Activities:

   Closure:

   Resources:

   Homework:

Student Reflection (optional):

Teacher Reflection:

1. Identify Desired Results

Standards: Check out national, state, or district guidelines regarding the content you are expected to address. Generally speaking, standards describe what students should know and be able to do. Academic or content standards provide a clear description of the knowledge and skills students should be developing through instruction in specific content (or academic) areas. Performance standards describe what it will take for a student to demonstrate mastery of a standard (sometimes called benchmarks).

Ultimate Goal(s): In this section you will state the specific goal you are aiming for. What should students know, understand, and be able to do? What is worthy of understanding? What endearing understandings are desired? Here are two examples: a) "Students will use an understanding of phonemic awareness to read rhyming words." b) "Students will be able to design a medieval castle based on an understanding of the architecture of the Middle Ages."

Specific Lesson Objectives: Your lesson plan's objectives describes what the students will be able to do upon completion of the instructional experience. To take the analogy one step further, objectives are what drive a lesson. They power it forward. Most important, everything you do in a lesson must be tied to one or more objectives. Every activity, every instructional devise, every teaching resource, and every means of evaluation and assessment must be linked to the lesson's objective(s).

A Word of Advice

"Having objectives posted for the children to see in the classroom sets the stage for instruction throughout the day. Post them each day. It not only provides the students with insight as to what they will learn each day, but they will also help keep you in check."

—Morgan Lanzalotti, current elementary teacher

2. Determine Acceptable Evidence

Assessment of prior knowledge: Students bring a certain amount of background knowledge or prior experiences to any lesson. Use this opportunity to find out what students know before beginning any lesson. Don't make the mistake of assuming what students know. Take the time to assess their background knowledge, and you'll be rewarded with more successful lessons. For example, just because students studied American history in elementary school, had a basic history course in middle school, and are now in your high school history class, don't assume they know all there is to know about American history. Take the time to find out. Bottom line: Always know what your students know!

Assessments (throughout the lesson): The bottom line of assessments is this: what do you need to know about your students, and when do you need to know it? The well-designed lesson will provide opportunities for both you and your students to evaluate progress within the lesson. Any and all assessment tools must be designed and placed within a lesson to determine if your students are mastering the objectives or are in the process of learning those objectives.

3. Plan Learning Experiences and Instruction

Motivational Opening: This stage of a lesson is critical! It's how you stimulate students' interest in a topic or subject. It may involve asking students a thought-provoking question such as, "How would you like to sleep for four months every year?" or "Did you know we can measure the height of any tree on the playground without climbing it?" Other attention-gaining devises can include models, maps, a piece of apparatus, or a demonstration. It is important that each and every lesson include some method to stimulate students' interests.

Direct Instruction + Methods: Not only is it important to give some thought as to what you're going to teach, it is equally significant that you consider the methods of presentation as well. I'm sure you've been in a class where the only method of instruction was dry, stale lectures. You undoubtedly found the class boring and wearying. The same fate awaits your students if you provide them with an overabundance of one type of teaching methodology to the exclusion of others (see Chapter 14).

Student Activities + Strategies: This is the heart of any lesson—that portion where you teach and where students learn. This is where students obtain valuable information, manipulate data, and engage in active discovery through total involvement. Include some of the following elements in this stage: problem-solving, creative thinking, hands-on activities, and student engagement.

Alternative Activities: As you'll discover in Chapter 17, you will undoubtedly have a wide variety of students who will exhibit various talents, skills, emotions, physical and mental attributes, languages, and perceptions. You'll need to make accommodations or create specialized learning opportunities for some of those students. You should include any special materials, procedures, or techniques in this section of a lesson plan.

Closure: Effective public speakers always follow three essential rules of a good presentation:

- Tell the audience what you're going to tell them.
- Tell them.
- Tell them what you've told them.

Those same rules are important in the well-designed lesson, too. It's essential that you incorporate some sort of closure into the lesson. This might mean a few minutes at the end of the lesson during which you or your students summarize some of the significant points, an activity in which students share perceptions with each other, or a time during which students recall their positive or negative perceptions of a lesson.

Resources: In this section of your lesson plan, you need to list all the materials and resources you want to use in teaching the lesson. You will undoubtedly discover that your biggest decision when planning your lesson is deciding which resources to use from the hundreds available. Effective lessons combine several different resources to provide for a variety of learning (and teaching) opportunities.

Homework: Homework assignments should be a natural extension of any lesson you teach. They are not "add-ons," but rather an authentic opportunity to practice and incorporate the skills and procedures of a designated lesson. At all costs, you'll want to stay away from "busy-work" assignments, those that simply take up valuable time without reinforcing anything (see Chapter 16).

Student Reflection: Let students (at any age) know that they have an active role and certain responsibilities in any designated lesson. Invite them to share some feedback and insights about what went on in the classroom and you will be expanding the possibilities for an invitational classroom.

Teacher Reflection: As you write lessons, include a brief section at the end that allows you to self-evaluate. This will be important when and if you decide to teach the lesson again. It will also provide you with some important insights relative to your perceived level of success. You might consider some of these self-evaluative questions:

- "How was my pacing?"
- "Did students understand the content?"
- "Did students understand the important concepts?"
- "Did I use my time appropriately?"
- "What changes should I make the next time I teach this lesson?"
- "Were students engaged and involved?"
- "What new activities or procedures could I include?"
- "Did I present the lesson well?"

Good lesson planning is an evolutionary process - one learned through lots of practice and lots of repetition. There will be inevitable bumps and hiccups along the way as you begin drafting your own lessons. And, you know what, that's OK. None of us crafted perfect lesson plans the first few times we did them. But we learned! We learned from our students, from our colleagues, and from the numerous teacher resources available to us (now, more than ever, with the resources available on the internet). And, so will you! Stay with the process and you'll see some incredible magic taking place in your classroom.

What a Great Idea!

<u>Student Reflection Questions for the Conclusion of a Lesson</u>

1. What is an unanswered question you have about today's lesson?

2. How could you expand your learning about this concept?

3. Why do you think the instructor spent time on this concept?

4. What was the most interesting part of this lesson?

5. What is something that still challenges you?

6. What is one thing you learned today?

7. Please provide a brief summary of today's lesson.

8. What was the most important thing you learned today?

9. What was the key insight that emerged for you today?

10. What part of today's lesson needs more explanation?

11. Why do you think this lesson/issue/concept is important?

QUOTABLE QUOTE

"Learning has nothing to do with what the teacher covers; learning has to do with what the student accomplishes."

—Harry K. Wong

What a Great Idea!

There are scores of online sites that offer a wealth of prepared lesson plans for teachers in grades K-12. All content areas and all grade levels are addressed on these sites, allowing you to tap into the collective wisdom of thousands of teachers all across the country. While it would be impossible for me to list all the sites here, the ones included below will get you started on an incredible journey of discovery. (Please note: At the time of the publication of this book, all these sites were active. Be aware that the ever-evolving nature of the internet may affect this listing.)

A to Z Teacher Stuff (www.atozteacherstuff.com)

Discovery Education (www.discoveryeducation.com)

ForLessonPlans (www.forlessonplans.com)

Lesson Plans Page (http://lessonplanspage.com)

Lesson Planet (www.lessonplanet.com)

Lessonplans.com (www.lessonplans.com)

Share My Lesson (www.sharemylesson.com)

Teacher Network (http://teachersnetwork.org)

Good lesson planning is an evolutionary process - one learned through lots of practice and lots of repetition. There will be inevitable bumps and hiccups along the way as you begin drafting your own lessons. And, you know what, that's OK. None of us crafted perfect lesson plans the first few times we did them. But we learned! We learned from our students, from our colleagues, and from the numerous teacher resources available to us (now, more than ever, with the resources available on the internet). And, so will you! Stay with the process and you'll see some incredible magic taking place in your classroom.

What a Great Idea!

If you'd like some additional information about Backward Design, I highly recommend the following resources:

Understanding by Design (2nd Ed.) by Grant Wiggins & Jay McTighe

Backwards Planning - Building Enduring Understanding Through Instructional Design - Grades K-12 by Harriet Isecke

Chapter 14

It's All About the Methods

It's important to give some thought as to what you are going to teach students; however, you must consider the methods of your presentation as well. You have undoubtedly been in a class that consisted of nothing more than dry, stale lectures. Chances are you found the class less than intellectually stimulating. The same fate awaits your students if you concentrate on one type of teaching methodology (only lectures, for example) to the exclusion of others.

The following charts list a wide variety of lesson methodologies appropriate for the presentation of material. Notice how these teaching methods move from Least Impact (Knowledge) to Greatest Impact (Synthesis).

KNOWLEDGE

How do you present basic information to your students? It makes no difference whether you're sharing consonant digraphs with your first-grade students or differential calculus with your twelfth-grade students; you must teach them some basic information. Knowledge is the basic information of a subject; the facts and data of a topic. You have several options for sharing that information.	
LEAST IMPACT ↓ ↓ ↓ ↓ ↓ ↓ ↓ ↓ **MINIMAL IMPACT**	1. Lecture 2. Reading information 3. Webquests 4. Demonstrations 5. Observations 6. Blended learning 7. Contract learning 8. Interviewing 9. Brainstorming 10. Socratic seminars

SYNTHESIS

One of the objectives of any lesson is to provide opportunities for students to pull together various bits of information to form a new whole or basic understanding of a topic. Synthesis is the combination of knowledge elements that form a new whole. This process underscores the need for students to do something with the information they receive.

MINIMAL IMPACT	11. Reflective discussions
↓	12. Experimenting
↓	13. Graphic organizers
	14. Problem-solving activities
MODERATE IMPACT	15. Cooperative learning

PERFORMANCE

Having a lot of knowledge is one thing. Being able to pull together bits and pieces of knowledge is another thing. But, the crux of a good lesson is the opportunities for students to use their knowledge in meaningful, hands-on learning tasks. Performance refers to the ability to effectively use new information in a productive manner.

MODERATE IMPACT	16. Interactive learning
↓	17. Flipped learning
↓	18. Role playing
↓	19. Modeling
↓	20. Simulations
	21. Projects
	22. Reciprocal teaching
MAXIMUM IMPACT	23. Reflective inquiry

As you look at the charts, you'll notice that lecture (Knowledge), for example, has the least impact on students (in addition to having the lowest level of student involvement). As you move up through each successive chart you'll note how successive methods (#1 ➔ #23) increase the level of impact (and level of involvement) for students. In the third chart (Performance), reflective inquiry (#23) has the highest level of impact (and involvement) on students of all the methods listed.

QUOTABLE QUOTE

"Great teaching—just plain old knock 'em dead, get it right, make 'em laugh, make 'em wonder instruction—is always going to be rare. Good teachers abound. Great ones are special."

—Robert Krulwich

Now let's take a closer look at each of those three major categories and the methodologies that are part of each one.

Knowledge

<u>1. Lecture</u>

Lecture is an arrangement in which teachers share information directly with students, with roots going back to the ancient Greeks. Lecture is a familiar form of information-sharing, but it is not without its drawbacks. It has been overused and abused, and it is often the method used when teachers don't know or aren't familiar with other avenues of presentation. Also, many lecturers might not have been the best teacher role models in school.

Often, teachers assume that lecturing is nothing more than speaking to a group of students. Wrong! Good lecturing also demonstrates a respect for the learner, a knowledge of the content, and an awareness of the context in which the material is presented.

Good lectures must be built on three basic principles:

1. Knowing and responding to the background knowledge of the learner is necessary for an effective lecture.

2. Having a clear understanding of the material is valuable in being able to explain it to others.

3. The physical design of the room and the placement of students impact the effectiveness of a lecture.

It's important to keep in mind that lecture need not be a long and drawn-out affair. For example, the "10-2" strategy is an easily used, amazingly effective tool for all grade levels. In this strategy, no more than ten minutes of lecture should occur before students are allowed two minutes for processing. This is also supportive of how the brain learns. When "10-2" is used in both elementary and secondary classrooms, the rate of both comprehension and retention of information increase dramatically.

During the two-minute break, you can ask students several open-ended questions, such as the following:

- "What have you learned so far in this lesson?"
- "Why is this information important?"
- "How does this information relate to any information we have learned previously?"
- "How do you feel about your progress so far?"
- "How does this data apply to other situations?"
- "Where else could this be used?"
- "What do you think might happen next?"
- "How do you think this lesson will turn out?"
- "Is there something you don't understand at this point?"
- "What are three new things you just learned?"

These questions can be answered individually, in small group discussions, or as part of whole class interactions.

Lectures are information-sharing tools for any classroom teacher. However, it's critically important that you not use lecture as your one and only tool. You must supplement it with other instructional methods to achieve the highest levels of comprehension and utility for your students.

2. Reading Information

With this method, you assign material from the textbook for students to read independently. You may also choose to have your students read other supplemental materials in addition to the textbook. These may include, but are limited to children's or adolescent literature, brochures, flyers, pamphlets, and information read directly from various publications.

3. Webquest

Webquests are often used at the beginning of a lesson to stimulate interest in a topic. By definition, they involve activities in which students solve problems, investigate background information, and generate questions using various online sites. In most cases, students are given an introductory problem or challenge and then encouraged to investigate it (either independently or in small teams) via a collection of pertinent web sites.

4. Demonstration

In this format, students witness a real or simulated activity in which you use materials from the real world. These materials may include artifacts and objects used by individuals in a specific line of work, for example: microscopes (biologists), barometer (meteorologists), transit (surveyors), or word processing program (writers).

5. Observation

This format allows students to watch an event or occurrence take place firsthand (e.g. videos). The only drawback is that sometimes unexpected and unplanned events happen over which you may have little control.

6. Blended learning

Blended learning is simply the combination of regular classroom instruction in concert with computer or other digital activities. Those devices may include (but are not limited to) computers, iPads, iPhones, blogs, podcasts, or interactive whiteboards. Basic information is shared with students and then those students (individually or in small groups) pursue the topic via a range of technology.

7. Contract learning

This form of learning involves a written document agreed to by both the teacher and an individual student. How a student masters the content of a lesson and how that same student will indicate a pre-established level of proficiency are both spelled out on the contract. Contract learning is most often used for individual students in need of specific remedial work or those individuals who require advanced enrichment work. The advantage is that contracts allow teachers to emphasize a differentiated curriculum, focusing on the specific learning needs of selected students. For students, contracts are motivational because they have been given an opportunity to "buy into" the lesson through a mutually agreeable plan of action.

8. Interviewing

This format may include the personal interview, in which one person talks with another person. It may also involve the group interview, in which several people talk with a single individual.

Depending on the subject matter, it's often advisable to encourage students to interview members of the local community and solicit specific types of information. For example, students in a high school history course can interview veterans and obtain their views and perspectives on a recent conflict. Elementary students could interview their parents and relatives about the duties and responsibilities of various occupations for a lesson on vocations.

9. Brainstorming

Brainstorming can be a valuable instructional tool which you can incorporate into almost any lesson. Simply defined, it is the generation of lots of ideas (without regard for quality) about a single topic. This method is particularly appropriate at the start of a lesson to tap into the background knowledge students may or may not have about a topic.

Effective brainstorming is governed by four basic rules:

- Generate as many ideas as possible—the more the better.
- There is no evaluation of any single idea or group of ideas. There is no criticism about whether an idea is good or bad.
- Zany, wild, and crazy ideas are encouraged and solicited.
- Individuals are free to build upon the ideas of others.

10. Socratic seminars

A Socratic seminar is a learning opportunity that places responsible questioning in the hands of students. Most often used with middle school and high school students a specified topic is shared in a small group setting. Students are asked to generate questions related to that topic and be prepared to pose those questions to other members of the group. The foundation for appropriate questions may be initiated by teacher modeling or may be explicitly taught to the class. Students may also be given to opportunity to respond to a set of written questions previously designed by the teacher (again, using a hierarchy of question types). Eventually, the teacher slowly pulls back from the discussion and allows students to take over the conversation.

Synthesis

11. Reflective Discussions

Reflective discussions are a useful strategy for stimulating thought as well as providing students with opportunities to defend their position(s). Your role in these discussions is that of a moderator.

You can pose an initial question, supplemental questions when the discussion falters, or review questions for a group to consider at the end of a discussion. It's important that you not take an active role in the discussions, but rather serve as a facilitator. Try these suggestions for making small group discussions successful:

- Place members of a group into a circle so everyone can see (and listen to) everyone else.
- Craft a few introductory questions to get a group started, but then stand back and let the group interact without your intervention.
- Be sure group members know the purpose of the discussion. What answers or resolutions are they trying to reach?
- Keep the groups at manageable levels. Groups larger than five tend to be nonproductive.
- Emphasize the value of a free and open discussion in any group. No one should be criticized for offering an opinion.
- Groups may either be convergent (specifically focused on a single topic) or divergent (discussing any and all elements about a general idea). Be sure the group is aware of any conversational limitations.

- Take time to acknowledge the contributions of everyone in a group. Generally, group work should not be graded, but it should be celebrated.

Some teachers think small group discussions are nonproductive because no actual teaching takes place. In actuality, though, small groups are highly productive. They allow for the absorption of valuable material, a reflection on different points of view, and an informal means of assessing students' comprehension of material.

12. Experimenting

Through experimenting, ideas are proved or disproved, and predictions confirmed or denied. Experimentation involves manipulating data and assessing the results to discover some scientific principle or truth. Students need to understand that they conduct experiments every day, from watching ice cream melt to deciding on what clothes to wear outside based on the temperature. In the classroom, they need additional opportunities to try out their newly learned knowledge in a wide variety of learning tasks.

13. Graphic Organizers

A graphic organizer is a pictorial representation of the relationships that exist between ideas. It shows how ideas are connected and how ideas are related to each other. It is the basis for all forms of comprehension. By definition, comprehension is an understanding of how ideas or concepts are assembled into groups.

For example, if I asked you to assemble a list of vegetables ("vegetables" is the group) you might list some of the following: broccoli, squash, beans, peas, corn, pumpkins, etc. Each of these items is a member of the vegetable group. Thus, you comprehend vegetables because you understand how all those individual vegetables are related to each other.

Graphic organizers assist students in categorizing information. Most important, they help students understand the connections between their background knowledge and the knowledge they're learning in class.

14. Problem-Solving Activities

In this situation, the class, small groups, or individuals are given a problem or series of problems and are directed to find an appropriate solution. It is important to include an appropriate problem-solving model as part of the instruction. Here's one (based on the familiar K-W-L reading strategy) to consider:

K*: What do we already* **know** *about the topic? What's our prior knowledge?*

W*: What would we like to learn?* **What** *do we want to discover?*

H*: How will we conduct our investigation?* **How** *will we research our questions?*

L*: What are we* **learning** *about our question? How are we discovering answers?*

A*: Are we able to* **apply** *our answers? What are the applications of our research?*

Q*: What new* **questions** *have we generated? How might we discover those answers?*

R*: How is this* **relevant** *to our lives? Why do we need to know this?*

15. Cooperative Learning

Cooperative learning is a most effective instructional activity in which students—arranged in one of several different kinds of grouping patterns—tackle a topic or a set of questions together. Each person in a group has an assigned responsibility (e.g. "Recorder," "Moderator," "Researcher," "Summarizer"). Cooperative learning activities work best when students are taught the responsibilities of each group member and the ways in which everybody can contribute to that group. Many times, novice teachers make the mistaken assumption that students know how to work in a group (particularly in middle school and high school). When a group begins to disintegrate it's usually because members aren't aware of the responsibilities of each and every individual.

> ## A Word of Advice
>
> "Never, never, ever give up on your students or on yourself. There are days when everything will go right and there are days when you just want to crawl into bed and pull the covers over your head. Just remember what brought you to the classroom. Remember, you have the power to transform lives."
>
> —Anita Meinbach, former classroom teacher

Performance

16. Interactive learning

Students working together on a common goal or a common challenge is a most effective instructional strategy. It encourages them to solve problems, build teamwork, and engage in real-world interactions that extend beyond the classrooms. Examples may include:

- Creating a class blog together
- Producing a classroom newspaper
- Sharing a newsletter with parents
- Creating a group Prezi
- Class video or YouTube production
- Skype interviews
- Contributing to online discussion boards
- Sharing podcasts

While interactive learning opportunities should be part of almost every lesson shared with students (regardless of grade level) they also have an additional instructional advantage—they allow students the opportunity to connect with other students or individuals around the world—thus expanding the classroom beyond its four walls.

17. Flipped learning

Flipped learning is a strategy in which a teacher assigns online work to be completed outside of class. Often, this online work will involve videos created by the teacher for the express purpose of introducing a specific topic to the class. Students watch and take notes on the video (typically as a homework assignment) and then come to class ready with specific questions or extending activities designed by the teacher. Often used for specific math topics it fosters higher levels of academic responsibility on the part of students as they (not the teacher) are in charge of the introductory material with the teacher expanding and reinforcing that material in class.

18. Role-Playing

In this event, a student (or students) takes on the role of a specific individual (a historical person, for example) and acts out the actions of that person as though he were actually that person. The intent is to develop a feeling for and an appreciation of the thoughts and actions of an individual.

Role-plays are typically short, lasting for a maximum of fifteen minutes. The best ones are those in which two or more students engage in a dialogue about a specific event or circumstance. This is a wonderful opportunity for students to capitalize on their creativity.

19. Modeling

In this method, you model the behavior students are to duplicate within an activity and encourage students to parallel your behavior in their own activity. Students may model appropriate behavior for each other, too.

20. Simulations

Simulations are activities in which students are given real-life problem situations and asked to work through those situations as though they were actually a part of them. Every simulation has five basic characteristics:

1. They are abstractions of real-life situations. They provide opportunities for you to bring the outside world into the classroom.

2. The emphasis is on decision-making. Students have opportunities to make decisions and follow through on those decisions.

3. Students have roles that parallel those in real life (mother, father, child).

4. The rules are simple, uncomplicated, and few in number.

5. A simulation has two or more rounds—opportunities to make decisions more than once.

6. If you've ever played the board games Monopoly, Clue, or Life, you have been part of a simulation.

What a Great Idea!

The author of this book has written over fifteen teacher resource books on readers theatre—a wonderful way to integrate role-playing into any classroom curriculum. Here are just a few of those titles:

- African Legends, Myths, and Folktales for Readers Theatre (Grades 4-8)
- American Folklore, Legends, and Tall Tales for Readers Theatre (Grades 4-8)
- Fairy Tales Readers Theatre (Grades 3-6)
- Readers Theatre for American History (Grades 4-8)
- Science Fiction Readers Theatre (Grades 4-8)
- Songs and Rhymes Readers Theatre for Beginning Readers (Grades 1-2)

Check out additional readers theatre titles and teacher resources at: www.anthonydfredericks.com

---

21. Projects

Students are allowed to create their own original designs, models, or structures to illustrate an important point or content fact. These can take many forms and formats:

• Mobiles	• Dioramas	• Shadow boxes
• Posters	• Newspapers	• Brochures
• Flyers	• Letters to the editor	• Collages
• 3-dimensional models	• Play/skit	• Song
• Diary	• Web Quest	• Prezi
• Blog	• Simulation	• Bulletin board
• Calendar	• Book	• Newsletter
• Sculpture	• Puzzle	• Experiment

22. Reciprocal teaching

In this strategy, students take over the responsibility of teaching material to other individuals or a small group of fellow students. In many cases, teachers will invite a student to read a selected piece of text and then invite that same student to teach the basic elements of that text to a group of classmates. The student-leader (teacher) may be asked to generate appropriate questions or initiate an in-depth discussion about the material. One of the biggest advantages of this strategy is that students—when they are in charge of teaching others—engage in metacognitive reflection that has a direct and positive impact on their learning.

23. Reflective Inquiry

This method is student-initiated and student-controlled. Individual students are encouraged to select a topic they want to investigate further. In so doing, they pose a series of questions that they want to answer on their own. The questions are typically higher-order questions and emphasize a variety of divergent thinking skills.

Vary Your Lessons

If you'd like to make every lesson successful, you must do one thing: include a variety of teaching and learning methodologies in every one. If variety is the spice of life, then fill your lessons with lots of spice as you incorporate multiple teaching strategies. Think of a boring class or presentation you recently experienced. I'm sure one of the primary reasons why that presentation was so boring was simply because the instructor did not take advantage of multiple teaching and learning methodologies. By using a variety, you can help create enthusiastic and involved students.

What a Great Idea!

Here's a good rule of thumb: For every lesson, try to include at least:

- one Knowledge method,
- one Synthesis method, and
- one Performance method.

That way, your students are getting the necessary information; they're pulling together that information into a comprehensible whole; and they're afforded opportunities to use that information in a creative and engaging way. I often refer to this as a "hands-on, minds-on" curriculum. This is a curriculum in which students do something with what they are learning. Best of all, students walk out of a classroom with a positive attitude about themselves and the information they just learned.

Chapter 15

<u>Your Most Powerful Teaching Tool:</u>
<u>Questions</u>

Allow me to take you back in time to a time in either middle school or high school. Imagine, if you will, an American history class. The teacher ("Miss Boring") is leading the class in a discussion of The Underground Railroad.

"Who can tell me what the Underground Railroad was?" Miss Boring asks the class.

No response.

"Doesn't anybody remember what we talked about two days ago?" she inquires.

Still no response.

"Once again, what was the Underground Railroad?" she asks.

By this time, most of the eyes are at "half-mast" as students are struggling to stay awake, even though the period started a mere five minutes ago,

"Okay, Sarah, can you tell me a famous person associated with the Underground Railroad?"

"I dunno," Sarah replied.

"Jackson, what about you?"

"I can't remember," Jackson mumbles while texting his girlfriend.

"Ashton, can you tell us one significant fact related to the Underground Railroad?" Miss Boring asks.

The question catches Ashton unawares, as he is doodling in the margin of his history book. "I really don't know," he replies.

"Justine, how about you?'

"Harriett What's-her-name," she guesses.

"Well, almost," Miss Boring replies.

The painful and tortuous scenario continues until Miss Boring, frustrated at all the "non-answers," finally tells everyone that Harriett Tubman was one of the pivotal figures in the Underground Railroad movement. Some of the students dutifully write the name in their notebooks, while others force themselves to stay awake for the next round of (boring) questions.

This classroom scene might be more prevalent than we like to admit. It depicts a teacher asking inane questions, students with little or no involvement in the lesson, and a kind of verbal ping-pong in which the teacher keeps asking low-level questions of various students until one student "gets" the right answer or until the teacher is forced to "give" the answer to a class of uninterested and uninvolved students.

As you might imagine, no instruction has taken place. The only objective in this scene is to obtain an answer to a predetermined question. It's a guessing game between students and the teacher. Students try to guess at the answers imbedded in the teacher's head. If they get it, the game moves on to the next question; if they don't get it, the teacher keeps asking until someone does or until the teacher gives the correct answer.

Unfortunately, most of the questioning that takes place in a classroom is trivial, with the emphasis on memory and information retrieval. Seldom are students given opportunities to think about what they're reading or doing, and rarely are they invited to generate their own questions for discovery. Yet good questioning is one of the most significant teaching skills you can acquire. And take it from me: it is also one of the most challenging!

Why Ask Questions?

Teachers ask questions for several reasons. These include:

1. Tapping into background knowledge (to find out what students know before the lesson begins) with questions such as "Before

we begin the lesson, why do you think plants are useful to humans?" This is critical because you always want to know both the depth and breadth of background knowledge students bring to a lesson.

2. Evaluating student progress or performance during a lesson with questions such as "How would you summarize what we have discussed so far on the Trojan Wars?" These are often called criterion checks and are a way of monitoring how well students are understanding a lesson. Stop every ten to fifteen minutes and ask students a question about how well they comprehend the material.

3. Evaluating student understanding at the end of a lesson with questions such as "What are the three types of rocks?" Unfortunately, this may be the most overused function of questions. Yes, you need to know if students mastered the objectives of the lesson, but to always end a lesson with a barrage of short-term memory questions is a sure way to make your lessons dull and boring.

4. Getting students involved in the lesson. Questions can be used as effective motivational tools that assist students in becoming actively involved in the dynamics of a lesson. For example, "Now that we have discussed latitude and longitude, how can we use those terms on this map of the world?"

5. Questions can be used to stimulate students to ask their own questions. When students self-generate questions they will be more inclined to pursue the answers to those questions simply because they *own* the queries. For example, "How many different questions can you come up with regarding the destruction of the Amazon rain forest?"

6. Moving student thinking to a higher level. It doesn't make any difference whether you're teaching kindergarten or twelfth-grade history; all students can benefit from the use of higher-level thinking questions. Stay tuned, and I'll share one of the most powerful teaching statements a little later in this chapter.

A Taxonomy of Questions

Here's something important you need to consider. That is, the goal of classroom questioning is not to determine whether students have learned something (as would be the case in tests, quizzes, and exams), but rather to guide students to help them learn necessary information and material. Questions should be used to <u>teach</u> students rather than to just <u>test</u> students!

Teachers frequently spend a great deal of classroom time testing students through questions. In fact, observations of teachers at all levels of education reveal that most spend more than 90 percent of their instructional time testing students (through questioning). And most of the questions teachers ask are factual questions that rely on short-term memory.

Although questions are widely used and serve many functions, teachers tend to overuse factual questions such as "What is the capital of North Dakota?" Not surprising, many teachers ask upward of 400 questions each and every school day. And approximately 80 percent of the questions teachers ask tend to be factual, literal, or knowledge-based questions. The result is a classroom in which there is little creative thinking taking place.

It's been my experience that one all-important factor is key in the successful classroom:

> **Students tend to read and think based on the kinds of questions they anticipate receiving from the teacher.**

If students are constantly bombarded with questions that require only low levels of intellectual involvement (or no involvement whatsoever), they will tend to think accordingly. Conversely, students who are given questions based on higher levels of thinking will tend to think more creatively and divergently.

In 1956, an educator named Benjamin Bloom developed a classification system we now refer to as Bloom's Taxonomy to assist teachers in recognizing their various levels of question-asking (among other things). The system (revised in 2001) contains six levels, which are arranged in hierarchical form, moving from the lowest level of cognition (thinking) to the highest level of cognition (or from the least complex to the most complex). The six levels are: Remembering, Comprehending, Applying, Analyzing, Evaluating, and Creating.

Remembering

This is the lowest level of questions and requires students to recall information. Knowledge questions usually require students to identify information in basically the same form it was presented. Some examples of knowledge questions include:

- "What is the biggest city in Japan?"
- "Who wrote War and Peace?"
- "How many ounces in a pound?"

Words often used in knowledge questions include know, who, define, what, name, where, list, and when.

Observations of both elementary and secondary classrooms has shown that teachers significantly overuse remembering questions. In fact, during the course of an average school day, many teachers will ask upward of 300 or more remembering-based questions.

Comprehending

Simply stated, comprehension is the way in which ideas are organized into categories. Comprehension questions are those that ask students to take several bits of information and put them into a single category or grouping. These questions go beyond simple recall and require students to combine data together. Some examples of comprehending questions include:

- "How would you illustrate the water cycle?"
- "What is the main idea of this story?"
- "If I put these three blocks together, what shape do they form?"

Words often used in comprehending questions include *describe, use your own words, outline, explain, discuss, and compare.*

Applying

At this level of questioning, teachers ask students to take information they already know and apply it to a new situation. In other words, they must use their knowledge to determine a correct response. Some examples of applying questions include:

- "How would you use your knowledge of latitude and longitude to locate Greenland?"

- "What happens when you multiply each of these numbers by nine?"

- "If you had eight inches of water in your basement and a hose, how would you use the hose to get the water out?"

Words often used in applying questions include *apply, manipulate, put to use, employ, dramatize, demonstrate, interpret*, and *choose*.

What a Great Idea!

Never end a presentation by asking, "Are there any questions?" This is the surest way to turn off students. Instead, say something like, "Take five minutes and write down two questions you have about the lesson. Share those questions and discuss possible answers with a partner."

Analyzing

An analyzing question is one that asks a student to break down something into its component parts. To analyze requires students to identify reasons, causes, or motives and reach conclusions or generalizations. Some examples of analysis questions include:

- "What are some of the factors that cause rust?"

- "Why did the United States go to war with England?"

- "Why do you think the author wrote this book?"

- "Why do we call all these animals mammals?"

Words often used in analyzing questions include *analyze, why, take apart, diagram, draw conclusions, simplify, distinguish,* and *survey.*

Evaluating

Evaluating requires an individual to make a judgment about something. We are asked to judge the value of an idea, a candidate, a work of art, or a solution to a problem. When students are engaged in decision-making and problem-solving, they should be thinking at this level. Evaluation questions do not have single right answers. Some examples of evaluating questions include:

- "What do you think about your work so far?"
- "What story did you like the best?"
- "Why do you think the pioneers left the Oregon Trail?"
- "Why do you think Benjamin Franklin is so famous?"

Words often used in evaluating questions include: *judge, rate, assess, evaluate, What is the best, value, criticize,* and *compare.*

Creating

Creating questions challenge students to engage in creative and original thinking. These questions invite students to produce original ideas and solve problems. There's always a variety of potential responses to synthesis questions. Some examples of creating questions include:

- "How would you assemble these items to create a windmill?"
- "How would your life be different if you could breathe under water?"
- "Construct a tower one foot tall using only four blocks."
- "Put these words together to form a complete sentence."

Words often used in creating questions include *compose, construct, design, revise, create, formulate, produce,* and *plan.*

What's It All About

OK, what does all this mean? Several things, actually! It means you can ask your students several different kinds of questions. If you only focus on one type of question, your students might not be exposed to higher levels of thinking necessary to a complete understanding of a topic. If, for example, you only ask students remembering questions, then your students might think that learning (a specific topic) is nothing more than the ability to memorize a select number of facts.

You can use this taxonomy to help craft a wide range of questions—from low-level thinking questions to high-level thinking questions. If variety is the spice of life, you should sprinkle a variety of question types throughout every lesson, regardless of the topic or the grade level you teach.

However, Bloom's Taxonomy is not grade-specific. That is, it does not begin at the lower grades (kindergarten, first, second) with knowledge and comprehension questions and move upward to the higher grades (tenth, eleventh, twelfth) with synthesis and evaluation questions. The six levels of questions are appropriate for **all** grade levels. For example, many elementary teachers mistakenly think primary-level students (kindergarten through grade two) cannot "handle" higher-level thinking questions (applying, analyzing, evaluating, and creating). Nothing could be further from the truth! Challenging all students through higher-order questioning is one of the best ways to stimulate learning and enhance brain development regardless of age.

Remember, <u>students tend to read and think based on the types of questions they anticipate receiving from the teacher</u>. In other words, students will tend to approach any subject as a knowledge-based subject if they are presented with an overabundance of knowledge-level questions throughout a lesson. On the other hand, students will tend to approach a topic at higher levels of thinking if they are presented with an abundance of questions at higher levels of thinking.

Dynamic Questioning Strategies

Questioning can certainly be much more than a teacher asking a question and a student answering that question correctly (or incorrectly). It sends the wrong message to students that teachers are in control of the information simply because they are in control of the questions. More important is the concept that questioning is a way to enlarge, expand, and diversify our thinking in new and creative ways. We can look at ideas in fascinating and interesting ways; we can expand our intellectual horizons; and we can develop higher levels of comprehension at any grade and in any subject area.

Following are some of my favorite strategies. I've used them as a former elementary teacher, a former secondary teacher, and certainly in my current role as an education professor. Consider these strategies as part of your teaching retinue and, you too, will see some magical (intellectual) events taking place in your classroom.

1. Wait Time

Listen in on many classrooms at all levels, and you'll probably hear teachers asking question after question. With so many questions coming at them, students have little time to think. Looking at it another way: the more questions that are asked, the less thinking occurs. Classroom observations reveal that teachers typically wait less than one second for students to respond to a question. Teachers often conclude that students don't know the answer to a question if they don't respond quickly. And when they do respond, they usually use remembering-level responses.

Classroom observations also reveal that if a student manages to get a response in, most teachers tend to ask another question within an average time span of nine-tenths of a second! In classrooms where students are bombarded with questions (this is the norm, not the exception), students have little time to think.

Is this a problem? Yes! But here's an interesting solution: increase the time between asking a question and having students respond to that question from the typical one second to five seconds. This is known as "wait time." Believe it or not, this simple act produces significant and profound changes in the classroom, including:

- The length of student responses increases 400 to 800 percent.
- The number of unsolicited but appropriate responses increases.
- Failure to respond decreases.
- Student confidence increases.
- Students ask more questions.
- Student achievement increases significantly.

What a Great Idea!

Here's a super tip: when you ask a question, don't preface it with a student's name. For example, "Marsha, what are some of the reasons why Leonardo da Vinci is considered a genius?" As soon as you say one student's name, all the other brains in the room immediately shut down. Often, the other students will be saying to themselves, "We don't have to think now because Marsha is going to answer the question."

Instead, ask the question, wait, and then ask for a response (For example, "What are some of the reasons why Leonardo da Vinci is considered a genius?" [Five second pause] "Marsha?") Interestingly, you'll discover a heightened level of involvement. Everyone has to think about a response because nobody knows who will be called on to respond. And, the responses you receive will be considerably better and more thoughtful.

Wait time provides students with time to think and time to create an appropriate response. Imagine if you went to your local coffee shop, ordered a latte, and the clerk reached under the counter and handed one to you immediately. Wouldn't you be just a little suspicious of the quality of that brew? You expect that, after you place your order, the coffee shop employee would take some time to brew your beverage and serve it to you a minute or two later when it's done. You're willing to wait because you know you'll be getting a beverage that has gone through an extensive brewing process rather than one that has been whipped out of an assembly line.

Wait time is the same thing. After you ask a question, let it percolate in students' heads for a while. And after a student responds, let the response percolate as well. Believe me, you'll wind up with a much better "brew" in your classroom.

Adding wait time to your teaching repertoire will, perhaps more than any other teaching strategy, have the greatest impact on student performance. However, it's only fair to tell you that it looks simpler than it is. It may be for you, as it has always been for me, one of the greatest teaching challenges you will ever face simply because teachers are uncomfortable with classroom silence. We tend to abhor it, often believing that learning can't really be going on in a quiet classroom. But with practice, you'll begin to see its incredible benefits!

2. Expanding

Remember Miss Boring from the beginning of the chapter? Miss Boring and thousands of other teachers engage in a practice I refer to as "verbal ping-pong." Here's how it goes:

- Teacher asks a question.
- Student responds.
- Teacher asks a question.
- Another student responds.
- Teacher asks a question.
- Another student responds.
- And so on and so on….

Not very exciting. But it happens all the time. When a student answers a question, there's absolutely no response from a teacher. Most teachers tend to accept student answers without any sort of elaboration or expansion. In short, we become "satisfied" with any correct response a student shares and then quickly move on to the next query. There is virtually no intellectual stimulation!

If all we do after getting an answer to a question is mumble "Uh-huh" or "Okay" and then move on to the next question, our students get the message that the sole object of those questions is to identify correct responses (a focus on the lowest level of cognition). Equally important, this "verbal ping-ponging" inhibits both the quality of responses as well as higher-level thinking abilities. A much more powerful response is to use the student's answer as part of a series of follow-up questions. Here's a scenario:

Teacher: How are these insects able to walk on the surface of the water?

Student: They use surface tension.

Teacher: So you think they use the natural surface tension of water to stay on top?

Student: Yeah. You know we learned that the water molecules at the surface of water form a strong attraction.

Teacher: Are you saying, then, that the insects use that attraction to walk on the water?

Student: Yes, but the insect has to be a certain weight or it will fall through.

Notice what happened here. For each response the student provided, the teacher used some of the student's words to craft a follow-up response or question. This process accomplished several things:

- It recognized that the teacher was actually listening to the student.
- It provided the teacher with an opportunity to have the student clarify her or his thinking.
- It provided a motivation to keep the conversation going.
- It celebrated the student's participation in the lesson.

What results is an emphasis on, not just answering a question, but an active process of thinking, expanding, and elaborating on the answer(s). Students get the idea that answering questions is not simply about right answers, it is also an opportunity to engage in an active dialogue with someone to further comprehension about a topic or area of study.

3. Prompting

Prompting involves assisting students in thinking beyond their responses to a question. It stimulates and encourages students to investigate and rationalize their answers and can enhance classroom dialogue.

Prompting questions such as these should be dropped into a discussion periodically:

- "How did you know it was _____?"
- "What do you know that isn't right?"
- "What do you think this should be?"
- "Why do you think your answer is correct?"
- "What do you think will happen next?"

Notice that these questions do not have right or wrong answers. Rather, they are designed to help students think about, defend, and rationalize their responses. Best of all, they ask for students' opinions and reactions. This is a sure way to increase student involvement and understanding of any topic.

4. Probing

Good teachers invite students as active participants in the dynamics of a lesson by probing. Simply stated, probing is a series of teacher statements or questions that encourage students to elaborate on their answers to previous questions. Probing is a way of shifting an individual conversation or class discussion to a higher level.

Good teachers use some of these probing questions frequently throughout a lesson:

- Clarification. "What do you mean by that?"
- Obtaining more information. "What's another word for that?"
- Making connections. "Is this like anything else you're familiar with?"
- Comparison. "How is your idea similar to or different from _____'s?"
- Expansion. "Is there any other information you can add to that?"
- Validation. "Why do you believe your response is correct?"

5. Reducing the "Dunno" Syndrome

There's something that happens in almost every classroom almost every day. Questions are asked and students (who are either bored, frustrated, distracted, or unprepared) answer "I don't know" or "Dunno." It's a common enough occurrence in any classroom that it is quite easy to recognize (I am certain, that you and me and hundreds of millions of other students have used this "cop out" more than once sometime in our educational careers.).

When students respond with "I don't know" they are effectively saying that they don't want to make any kind of intellectual investment in the topic under discussion. It's a convenient way of escaping from any intellectual pursuit—a way of telling the teacher, "I'm not responsible and I don't want to get involved." In many ways, the student is telling the teacher, "I'm done here, go ahead and move on to someone else."

I find this common occurrence unacceptable. I don't ask questions to waste students' time, rather I ask questions to help students understand the ramifications of a concept, expand their thinking horizons, and engage in a supportive conversation that is both respectful and educational. To do that, I don't allow students to escape from a question, I always pursue some form of dialogue—some form of intellectual discovery. "I don't know" is never an acceptable response. Here's a scenario:

> **Teacher** (to Becky): What do you think are some of the consequence of oil pollution?
>
> **Becky**: I dunno
>
> **Teacher** (to Stewart): Stewart, what's your thinking about the effects of oil pollution?
>
> **Stewart:** Well, it severely alters the environment for wildlife. Animals can't find the food they need to survive and their habitats are often damaged.
>
> **Teacher** (back to Becky): Now, Becky, what do you think about oil pollution?
>
> **Becky**: It's dangerous for animals. They often can't find food or a place to live.
>
> **Teacher**: How would you feel if you couldn't find any food or didn't have a place to live?
>
> **Becky**: I'd be pretty bummed out. I'd probably have to move out of the area.

In this scenario, Becky responded to the initial question with an "I don't know." The teacher then turned to another student and invited him to respond to the same inquiry. Then, the teacher came back to Becky and asked the same question (although in a different format). Becky knew that she wasn't going to "escape." If necessary, the teacher could have turned to yet another student, asked for a response, and, once again returned to Becky.

What is important about this questioning sequence is the fact that students realize that their mental presence in a subject is not optional —it is required. As teachers, we need to provide opportunities for ALL students to become engaged in learning a planned topic. What you will discover, as I did many years ago, is that over time the number of "I don't knows" decreases significantly to the point where they almost become non-existent.

Here's another scenario:

> **Teacher** (to Terry): Why do you think Benjamin Franklin was so famous?
>
> **Terry**: I don't know.
>
> **Teacher** (reworking the question): If you could be famous for something, what would it be?
>
> **Terry**: I guess my model trains.
>
> **Teacher**: Why your model trains?
>
> **Terry**: Because I spend a lot of time working with them.
>
> **Teacher:** Was there something Benjamin Franklin spent a lot of time on?
>
> **Terry**: Yeah, he spent a lot of time working on spectacles—those weird-looking glasses.
>
> **Teacher**: So, what is one thing that made Benjamin Franklin so famous?
>
> **Terry**: He invented bifocals.

Notice in the sequence above that the teacher didn't give up on Terry. It would be quite easy whenever getting an "I don't know" response to end the conversation with one student and move on to another student. Don't do it! Rework, revise, or reconfigure your original question in a way that taps into something you know the student enjoys or is familiar with. Use that background knowledge to help the student eventually arrive at an appropriate response to the original question.

Here's something else you may have noticed. In both of the scenarios above, the questions asked by the two teachers were all at higher levels of cognition. They were not, as is often typical in most classrooms, primarily *remembering* questions. And, here's why that is so important: By focusing more on higher level cognitive questions you give yourself more options for ensuring student responses than you would if using a preponderance of low-level or *Remembering* questions. In other words, you limit your opportunities for engaging students with low-level queries; you significantly increase those opportunities with questions higher on the taxonomy.

6. Everybody In

I'm going to suggest something radical—something that will go against the status quo. Yet, it's a procedure that can produce some dramatic and dynamic results. Simply, when I ask a question, I don't ask for a show of hands. In fact, I frequently discourage the common practice of "raising your hand to answer a question." Here's why. Often (as you might imagine) it's always the same students who raise their hands in any classroom. And, it's always the same students whom the teacher recognizes to answer those questions. As a result, students quickly learn that it is possible to "hide" in the classroom simply by never raising their hands during any inquiry process. They never have to participate.

Instead, I want everyone in the room to accept the responsibility of answering any and all questions that might be posed. In short, there are no "innocent bystanders." I want everyone to be intellectually engaged and ready to contribute at a moment's notice. Here's a typical scenario:

> **Teacher**: What do you think the "Founding Fathers" would have thought about how the second amendment is being interpreted today?

(Pause for five seconds)

> **Teacher**: Kayla, what do you think?

Notice that the teacher didn't ask for any hands to be raised. She asked the question and allowed it to seep into everyone's brain. Then, she called on a random student. In other words, everybody was "asked" to consider and process the question. Then, after a short period of time, one individual, selected arbitrarily, was invited to answer. You will quickly notice that this is a reaffirmation of "Wait Time" —a strategy that will dramatically and positively influence the dynamics of your lessons.

What a Great Idea!

At the beginning of the year I invite students to each write their name on a colored craft stick or tongue depressor (available at my local arts and crafts store). I then collect all those sticks and place them in a small glass jar. When I ask a question of the class I allow the question to percolate for a while and then randomly select one of the craft sticks from the jar. The student whose name is on that stick gets "first crack" at answering the question. Then another stick is selected, and another, and so on. Not only does this help me quickly learn student names early in the year, but it also ensures that the student answering process is completely random and by chance. Students don't have to raise their hands, but they are all potential "subjects" for a teacher/ student interaction.

Something to Think About

There is a long-standing "tradition" among teachers to use questions as a way of *testing* students, finding out what they read or learned. But, the real value of questions is as a *teaching* tool—one that helps students comprehend and master material. That comes about when you place a value on:

- Using questions as a natural and normal part of EVERY classroom lesson

- Helping students understand that questions are always a part of good lesson
- Asking higher-level questions more so than lower-level queries
- Providing opportunities for all students to take part in the cognitive processes required to answer those questions
- Working to eliminate any and all "I don't knows"

Always include questions in any kind of classroom presentation—old material or new material. Help students understand that questions are always a part of learning. Just as the kinds of questions are important; so too, is how we process information after a question has been asked. You want to let students know that learners—good learners—are always responding to questions. The ultimate goal is students who begin asking their own self-initiated questions as a result of the models you provide in the classroom.

Any questions?

Chapter 16

Taming the Homework "Monster"

Mention the word "homework" to most students, and you'll probably get a series of groans, yawns, and other verbal reactions - most of which I can't print in the pages of this book. It seems as though homework is something done to students for reasons that may range from reinforcement of classroom concepts to punishment. Ask the average teacher why he or she assigns homework, and you may hear, "It's required by the administration," "I've always done it," or "It's good for the students: it teaches them responsibility and discipline."

Teachers often report that the value of homework is threefold:

- It helps develop good study habits.
- It fosters positive attitudes toward school.
- It communicates to students that learning happens in places outside of school as well as in school.

From studies of effective teaching, we know there is a positive correlation between homework as a learning tool and student achievement in the classroom. Some educators argue that homework does not have as much of an effect on the scholastic achievement of elementary students as it does on secondary students. Nevertheless, we know there are measurable gains at both levels. That statement comes with a caveat, however; that is, the amount of homework assigned needs to be tailored to the students' age and grade level.

The burning question is: how much homework should teachers assign to students? There is no clear answer to that query, but I'd like to offer the following simple formula, which has been suggested by many teachers:

Homework = Grade level X 10

This means that the amount of after-school homework (in minutes) is equivalent to the grade you teach times ten. For example, if you teach fifth grade, you would assign fifty minutes of homework per evening

(5th grade X 10 = 50). Here's a sampling:

Grade Level	X	Minutes of Homework (per evening)
2	10	20
4	10	40
6	10	60
8	10	80
10	10	100

As you'll quickly note, the amount of homework assigned is grade-specific. Students in the lower grades should receive less homework than students in the higher grades.

The "Homework = Grade level X 10" formula refers to the total amount of homework per student, not the amount of homework per subject. Consequently, if you are a middle school or high school teacher, you will need to coordinate your homework assignments with other teachers so you don't overload your students. By the same token, students in kindergarten and first grade should not receive any homework. No research suggests that homework at these levels is necessary or productive.

How Involved Should Parents Be?

Some schools and many districts have written policies regarding the degree of involvement parents should have in their children's homework. Based on a review of many of those documents, I'd like to offer the following suggestions regarding the role of parents in homework:

- Keep parents regularly informed about the amount of homework assigned to their children. (Check out www.schoolnotes.com as a way for parents and students to keep track of homework assignments in your class on a daily basis.)

- Parents should facilitate the completion of homework assignments. They should not do assignments for students; rather, they should provide the atmosphere and support system that will increase the likelihood of student completion (e.g. a quiet place to study, encouragement, and praise).

- Parents should have active and regular conversations with their children about homework assignments, concerns, and issues. A solid interest in homework helps support the completion of that homework.

- Be sure parents understand the purposes of homework, the amount of homework assigned, consequences for non-completion of homework, and a list of the types of suggested or acceptable parent involvement.

What a Great Idea!

In my elementary classroom, we had a "Homework Council" composed of several parent volunteers. We would meet periodically throughout the year and establish policies and practices regarding homework assignments. Decisions included how much homework, what subjects to emphasize, grading practices, and other similar issues. As a result, parents had a sense of ownership and were highly supportive of any assignments made.

Teachers will say that homework, if it is to be effective, must serve one of two purposes. The first is for the general purpose of practice. Homework cannot be used to introduce a new concept; it should be used to provide students with necessary practice to help them master a concept presented in the classroom.

Although practice is both important and necessary, I'd like to suggest that the practice has to be realistic. For example, assigning students a hundred three-digit addition problems as a homework assignment may be overdoing it. There's nothing to suggest that a hundred is any better than twenty (for example). If twenty gives your students the necessary practice time, why extend it even further?

The second general purpose of homework would be to prepare students for a forthcoming presentation or new topic. For example, before you introduce the topic of desert animals to your first-grade students, you may ask them to read the children's book *Desert Night, Desert Day,* by

Anthony D. Fredericks as a homework assignment the night before. Or, before you lecture your eleventh-grade students about small-business economics, you might want them to interview one or more small business owners in the local community beforehand about the challenges they face with supply and demand issues.

Doing a homework assignment and turning it in without receiving any feedback is nonproductive as well as demoralizing. My own experience, as well as those of teachers at all grade levels, has shown that the impact of a homework assignment is directly proportional to the immediacy and nature of any resulting feedback. Simply stated, students need feedback and comments as soon as possible after turning in a homework assignment. Here is a list of teacher responses (or nonresponses) to homework - ranging from least impact on academic achievement to greatest:

1. Assigned, but not graded

2. Assigned, graded, but no verbal comments

3. Assigned, graded, and verbal comments

4. Assigned, graded, and written comments

5. Assigned, graded, and verbal and written comments

6. Assigned, graded, verbal and written comments, and a direct connection to classroom work

Here's the bottom line: if you assign homework, grade it, comment on it, and get it back to students as quickly as you can. Timely, frequent, and specific feedback to students has been proven to be the most powerful academic motivator (for the completion of that homework) and has a greater impact on learning.

Many students at the secondary level hold part-time jobs and are involved in after-school sports or a variety of extra-curricular activities. All these compete for a student's time. Be sensitive to all the outside influences in students' lives, and adjust your homework assignments accordingly.

It's Your Choice

As appropriate, offer students several choices within a homework assignment. Of course, not every assignment will lend itself to choice-making. However, when the teacher gives students the option of making some choices, they will be more motivated to complete those assignments. Here are a few possibilities:

- Do the even-numbered or odd-numbered problems.
- Select any four of the following nine questions.
- Select any two of the following eight multiple intelligence activities.
- Work alone or work with a buddy.
- Select an appropriate due date from one of the following.

By providing students with choices, you are also providing them with a sense of ownership in their homework assignments. As a result, they will be more invested in those tasks.

Final Tips

Here's an assembly of tips and suggestions from teachers who have wrestled with the homework "monster" for years. Tap into their expertise, and incorporate some of these ideas into your classroom routines.

1. Many teachers give homework passes. Students earn these special certificates after accomplishing certain tasks in the classroom. Students can then use these passes to opt out of homework for a day or several days. I don't like these simply because they tend to diminish the value of homework. The message is that homework isn't very important. Instead, use a "Homework Extension Card." Students can earn and use this certificate to extend the deadline for a specific homework assignment by one, two, or three days and still receive full credit.

2. Students have other obligations in their lives besides school. For that reason, I'm a firm believer in not assigning any homework over the weekend. Students need opportunities to be with their families, play, or just "chill out" from all the demands of the academic world. Scheduling a homework assignment to be due on Monday morning puts an additional burden on students that just isn't fair or necessary. Let kids be kids on the weekends - there's plenty to do from Monday through Friday. The same rule holds true for holidays and vacation periods. These are

times away from the academic rigors of classroom life. Let your students enjoy these breaks free of the anxiety of an impending assignment or fast-approaching due date. You'll see higher levels of motivation as a result.

3. At the beginning of the year, assign each student a "Homework Buddy." If one partner is absent, the other can gather assignments and call or visit her or his buddy to let them know what was missed.

4. Keep a homework notebook, with a separate section for each class. Each day, record the homework assignment with any necessary directions. Include copies of any handouts. When students return from an absence, they are responsible for checking the notebook and obtaining the necessary information.

5. Remember, outside factors may affect a student's ability to do homework. After-school jobs and family issues are often a greater concern for some students than research on the sonnets of William Shakespeare or a summary of Southwestern desert habitats. Be sensitive to individual student responsibilities outside of school.

6. Be sure to share any homework assignments in both verbal and written form. For each subject or class, post the homework assignments on individual clipboards attached to the wall. Post them, too, on a class blog or web page. Consider audio recordings of assignments for physically challenged students in your class.

7. Always put a date on every homework assignment. That way, students who are absent for extended periods of time can retrieve the necessary assignments by date.

Homework doesn't have to be a "monster." It can be a positive component of your overall curriculum and a way to help students develop appropriate work habits—habits that will serve them throughout their educational career.

Chapter 17

<u>Meeting All Their Needs</u>

For many years, teachers and administrators provided for special needs children by removing them from the regular classroom and isolating them in classrooms staffed by one or more specialists. These students were all grouped together in one classroom and provided with instructional procedures and materials that could be similar to, or completely different from, those used in the regular classrooms. This pull-out, or tutorial, approach to education was deemed educationally sound because the specialist teacher could meet the special needs of the students on an individual basis.

As a classroom teacher, you will have a wide diversity of children exhibiting various talents, skills, emotions, physical and mental attributes, languages, and perceptions. Although all this diversity may, on the surface, seem overwhelming to you, it needn't be. I believe this variety offers some unique opportunities for every class you teach.

In the latter half of the twentieth century, a number of court cases and legal challenges were held regarding educational issues. Then, in 1975, Congress passed the Education of All Handicapped Children PL 94-142 law. This law provided for inclusion of all students in "the least restrictive environment." This environment included "the use of supplementary aids and services."

In 1990, the original law and its amendments merged into the Individuals with Disabilities Education Act (IDEA), which was reauthorized in 1997. Sometimes called the mainstreaming law, the IDEA "requires students with disabilities to be educated with their nondisabled peers to the maximum extend appropriate, with the supplemental aids and services needed to help them achieve." The law also requires schools to have alternative placements available (special classroom, residential institution, etc.) if selected students cannot be educated in the general education setting. The IDEA identifies thirteen categories of disabilities:

1. Mental retardation (pending language change to "intellectual disability")

2. Hearing impairment

3. Speech or language impairment

4. Visual impairment (including blindness)

5. Emotional disturbance

6. Orthopedic impairment

7. Autism

8. Traumatic brain injury

9. Other health impairment

10. Specific learning disability

11. Deafness

12. Deaf-blindness

13. Multiple disabilities

One of the provisions of PL 94-142 is that an Individualized Education Plan (often referred to as an IEP) be developed for each and every special needs student. This plan is written in consultation with a multidisciplinary team (MDT) of administrators, teachers, special education specialists, school counselors, and parents.

It is quite common, therefore, to find many classrooms with students of all ability levels working and learning together. The notion that special needs children, whenever and wherever possible, should be included in all activities and functions of the regular classroom is known as **inclusion**.

Inclusion is involving all students in the regular educational setting that best meets their needs. It also means that significant efforts are made to include special needs students in regular public school classrooms to the fullest extent possible.

Educators at all levels refer to special needs students as those with disabilities. In general, disabilities fall into two broad categories:

1. High-incidence disabilities (those most commonly seen in a public school) include, but are not limited to, communication disorders (such as speech and language impairments), emotional or behavioral disorders, mild-moderate intellectual delays, specific learning disabilities and other health impairments. About 12 percent of the school age population has a high-incidence disability.

2. Low-incidence disability include, but are not limited to: blindness/low vision, hard-of-hearing, deafness, deaf-blindness, orthopedically-impaired and multiple disabilities. About one percent of the school-age population has a low incidence disability.

Most educators prefer not to use the term "handicapped" because of its negative implications. You'll more often see terms like "students in need of specially designed instruction (SDI)" which has more positive implications. In an average-size classroom of twenty-five students, it is conceivable that three or four individuals will exhibit one or more disabilities.

It is quite likely that you will have a diversity of students in your classroom representing a variety of talents and abilities. With this in mind, I suggest some generalized strategies for you to consider as you work with all special needs students:

- Be aware that special needs students may not want to be singled out for any special treatment. To do so may identify their disability for other students and cause them to receive some form of attention they may not be able to handle.

- Ensure that your attitude and responses to special needs students are identical to those to other students. View all students as contributing students.

- Consider learning over a long period of time. Special needs students may require extended periods of time to master a concept or learn a specific skill. You may need to repeat information several times and reinforce it in many ways.

- It is quite easy to fall into the trap of focusing on the weaknesses of special needs students. Yet it is vitally important that you be aware of and seek to identify the individual strengths of each and every student in your classroom.

- Help students understand that grading, evaluation, and assessment is based on identifiable objectives in accordance with individual potential. Evaluation should not be coupled with the limitations of students but rather to their expectations.

- Provide significant opportunities for students of all abilities to learn from each other. Structure a variety of learning activities in which the social climate of the classroom is both promoted and enhanced. It is important that everyone feels like he's contributing.

- Do not make inappropriate assumptions based on students' exceptionalities. For example, don't assume that a student who is confined to a wheelchair is an unhappy child. Don't assume that a learning disabled student is not gifted in the visual arts. Also, don't assume that children with disabilities are disabled in all areas.

When working with special needs students, two terms you are sure to encounter are accommodation and modification. An accommodation is a device, material, or support process that will enable a student to accomplish a task more efficiently. Typical accommodations include computers, changes to a desk, a wheelchair ramp, preferential seating, a study guide, enlarged print, color-coded materials, tests read aloud, or e-books. Modification refers to changes to the instructional outcomes; a change or decrease in the course content or outcome. Typical modifications include adjusted expectations, fewer problems, and an emphasis on functional tasks.

Acronyms

- ADA - Americans with Disabilities Act
- ADD - Attention deficit disorder
- ADHD - Attention deficit hyperactive disorder
- ESE - Exceptional student education
- ESL - English as a second language
- FAPE - Free appropriate public education

- IDEA - Individuals with Disabilities Education Act. The purpose of the IDEA is to allow those students who have disabilities to acquire the same level of education as students without disabilities. To achieve this. Students are to be placed in the least restrictive environment (LRE). Further, each student is required to have an individual education plan (IEP) that would lead to substantive learning.

- IEP - Individual education plan. The IEP is a plan that must be followed by the school, special education staff, and regular teachers. The implication is that with an IEP, there is an increase in accountability.

- LD - Learning disabled

- LEP - Limited-English proficient

- LRE - Least restrictive environment

QUOTABLE QUOTE

"I have come to believe that a great teacher is a great artist and that there are as few as there are any other great artists. Teaching might even be the greatest of the arts since the medium is the human mind and spirit."

—John Steinbeck

Learning Disabled Students

Learning disabled students are those who demonstrate a significant discrepancy, which is not the result of some other handicap, between academic achievement and intellectual abilities in one or more of the areas of oral expression, listening comprehension, written expression, basic reading skills, reading comprehension, mathematical calculation, mathematics reasoning, or spelling.

Following is a list of some of the common indicators of learning disabled students. These traits are usually not isolated ones; rather, they appear in varying degrees and amounts in most learning disabled students. A leaning disabled student:

- Has poor auditory memory, both short term and long term.

- Has a low tolerance level and a high frustration level.

- Has a weak or poor self-esteem.

- Is easily distractible.

- Finds it difficult, if not impossible, to stay on task for extended periods of time.

- Is spontaneous in expression; often cannot control emotions.

- Is easily confused.

- Is verbally demanding.

- Has some difficulty in working with others in small or large group settings.

- Has difficulty in following complicated directions or remembering directions for extended period of time.

- Has coordination problems with both large and small muscle groups.

- Has inflexibility of thought; is difficult to persuade otherwise.

- Has poor handwriting skills.

- Has a poor concept of time.

Teaching learning disabled youngsters will present you with some unique and distinctive challenges. Not only will these students demand more of your time and patience; so, too, will they require specialized instructional strategies in a structured environment that supports and enhances their learning potential. It is important to remember that learning disabled students are not students who are incapacitated or unable to learn; rather, they need differentiated instruction tailored to their distinctive learning abilities. Use these appropriate strategies with learning disabled students:

- Provide oral instruction for students with reading disabilities. Present tests and reading materials in an oral format so the assessment is not unduly influenced by lack of reading ability.

- Provide learning disabled students with frequent progress checks. Let them know how well they are progressing toward an individual or class goal.

- Give immediate feedback to learning disabled students. They need to see quickly the relationship between what was taught and what was learned.

- Make activities concise and short, whenever possible. Long, drawn-out projects are particularly frustrating for a learning disabled child.

- Offer learning disabled students a multisensory approach to learning. Take advantage of all the senses in helping these students enjoy, appreciate, and learn.

- Learning disabled youngsters have difficulty learning abstract terms and concepts. Whenever possible, provide them with concrete objects and events: items they can touch, hear, smell, etc.

- Learning disabled students need and should get lots of specific praise. Instead of just saying, "You did good," or "I like your work," be sure you provide specific praising comments that link the activity directly with the recognition; for example, "I was particularly pleased by the way in which you organized the rock collection for Karin and Miranda."

- When necessary, plan to repeat instructions or offer information in both written and verbal formats. Again, it is vitally necessary that learning disabled children utilize as many of their sensory modalities as possible.

- Encourage cooperative learning activities when possible. Invite students of varying abilities to work together on a specific project or toward a common goal. Create an atmosphere in which a true "community of learners" is facilitated and enhanced.

For additional information on teaching learning disabled students, contact the Learning Disabilities Association of America at:

4156 Library Road
Pittsburgh, PA 15234
412-341-1515
www.ldanatl.org

A Word of Advice

"Keep your principal informed of any incidents, situations, challenging students and/or parents. It is so very important to keep your principal 'in the loop' so he/she can assist you with any additional issues that may arise."

—Jane Piepmeier, former elementary teacher

Students Who Have Hearing Impairments

Hearing impairment may range from mildly impaired to total deafness. Although it is unlikely that you will have any deaf students in your classroom, it is quite possible that you will have one or more who will need to wear one or two hearing aids. Here are some teaching strategies:

- Provide written or pictorial directions.

- Physically act out the steps for an activity. You or one of the other students in the class can do this.

- Other students can be responsible for taking notes (on a rotating basis) for a hearing impaired student.

- Seat a hearing impaired child in the front of the classroom and in a place where he or she has a good field of vision of both you and the white board.

- Many hearing impaired youngsters have been taught to read lips. When addressing the class, be sure to enunciate your words (but don't overdo it) and look directly at the hearing impaired student or in his or her general direction.

- Provide a variety of multi-sensory experiences for students. Allow students to capitalize on their other learning modalities.

- It may be necessary to wait longer than usual for a response from a hearing impaired student. Be patient.

- Whenever possible, use lots of concrete objects such as models, diagrams, realia, samples, and the like. Try to demonstrate what you are saying by using touchable items.

Students Who Have Visual Impairments

All students exhibit different levels of visual acuity. However, it is quite likely that you will have students whose vision is severely hampered or restricted. These students may need to wear special glasses and require the use of special equipment. Although it is unlikely you will have a blind student in your classroom, it is conceivable that you will need to provide a modified instructional plan for visually limited students. Consider these tips:

- Make audio recordings of portions of textbooks, trade books, and other printed materials so students can listen (with earphones) to an oral presentation of necessary material.

- When using the white board, use black markers and bold lines. Also, be sure to say out loud whatever you write on the white board.

- As with hearing impaired student, it is important to seat the visually impaired student close to the main instructional area.

- Provide clear oral instructions.

- Be aware of any terminology you may use that would demand visual acuity the student is not capable of. For example, phrases such as "over there" and "like that one" would be inappropriate.

- Partner the student with other students who can assist or help.

Students Who Have Physical Impairments

Physically challenged students include those who require the aid of a wheelchair, canes, walkers, braces, crutches, or other physical aids for getting around. As with other impairments, these youngsters' exceptionalities may range from severe to mild and may be the result of one or more factors. What is of primary importance is the fact that these students are no different intellectually than the more mobile students in your classroom. Here are some techniques to remember:

- Be sure there is adequate access to all parts of the classroom. Keep aisles between desks clear, and provide sufficient space around demonstration tables and other apparatus for physically disabled students to maneuver.

- Encourage students to participate in all activities to the fullest extent possible.

- Establish a rotating series of "helpers" to assist any physically disabled students in moving about the room. Students often enjoy this responsibility and the opportunity to assist whenever necessary.

- Focus on the intellectual investment in an activity. That is, help the child use his or her problem-solving abilities and thinking skills in completing an assignment without regard to his or her ability to get to an area that requires object manipulation.

- When designing an activity or constructing necessary equipment, be on the lookout for alternative methods of display, manipulation, or presentation.

- Physically impaired students will, quite naturally, be frustrated at not being able to do everything the other students can accomplish. Be sure to take some time periodically to talk with those students and help them get their feelings and/or frustrations out in the open. Help the child understand that those feelings are natural but also that they need to be discussed periodically.

Students Who Have Emotional Problems

Students with emotional problems are those who demonstrate an inability to build or maintain satisfactory interpersonal relationships, develop physical symptoms or fears associated with personal or school problems, exhibit a pervasive mood of unhappiness under normal circumstances, or show inappropriate types of behavior under normal circumstances.

Although you won't be expected to remediate all the emotional difficulties of students, you need to understand that you can and do have a positive impact on students' ability to seek solutions and work in concert with those trying to help them. Here are some guidelines for your classroom:

- Whenever possible, give the student a sense of responsibility. Put the student in charge of something (operating an overhead projector, cleaning the classroom aquarium, re-potting a plant), and be sure to recognize the effort the student put into completing the assigned task.

- Provide opportunities for the student to self-select an activity or two he or she would like to pursue independently. Invite the student to share his or her findings or discoveries with the rest of the class.

- Get the student involved in activities with other students, particularly those students who can serve as good role models for the child. It is important that the emotionally disturbed child has opportunities to interact with fellow students who can provide appropriate behavioral guidelines through their actions.

- Discuss appropriate classroom behavior at frequent intervals. Don't expect students to remember in May all the classroom rules that were established in September. Provide "refresher courses" on expected behavior throughout the year.

- Emotionally disabled students benefit from a highly structured program - one in which the sequence of activities and procedures is constant and stable. You will certainly want to consider a varied academic program for all your students, but you will also want to think about an internal structure that provides the support emotionally impaired youngsters need.

- Be sure to seat an emotionally impaired child away from any distractions (highly verbal students, equipment, tools, etc.).

- Whenever possible, keep the activities short and quick. Provide immediate feedback, reinforcement, and a sufficient amount of praise.

Students Who Have Attention-Deficit/Hyperactivity Disorder

Students with Attention-Deficit/Hyperactivity Disorder (ADHD) offer significant and often perplexing challenges for many teachers. However, it is interesting to note that the IDEA's definition of students with disabilities does not include students with ADHD. For this reason, ADHD students are not eligible for services under IDEA unless they fall into other disability categories (hearing impairment, learning disability, etc.). However, they can receive services under Section 504 of the Rehabilitation Act of 1973.

Section 504 of the Rehabilitation Act of 1973 is a civil rights law requiring that institutions not discriminate against people with disabilities in any way if they want to receive federal funds. It requires that a school create a special plan to accommodate students' learning needs. However, the law provides no funding to do so.

ADHD students comprise approximately 3 to 5 percent of the school-age population. This may be as many as thirty-five million children under the age of eighteen. Significantly more boys than girls are affected, although reasons for this difference are not yet clear. Students with ADHD generally have difficulties with attention, hyperactivity, impulse control, emotional stability, or a combination of those factors.

As you consider this list of signs of ADHD, know that several of these traits must be present in combination before a diagnosis of ADHD is made. A student who has ADHAD:

- Has difficulty following directions.
- Has difficulty playing quietly.
- Talks excessively.
- Fidgets or squirms when sitting.
- Blurts out things.
- Is easily distracted.
- Often engages in dangerous play without thinking about the consequences.
- Has difficulty awaiting turns.
- Interrupts or intrudes.
- Doesn't seem to listen.
- Has difficulty paying attention.
- Has difficulty remaining seated.
- Often shifts from one activity to another.

When working with ADHD students in your classroom, keep the following in mind:

- Make your instructions brief and clear, and teach one step at a time.
- Be sure to make behavioral expectations clear.
- Carefully monitor work, especially when students move from one activity to another.
- Make frequent eye contact. Interestingly, students in the second row are more focused then those in the first.
- Adjust work time so it matches attention spans. Provide frequent breaks as necessary.
- Provide a quiet work area where students can move for better concentration.
- Establish and use a secret signal to let students know when they are off task or misbehaving.
- Use physical contact (a hand on the shoulder) to focus attention.
- Combine both visual and auditory information when giving directions.
- Ease transitions by providing cues and warnings.
- Teach relaxation techniques for longer work periods or tests.
- Each day be sure students have one task they can complete successfully.
- Limit the amount of homework.
- Whenever possible, break an assignment into manageable segments.

You are not alone when you're working with special needs students. Often specialists, clinicians, and other experts are available in the school as part of an educational team. Included on the team may be special education teachers, diagnosticians, parents, social workers, representatives from community agencies, administrators, and other teachers. By working in concert and sharing ideas, you can provide a purposeful education plan for each special needs student.

A Word of Advice

"Invite the children into the classroom to eat lunch with you, or more importantly, eat lunch with them in the cafeteria. It creates a bond beyond measure, and those children who are unmotivated will connect with you and be more willing to make an extra effort."

—Morgan Lanzalotti, current elementary teacher

English as a Second Language

The education of students whose dominant language is not English and who are ELLs is the responsibility of every Local Education Agency (LEA). The law requires the LEA to provide a program for every student who is limited English proficient (LEP) or an English language learner (ELL).

Some estimates indicate that approximately 10 percent of the school-age population in this country speak languages other than English as their primary language. Obviously, not all the children in our classrooms are able to speak English as their second language. They may be recent arrivals to this country; they may use their native language exclusively at home; or they may not understand some of the patterns and grammar of English sufficiently to speak it with any degree of competence.

Bilingual education refers to a mix of instruction through the medium of two languages. The primary goal of bilingual education is to teach concepts, knowledge, and skills through the language the learner knows best and then to reinforce this information through the second language in which the learner is less proficient. When working with bilingual learners, follow these instructional principles:

1. Lessons Should Proceed from Whole to Part

It is important for second language learners to see the big picture. They can develop concepts when they are able to start with the general ideas and fill in "gaps" with specific details.

Instructional strategies and activities include the following:

- Reading to students
- Students listening to tape-recorded texts
- Students reading to students
- Students dictating stories that are recorded by a teacher

2. Lessons Should Be Learner-Centered

Students learn to become literate when instructional lessons begin with what they know (background knowledge) and build on those concepts. Learning is not the simple transmission of knowledge but rather the construction of knowledge based upon what learners bring to any learning situation.

Instructional strategies and activities include the following:

- Publication of a classroom newspaper
- Journal writing
- Self-initiated questions
- Interactive brainstorming
- Bringing in native language literature to share
- Publishing handmade books

3. Lessons Should Have Meaning and Purpose for Students Now

It is vital that students not only know why they are learning something but that they are also able to see some immediate relevance and applicability of that material to their daily life.

Instructional strategies and activities include the following:

- Student to student e-mails; pen pals
- Survival words and phrases (Men, Stop, Don't Walk)
- Vocabulary charts and graphs
- Daily journaling

4. Lessons Should Engage Groups of Students in Social Interactions

Collaborative work can be a powerful stimulus to learning. When children have opportunities to interact with each other—sharing ideas and concepts—learning becomes a social function, a function of support and camaraderie. Instructional strategies and activities include the following:

- Cooperative learning
- Small group and large group work
- Group problem-solving
- Pen pal e-mails or texts (Check out www.epals.com)
- Cross-age tutoring

5. Lessons Should Develop Both Oral and Written Language

True learning comes about when children are immersed in all the dimensions of language. Consequently, the development of oral and written language can happen simultaneously (each supporting the other) when students are provided with realistic opportunities to use those language arts in a productive learning environment. Instructional strategies and activities include the following:

- Student-dictated stories
- Word sorts
- Environmental print (menus, labels, billboards, etc.)
- E-books

6. Learning Should Take Place in the First Language to Build Concepts and Facilitate the Acquisition of English

Although this may be a difficult principle for you to embrace, particularly if you do not speak the native language(s) of your students, I submit that acquisition of English occurs when youngsters are encouraged to build concepts in their first language. Instructional strategies and activities include the following:

- Oral presentations
- Native language books (commercial and student-created)

- Teacher presentation of instruction in the native language
- Classroom aids who speak the native language
- Concepts taught in the first language followed by concepts taught in English
- Valuing students' language and culture (learning students' languages, learning about students' cultures, hiring bilingual staff, allowing students to speak their primary language)

Monolingual Teachers and Bilingual Students

At this point, you may be wondering how you will be able to teach bilingual students if you don't speak their language. The concern is a good one. However, you can employ a variety of techniques in your classroom to assist students whose native language is other than English, especially when yours may be strictly English. Consider these ideas:

- Arrange for bilingual aides or parent volunteers to read literature written in the primary language to the students.
- Plan for older students who speak the younger students' first language to come to class regularly to read to or talk with the younger students.
- Set up a system of pen pal communiques (written in the primary language) between students of different classes or different schools. (Again, check out www.epals.com)
- Have students who are bilingual pair up with classmates who share the same primary language but are less proficient in English. This buddy system is particularly helpful for introducing new students to class routines.
- Invite bilingual storytellers to come to the class and tell stories that would be familiar to all the students. Using context clues, these storytellers can convey familiar stories in languages other than English.
- Build a classroom library of books in languages other than English. At times, teachers within a school may want to pool these resources.
- Encourage journal writing in the first language. A bilingual aide or parent volunteer can read and respond to journal entries. Give

students a choice of languages to read and write in.

- Look around the room at the environmental print. Include signs in the first language as well as articles and stories in English about the countries the students come from.

- Have students engage in oral activities such as show-and-tell using their first language as they explain objects or events from their homelands.

- Student-dictated stories

- Word sorts

- Environmental print (menus, labels, billboards, etc.)

- E-books

Teachers of English to Speakers of Other Languages (TESOL) can provide you with a wealth of resources for teaching non-English speaking students in your classroom. Contact them at:

700 S. Washington Street, Suite 200
Alexandria, VA 22314
703-836-0774
www.tesol.org

Here's an important point: approach the teaching of bilingual students as a wonderful learning opportunity for you. Relish these students' involvement in your classroom, and provide them with active opportunities to participate in and contribute to that environment. You will grow, your English-speaking students will grow, and your bilingual students will grow as well.

Co-teaching

Many schools have a co-teaching model in place to work with students with disabilities. In this model, two certified teachers are in the classroom at the same time - one is the regular classroom teacher (who is ultimately responsible for the overall classroom curriculum) and the other is a special education teacher who works in concert with the regular teacher to ensure that lesson objectives are being met for all students. In many cases these co-taught classrooms are established for classes in which there is a higher than average number of disabled students.

The advantage, as you might imagine is that both teachers can work together in order to reach all students - something which may be difficult to do for a single teacher working solo. In order for this to happen, it is essential that both teachers have a positive working relationship and a camaraderie of shared responsibilities and educational philosophy. Open communication is essential in ensuring that these classrooms work effectively.

Here are some tips on working with a co-teacher (a special education teacher) in your classroom:

- This is not a "power struggle," it is an opportunity to reach more youngsters through the expertise of two certified teachers.
- Daily (or, at the very least, weekly) conferences are strongly suggested. Work to establish and maintain open lines of communication.
- Take time to discuss educational outlooks and pedagogical philosophies. Try to reach common agreement in cases where there may be some potential conflict or disagreement.
- Keep in mind that both of you are bound by a student's IEP. That is, you are BOTH responsible for ensuring that all elements of the IEP are satisfied. In other words, one teacher does not have more responsibility than does another.
- When modifications to IEPs are made, it is essential they be done in a spirit of shared cooperation.

Suffice it to say, you will have a range of learners in your classroom. Attending to all their needs may seem to be a daunting task at first. But, know that there are many resources and many people ready to assist you with insight and camaraderie.

Chapter 18

Assessing Student Progress

By some estimates, the average student will take nearly 2,500 tests, quizzes, and exams during her or his school years. For the most part, those measurement devices determine how much students know about a particular topic. However, they are often misused and overused— instruments that often waste time and yield imperfect results. Do we need to know how well students are learning? Absolutely! But, giving lots of tests because—well—because we've always given lots of tests is hardly a justification. Let's take a look.

> ## QUOTABLE QUOTE
> "Much education today is monumentally ineffective. All too often we are giving young people cut flowers when we should be teaching them to grow their own plants."
>
> —John W. Gardner

Assessment and Evaluation

Assessment and evaluation are not new concepts for you; however, in most previous academic environments you were probably the one being assessed or evaluated. As you move into your first-year teaching position, you will assume the responsibilities of an evaluator and an assessor. You will be required to determine how well your students are learning, gauge their performance, and measure the appropriateness of the content and the effectiveness of the methods and techniques utilized in your classroom.

So, before we go any further into this chapter, let's get a basic understanding of these two (frequently misused) terms:

1. Assessment: When you assess students, you gather information about their level of performance or achievement. We can further define this term according to type:

- Formative assessment. Formative assessment is used concurrently with instruction. It's used to determine student progress with the material being presented, as a diagnostic instrument to track student strengths and weaknesses, and to provide feedback for the student and teacher. It is the assessment that occurs between the introduction of a unit of work and its conclusion. The feedback provided by formative assessment will help you determine the effectiveness of the content with a series of questions; for example, "Is the material too difficult or too easy?" "Are there gaps that need to be covered before we move on?" and "Do any concepts or vocabulary need to be clarified?"

- Summative assessment. Summative assessment is used frequently at the conclusion of a unit of study. Basically, it serves three primary functions: 1) It assesses the extent of pupils' achievement or competency at the end of instruction, 2) It provides a basis on which grades or course marks can be fairly assigned, and 3) It provides the data from which reports to parents and transcripts can be prepared.

One way to distinguish between formative and summative assessment is based on the utilization of the data collected through the assessment instrument. If it is to be used to determine a final grade or assess the final achievement or performance of a student or a group of students, it is summative. If, however, the information is for planning purposes, it is formative.

Here are some criteria to consider for your own classroom:

- Effective assessment is a continuous, on-going process. Much more than determining the outcome of learning, it is rather a way of gauging learning over time. Learning and assessment are never completed; they are always evolving and developing.

- A variety of assessment tools is necessary to provide the most accurate measurement of students' learning and progress. Dependence on one type of tool to the exclusion of others deprives students of valuable learning opportunities and robs you of measures that help both students and the overall program grow.

- Assessment must be a collaborative activity between teachers and students. Students must be able to assume an active role in assessment so they can begin to develop individual responsibilities for development and self-monitoring.

- Assessment needs to be authentic. It must be based on the natural activities and processes students do both in the classroom and in their everyday lives.

2. Evaluation: When you evaluate students you compare one student's achievement with other students or with a set of standards. One very common example of formal evaluation is high-stakes testing. Simply stated, high-stakes testing is when students are given a standardized test, the results of which are rewarded in some way. Failing the test might have negative consequences (or rewards), too. For example, in California, students must pass the California High School Exit Examination to graduate. If they don't pass, they don't graduate. Thus, when some sort of reward system is attached to a standardized test, that test becomes a high-stakes test. SATs (Standardized Achievement Test) and ACTs (American College Testing) are good examples of high-stakes testing because the "reward" is often admission into college.

There are various types of federal legislation that require states to administer standardized tests to select groups of students. Often students' achievement on these tests determines the amount of funding or financial reimbursement a school, district, or state will receive from the federal government. As with just about everything else, high-stakes testing has arguments for and against. Here are some of the arguments against high-stakes testing:

- The content on the tests may not match the content taught in the classroom.

- Educational decisions are often based on how well students do on a single test.

- Students from lower socio-economic groups and from certain minority groups tend to do poorer on standardized tests.

- High-stakes testing often puts a lot of pressure on both teachers and students.

And some advantages of high-stakes testing include the following:

- Standardized testing holds teachers accountable for teaching what needs to be taught.

- The tests allow schools within a district to be compared with each other. Schools may be rated good, average, or poor based on test results.

- The public can get a sense of how well a school is doing by reviewing the results of these tests.

- Some people argue that the tests foster increased student motivation. For example, if students want to graduate from high school, they need to pass the state exam.

As a classroom teacher, you have little control over the use of high-stakes testing. You may be required to administer these tests whether or not you agree with them. In fact, in many districts, these tests are used to evaluate individual teacher performance. Suffice it to say, these tests will impact you and the kind of instruction you provide for a long time to come.

A Word of Advice

"Data is essential. Take the time to truly analyze student data, and develop a 'What's Next?' plan to address individual weaknesses and strengths. Learn how to analyze data and create an action plan."

—Morgan Lanzalotti, current elementary teacher

Effective Assessment Tools

Just as a carpenter has many tools in her or his collection; so too, do teachers have a wide variety of assessment options to use with students. It is highly likely you took a course on assessment as part of your teacher training program. I won't attempt to duplicate any of that information here. However, I would like to share a variety of assessment tools for you to consider as part of your teaching repertoire. This is not meant as an exhaustive list, but rather a collection of some of the most useful and informative instruments available.

1. Rubrics

A rubric is a one-page document that describes varying levels of performance, from high to low, for a specific assignment. Rubrics let students know the expectations for an assignment before they begin work on that assignment. They clearly define what a student must include in a piece of work to achieve a certain score. As such, they may be general in nature (all the homework assignments in math) or specific (an assignment that focuses on the use of details in an expository writing paper). Here's a brief example of a rubric that might be used in an English class.

	4 points	3 points	2 points	1 point
ACCURACY	Factual data is accurate	Most data is accurate	Some information is accurate	Little accurate information
ORGANIZA-TION	Material is presented logically	Material is reasonably logical	Material is minimally organized	Little or no organization is evident
CREATIVITY	High level of creativity and originality is evident	Moderate level of creativity and originality is evident	Some creativity and originality	Little or no creativity and originality
FOCUS	Project is focused and detailed	Project is moderately focused and detailed	Project is minimally focused and detailed	Project show little focus; unclear ideas

You can easily create a rubric for any assignment or instructional activity. Here are some steps to follow:

1. Determine the criteria by which you will grade a specific assignment.

2. What are the levels of mastery you want in that assignment? You can do this by determining to best and worst levels, and then determining the levels in between.

3. Create a rubric using the format in the sample above.

4. IMPORTANT: Show students models of both acceptable and unacceptable assignments. For example, show a paper that would get a high score and the rubric used to determine that score. Make sure students understand how each of the criteria was satisfied in the rubric.

5. You may wish to distribute several random papers and invite students (in groups, perhaps) to assess the assignment using a prepared rubric.

What a Great Idea!

There are several web sites that allow you to customize your own rubrics. These sites also have a plethora of prepared rubrics that you can use for any subject, any assignment, and any activity in any grade (yup, there are hundreds of them ready for you to use). Some are available in both English and Spanish:

4Teachers (www.4teachers.org)

Educator's Network (www.rubrics4teachers.com)

---

2. Anticipation Guides

Anticipation guides alert students to some of the major concepts in textual material before it is read. As such, students have an opportunity to share ideas and opinions as well as activate their prior knowledge about a topic before they read about that subject. It is also a helpful technique for eliciting students' misconceptions about a subject. Students become actively involved in the dynamics of reading a specified selection because they have an opportunity to talk about the topic before reading about it.

- Read the textual material and attempt to select the major concepts, ideas, or facts in the text. For example, in a selection on "Weather" the following concepts could be identified:

  ○ There are many different types of clouds.

Different examples of severe weather include tornadoes, hurricanes, and thunderstorms.

○ Precipitation occurs in the form of rain, snow, sleet, and hailstones.

○ Many types of weather occur along "fronts."

• Create five to ten statements (not questions) that reflect common misconceptions about the subject, are ambiguous, or are indicative of students' prior knowledge. Statements are written on the white board, developed as a PowerPoint presentation, or photocopied and distributed.

• Give students plenty of opportunities to agree or disagree with each statement. Whole class or small group discussions would be appropriate. After discussions, let each individual student record a positive or negative response to each statement. Initiate discussions focusing on reasons for individual responses.

• Direct students to read the text, keeping in mind the statements and their individual or group reactions to those statements.

• After reading the selection, engage the class in a discussion on how the textual information may have changed their opinions. Provide students with an opportunity to record their reactions to each statement based upon what they read in the text. It is not important for a consensus to be reached, nor that students agree with everything the author states. Rather, it is more important for students to engage in an active dialogue - a conversation which allows them to react to the relationships between prior knowledge and current knowledge.

As part of Ted Pringle's fifth grade unit on "Oceanography" students had expressed an interest in learning about some of the dangers facing the world's oceans. The effects of a recent oil spill off the New Jersey coast had received front page coverage in the New York Times and had sparked students' curiosity about how oil spills and other environmental hazards affected the local flora and fauna. In preparation for their study of pollution, Ted prepared the following Anticipation Guide:

DIRECTIONS: Look at the sentences on this page. The statements are numbered from 1 to 6. Read each sentence; if you think that what it says is right, print *"Yes"* on the line under the word "BEFORE." If you think the sentence is wrong, print "No" on the line under the word "BEFORE." Do the same thing for each sentence. Remember how to do this because you will do it again *after* you read the selection.

BEFORE   **AFTER**

_____   _____   1. There is only one way to clean up an oil spill.

_____   _____   2. An oil spill is dangerous to sea and land creatures, but not birds.

_____   _____   3. Untreated sewage is dumped directly into the ocean.

_____   _____   4. Bottom-feeding fish eat cigarette butts.

_____   _____   5. Laundry detergent is a pollutant.

_____   _____   6. The oceans of the world are in serious danger.

Working as a class, students responded to each of the statements on the Anticipation Guide (by recording a "Yes" or "No" on each line in the "BEFORE" column). Class discussion centered on reasons for their choices and predictions about what they might discover in the forthcoming chapter. Ted then provided multiple copies of a newspaper article to students and invited them to read and locate confirming data related to each of the identified statements. Afterwards, students completed the "AFTER" column of the guide and shared their reasons for placing "Yes" or "No" on each line. Follow-up discussions revealed some differences of opinion, yet the conversation was lively as well as supportive. Students found that they each brought different perspectives to the article, yet they could all benefit from those differences in a mutually stimulating learning environment.

3. Group Quiz

Here's an assessment tool that will reap untold benefits - not only in terms of your overall assessment of student progress in a class or subject, but also in terms of other essential factors critical to a well-run classroom environment. In fact, I've been using this strategy for many years with incredible success. It is appropriate for use with students in grades 3–12 and will help clarify (for them) critical concepts in your course while promoting an active learning environment.

Called "Group Quiz," here's how it works. Assign a specific reading assignment to your students. This can be a homework assignment or an in-class reading assignment. Let students know that after they have read the assigned text they will take a ten-item multiple-choice quiz.

Prepare a ten-item multiple-choice quiz on the reading selection with four choices for each of the ten questions. Type up the quiz, duplicate it, and distribute it to all the students in the room.

- **Phase A:** Invite each student to complete the quiz by circling the correct answer to each question according to what they read or understood from the assigned work.

- **Phase B:** After everyone has completed Phase A assemble the students into various groups of about 4–5 students each. The groups can be permanent groups or are assembled as ad-hoc groups on the spot. Distribute a Quiz Record Sheet to each group (see the sample below) and invite them to work together using their own individual quizzes as starting points to collectively determine an appropriate answer for each question. They may not use any notes or the actual text.

All responses are recorded on individual Quiz Record Sheets (one for each group). The initial responses for each group is recorded by hand in the "5 Points" column. After the answers to all ten questions have been recorded by a group, one person raises her or his hand and invites you (the teacher) to score the responses. If a response is correct, it is left intact. However, if a response to a question is incorrect an "X" is put over it. If a group gets all ten questions correct, they receive 50 points (5 points per question times ten questions).

However, if an answer is incorrect (an "X" was placed over the answer recorded on the sheet) the sheet is returned to the group and they are encouraged to select a response from the remaining items for that question. That new response is recorded in the "3 Points" column. Once again the sheets are handed in and immediately scored. If, again, a recorded response is incorrect an "X" is placed over it and the sheet is returned. The next response is then recorded in the "1 Point" column. If that answer is incorrect, the last (and the correct) answer is recorded in the final ("0 Points") column.

The overall scores for each group is tallied and recorded.

EXAMPLE:

You are a high school Biology teacher and are in the midst of a series of lessons on invertebrates. One of the "classic" invertebrates studied during these lessons are clams. You assign the following reading selection (from a popular nonfiction book) to your students to read as a homework assignment. You tell your students that the first thing they will do in class tomorrow will be to take a Group Quiz on the material in the assigned reading (NOTE: while they are doing the reading, you are putting together the ten-item Group Quiz for tomorrow's class.)

While clams are not endowed with a brain, they have what is often referred to as a "simplified brain," known to biologists as ganglia. While most creatures have a single brain, many species of clams have two coordinated ganglia. One, known as the pedal ganglia, is responsible for controlling the clam's foot. The other, known as the visceral ganglia, regulates the clam's internal organs.

Ask a zoologist for a definition of ganglia and he or she will tell you that it is "a biological tissue mass, or a mass of nerve cell bodies." Human brains, such as yours and mine, are capable of thought and reason; however, ganglia are only capable of controlling the most rudimentary of biological functions: moving the foot, for example, or moving food along the digestive tract. In short, clams cannot think, they can only do. It's a classic case of stimulus/response—no pondering, no thought, and no contemplation. Clams are essentially creatures without reason; organisms without a conscience.

Although clams do not possess thinking organs, they have the capacity to sense their surroundings. For example, many species of clams have a series of tentacles with chemoreceptor cells used to taste the surrounding water. By tasting the water a clam can determine if food is nearby or if a fellow clam is in the immediate area.

Another notable sensory organ is the clam's osphradium, a patch of sensory cells located below the posterior adductor muscle (the muscle that opens and closes a clam's two shells). A clam sometimes uses this organ to taste the water or measure its turbidity (the cloudiness or haziness of water due to particulate matter [dirt] suspended in the water).

Clams and their relatives also have an additional sensory feature, a collection of organs known as statocysts. These organs help the clam sense and correct its orientation, that is, is it right side up or upside down? And, if it is right side up, is it tilted to one side or the other? This orientation is critical in helping ensure that the clam is able to feed efficiently.[1]

Following are the first four questions (of the ten-question Group Quiz) you have developed for the assigned reading above. These questions have been typed and are distributed to every student in the class.

1. The clam's osphradium is used to:
   a. Measure the cloudiness of the surrounding water
   b. Taste the water
   c. Both A & B
   d. Neither A or B

2. The pedal ganglia controls the clam's
   a. Brain
   b. Foot
   c. Stomach
   d. Reproductive organs

3. In order to feed efficiently clams rely on their
   a. Statocysts
   b. Visceral organs

---

1 Excerpted from: Fredericks, Anthony D. *The Secret Life of Clams: The Mysteries and Magic of Our Favorite Shellfish* (New York: Skyhorse Press, 2014), pp. 110-111. Used by permission of the author.

    c.   Brains

    d.   Posterior adductor muscles

4.   "A mass of nerve cell bodies" refers to a clam's

    e.   Shells

    f.   Ganglia

    g.   Particulate matter

    h.   Foot

Each group records its answers on a Quiz Record Sheet. A partial one is illustrated below:

Group Quiz #_____

Group Members:

_____	_____
_____	_____
_____	_____
_____	_____

Group Name: _____

	5 points	3 points	1 point	0 points
1.				
2.				
3.				
4.				

As explained above, when the group completes answering all ten questions (recorded in the "5 Points" column) they submit the sheet to you. You quickly score it (By the way, for the four questions above the correct answers are: 1 - C; 2 - B; 3 - A; 4 - B). An "X" is over any incorrect answers and the sheet is returned to the group for them to make some decisions on more appropriate responses.

Group Quiz scores are recorded over the length of the school term and become part of the final grade. My own experience has shown that this is one of the most enjoyable assessment exercises students have experienced. It is non-stressful, engaging, and offers valid information necessary for you to ensure a well-focused lesson or unit. Other teachers from around the country have also seen some very positive benefits of this tool. Here are some of their insights:

1. This is an excellent way to ensure that students read the material assigned. They cannot actively participate in group discussions unless they have read the assigned text. Initially, some may be reluctant to do so, but if you make these a normal and regular part of your academic program (in my classes about 20% of the final grade is the results of these quizzes) you will notice, over time, more and more students reading the necessary material.

2. These Group Quizzes also serve as a way to determine the background knowledge of the class for a forthcoming topic. By giving a Group Quiz before launching into a formal lesson plan you can determine if students have sufficient prior knowledge to handle the material. If a significant majority of the class "bombs" the quiz, then you may need to revise a forthcoming lesson; on the other hand, if most groups "ace" the quiz, then you can feel comfortable in the fact that they are sufficiently prepared to handle the material.

3. The quizzes promote a sense of classroom community. Students are working together in a coordinated fashion to arrive at answers that are beneficial to the entire group. The individual groups are not competing against one another - they are only competing with themselves. When I debrief with students at the end of a course the one element they always mention is the value of the Group Quizzes in helping to form friendships, solidify class camaraderie, and cement a spirit of cooperation.

4. The Quizzes are never viewed as punitive in nature. Students see them as what they are - a way to actively assess their reading knowledge and comprehension about a specific topic. These are

not something "done by the teacher," but, rather are instruments that help clarify important concepts and clearly identify specific objectives for a lesson.

What a Great Idea!

Purchase several sheets of self-adhesive mailing labels and a clipboard. Identify the two to four students you will be observing on a particular day, and write each of their names and the date in the corner of separate mailing labels. As you walk around the room during a lesson, jot down observational notes for each student on his or her mailing label (use more than one label if necessary). At the end of the day, remove each student's label and place it on a sheet of paper you then store in the student's folder. This way you can transfer your observations to students' folders quickly and can easily keep track of each student's progress in a chronological fashion.

Alternate strategy: Use an iPad to record your notes and observations of each student as you walk around the room. At the end of the day, transfer those records into a spread sheet you maintain on your desktop computer.

- Record only what you saw and not the subjective reasons you think may have caused the behavior.

- Plan time at the end of the day to discuss your observations and anecdotes with each identified student. Let the students know what you have observed, and provide them with an opportunity to react and ask pertinent questions.

5. Most important, students don't see themselves as academic combatants. In many traditional classrooms students are evaluated on tests that rank order them from high to low; good to bad. Students (as did you) quickly learn how they rank on

the scholastic ladder. In many cases, they are permanently categorized. Group Quizzes, however, place more of the emphasis on a shared intellectual responsibility - an academic cohesiveness that is significantly more cooperative than combative. The result, I'm happy to report, is students more (successfully) engaged in their own learning.

4. Anecdotal Records.

As I alluded to earlier, assessment is not a "once-and-done" process. Rather, it occurs over time and tracks a student's development and competence over many days, weeks, or months. Anecdotal records, or narrative descriptions of students' behavior and academic performance, can be some of the most valuable evaluation tools available. Through anecdotal records, you can keep a running record of each individual student to determine likes and dislikes, advancement or regression, and growth and development.

By their nature, anecdotal records are subjective assessments of students. However, they have the advantage of "tracking" students over many occasions and many learning opportunities. In this way, they serve as an accurate record of performance that the teacher can share with administrators and parents. Here are some guidelines for using anecdotal records:

- Don't try to write a description of each student's behavior and performance every day. Identify four or five students a day, and concentrate on them.

- Keep your comments short and to the point. It's not necessary to write long, involved sentences about what you observe. To keep the notes short, invent your own method of shorthand.

- Maintain a file folder on each student. Store a student's anecdotal record in his or her folder at the end of the day.

5. Journal Entry Sheet

Whenever students work together in cooperative groups it may be appropriate for a designated member of each group to complete a survey form similar to the one below. Copies of completed sheets can be included as entries in each group member's personal folder.

Journal Entry Sheet

Topic/Subject: _____

Date: _____

What we knew: _____

_____

_____

What we discovered: _____

_____

_____

Books or media where information was found: _____

_____

_____

The most interesting fact we learned: _____

_____

Signed: _____ (Group Recorder)

---

6. Student Self-Assessment

I strongly believe that effective instruction is instruction that involves students in each and every aspect of that instruction including assessment. When students can participate in assessing their own progress they begin to develop an internal sense of responsibility which helps them assume control over their own learning. The Student Self-Report Form, indicated below, is one that can be shared with individual students - in either a written or verbal format - providing them with authentic opportunities to "look inward" and gauge their learning.

Student Self-Report Form

Name: _____   Date: _____

1. These are some of the things I learned this week: _____

_____

_____

2. These are some of the things that gave me trouble this week:

_____

_____

_____

3. I believe I have improved this week. Here's why: _____

_____

_____

4. Here are some things I'd like to learn more about: _____

_____

_____

5. Here is how I would rate my performance this week: _____

_____

_____

6. This is what I'd like to do next week: _____

_____

---

7. Attitudinal Assessment

Attention to your students' attitudes is and should be an important part of the overall evaluation process. It stands to reason that if a student enjoys a particular subject or topic, she or he will learn a great deal in that subject. Conversely, if a student dislikes a specific topic, it's doubtful that she or he will take advantage of the learning opportunities in that area. Knowing what your students think about a subject area provides you with valuable data on which to remedy weak areas of the curriculum or revise portions of your program in accordance with individual perceptions. That doesn't necessarily mean that all students must like the subject, but it can help you make a conscience effort at strengthening the affective dimensions of your classroom program.

You can assess your students' attitudes in any number of ways. Here's an example of a sentence completion form that could be used at the beginning of the school year in an elementary classroom. The subject is math, and the teacher is attempting to gauge the background knowledge of her students as well as their initial feelings about math.

Math Sentences

Name: _____

Date: _____

Directions: Complete each of the following sentence stems in your own words. There are no right or wrong answers.

Math is:

_____

_____

I don't think math is:

_____

_____

The thing I hate most about math is:

_____

_____

Instead of math class I'd rather:

_____

_____

When it's time for math, I:

_____

_____

I enjoy math when:

_____

_____

Most mathematicians are:

_____

_____

Math would be more interesting if:

_____

_____

Most of my friends think math:

_____

_____

When we do math activities, I often feel:

_____

_____

Final Thoughts

Overall, I like to think of assessment as a process that offers opportunities for growth- teacher growth, student growth, and program growth. It's one thing to assess student performance; it's quite another to do something with that information. If all you do is administer an endless bank of assessments and do nothing with the results, then your assessment protocol is close to worthless. The data you gather from all forms should be used productively to help students develop the skills, processes, and attitudes that help make learning an important part of their lives.

It's important to keep in mind that assessment, to be thorough, must occur before, during, and after instruction. One of the dangers of formalized tests is that it often take place at the conclusion of a lesson or activity. This tends to underscore learning as simply an accumulation of facts and figures to be memorized and regurgitated on various written instruments. Good assessment is not merely the attainment of high scores, but also an opportunity to improve your teaching skills to ensure student learning.

Chapter 19

<u>Motivating Your Students</u>

It seems that the topic of motivation is a constant in many teacher discussions. It makes no difference whether those conversations are taking place in elementary schools, middle schools, or high schools, there is a shared concern about why students aren't motivated and how teachers can motivate them to learn.

But, the reality is that teachers often ask the wrong kind of question about motivation. They ask, "How can I motivate my students?" That kind of question implies that motivation is something done to or created for students. That kind of thinking is dangerous. True, you will probably have unmotivated students in your classroom. Who knows, perhaps at some time in your educational career you were unmotivated in a particular class or course (hopefully, not one of mine). You may have been uninterested in a subject, uninspired to do the work, or uncaring about the topic or the way in which it was presented.

Make no mistake about it: motivation is a critical factor in how students learn. But, to be successful, we need to look at motivation from the other side, from the students' side. In this chapter, I'll show you how to do that.

QUOTABLE QUOTE
"We expert teachers know that motivation and emotional impact are what matter."

—Donald Norman

Understanding Motivation

Teachers often have some preconceived notions about what motivation is and how it's manifested in students. As teachers, we need to deal with those misperceptions first before we can discuss the ways in which we can enhance students' motivation. Here are a few:

- People are either motivated or they're not—in all tasks, assignments, or learning situations.

- Motivation is a constant, stable condition like the number of fingers on your hand or the color of your skin.

- We can enhance motivation for a learning task through rewards (or punishment).

- There are two types of students: those who are motivated (they will learn), and those who are not motivated (they will not learn).

As you look at these misconceptions, you might notice that most are couched in terms that imply that motivation is something controlled or managed from the outside. That is to say, motivated students are those who have been inspired by dedicated teachers and supportive parents. Often, when teachers talk about motivation, they talk about what they do to interest students in a topic or encourage them to participate willingly in the dynamics of a lesson. The assumption is twofold: teachers create motivational conditions in the classroom and students come to class motivated or unmotivated to work. Those assumptions imply that motivation is an external event or condition. That view often causes anxiety and frustration for many teachers.

One of the biggest misconceptions about motivation many new teachers have is that you can motivate your students by making learning fun. Teachers often define their colleagues' skill as educators in terms of their ability to make learning enjoyable and entertaining. Unfortunately, the "motivation = fun stuff" equation is one of the most common teaching myths. You probably remember fun and enjoyable activities or situations when you were in school; perhaps you learned something, too. But, learning doesn't have to be fun to be motivational.

The problem is one of perception. That is, teachers who strive to make every classroom activity fun are looking at motivation as an externally controlled condition—something teachers do to students to make them do something else. That sends the wrong message to students. Yes, learning can be amusing and enjoyable, but it doesn't need to be fun to be effective. Fun is a byproduct of learning, it is never a purpose for learning.

The Three Elements of Motivation

Motivation is defined as an emotion, desire, or psychological need that incites a person to do something. The word motive comes from a Latin root meaning "to move." At its simplest, motivation is comprised of three critical elements:

1. Expecting success

2. Developing a community of learners

3. Placing a value on learning

Your awareness of these three factors and your willingness to address these issues in your classroom will determine, to a large extent, how well your students will be motivated. Let's take a look at them in a little more detail.

1. Expectations of Success

Whether you're teaching a roomful of kindergarten students about the letter "B" or you're teaching adolescents about the social ramifications of Salvador Dali's painting *The Persistence of Memory*, you must provide instruction that will ensure a measure of success for every student. Each student must know that she or he can achieve a degree of success with an assignment or academic task.

Often, people don't try new things because they're afraid of failure. This fear of failure begins early in our academic careers and carries forward into our adult lives. As classroom teachers, we must establish and promote conditions that will emphasize and support an expectation of success for each student. Try these ideas:

- Offer differentiated instruction. Be aware that you'll have students of differing abilities in your classroom. Don't make the mistake of crafting a single lesson for everybody - without taking into consideration the different ability levels. Differentiated instruction is a respect for the different ability levels in your classroom and, therefore, a respect for each student's ability to succeed. You might provide one type of learning task for struggling students and another for independent students. You might need to adjust the time available for completion of an assignment or offer additional assistance for another.

What a Great Idea!

One of the most effective ways of offering differentiated instruction is via multiple intelligences. There is mounting evidence that learning experiences that involve a variety of intelligences allow students to extend, expand, and take advantage of their individual learning preferences. Here they are:

1. Verbal-Linguistic Intelligence - This intelligence involves ease in producing language and sensitivity to the nuances, order, and rhythm of words.

2. Logical/Mathematical Intelligence - This intelligence relates to the ability to reason deductively or inductively and to recognize and manipulate abstract patterns and relationships.

3. Musical-Rhythmic Intelligence - This intelligence encompasses sensitivity to the pitch, timbre, and rhythm of sounds as well as responsiveness to the emotional implications of these elements of music.

4. Visual-Spatial Intelligence - This intelligence includes the ability to create visual-spatial representations of the world and to transfer them mentally or concretely.

5. Bodily-Kinesthetic Intelligence - This involves using the body to solve problems, make things, and convey ideas and emotions.

6. Intrapersonal Intelligence - This entails the ability to understand one's own emotions, goals, and intentions.

6. Intrapersonal Intelligence - This entails the ability to understand one's own emotions, goals, and intentions.

7. Interpersonal Intelligence - This intelligence refers to the ability to work effectively with other people and to understand them and recognize their goals and intentions.

8. Naturalist Intelligence - This includes the capacity to recognize flora and fauna and to make distinctions in the natural world.

If you'd like additional information on "Multiple Intelligences" or would like to see it in action in a classroom environment, please check out the following YouTube videos:

- **Multiple Intelligences (by MsHMcKnight)**
- **Multiple Intelligences Thrive in Smartville**
- **How Do You Teach Multiple Intelligences**

- Provide feedback promptly, frequently, and efficiently. Students must be able to see a direct connection between any effort or completed task (such as homework) and a response from you. Here are some suggestions for providing successful feedback:

  ○ Make feedback immediate. ("I'm returning the social studies test you took yesterday.")

  ○ Never be sarcastic when giving feedback. ("Everybody must have had a 'brain freeze' when you did this assignment!")

  ○ Allow students to revise their incorrect responses. ("I'm not sure that's correct. Is there another way we could do this?")

  ○ Use verbal as well as written feedback. ("You must feel pretty good when you do work like this.")

  ○ Allow students to control some feedback. ("How do you think you did on the scooter test?")

  ○ Make comments specific, and suggest corrections. ("You provided a good rationale for Wilson's League of Nations, but you might want to look further into Congress's response.")

○ Offer feedback in terms of a student's progress, not her or his comparison with others. ("Look how you moved from 14 correct on the spelling test to 17 correct this week.")

• Students should have multiple opportunities to set their own academic goals. Invite them to establish obtainable goals for a lesson, a unit, or even for the whole year. Ask them what they would like to learn about a topic and what they think they must do to learn that material. Psychologists tell us that the goals we set for ourselves (as opposed to the goals others set for us) are intrinsically more motivational. We're more inclined to pursue those goals and relish in the success that comes about when we achieve them.

• Help students see the connection between effort and result. Let students know that the work they put into an assignment will result in the completion of a task or some new material learned. It's important that students understand that learning is work and that the more they work, the more they can learn.

A Word of Advice

"When dealing with an uninvolved student, I always find it helpful to make a personal connection with them. We've all been unmotivated at times. Let he/she know that you, too, have struggled with not feeling like doing something. Give him/her details and the process you used to persevere."

—Becky Glatfelter, current elementary teacher

2. Developing a Community of Learners

We spent considerable time in Chapter 4 on how to build an invitational classroom. There were several good reasons for that; one of which is that an invitational classroom is critical to the level of motivation (to learn) exhibited by students. I won't repeat all the "stuff" in that chapter; however, here are a few additional points to keep in mind as you consider the value of an invitational classroom in terms of overall student motivation.

- A feeling of "belongingness" precipitates motivation. When a group has common goals and common objectives they tend to work together. Members of that group have a commonality of purpose and, as a result, they have a cohesiveness that binds everyone together. That cohesiveness is intrinsically motivating.

- All students want and need to be respected members of a group. Effective group membership is essential to establishing positive learning environments where individual motivation is valued.

- A study from the University of Northern Iowa looked at the relationship between motivation and group membership. It was hypothesized that individuals would have higher levels of motivation and performance while working in groups. The results supported this hypothesis, demonstrating that individuals perform at higher levels and report having a higher level of motivation when completing tasks in groups.

- A study published in the March 2012 issue of the *Journal of Personality and Social Psychology* demonstrated that group membership is sufficient to increase feelings of motivation. According to the authors, "Ultimately, people seem wired to adopt the goals of the people around them." In short, positive group membership is a significant factor in motivating the members of that group.

- Several other research studies have demonstrated the connection between group membership and motivation. The results of those studies have supported the notion that "Individuals are motivated to achieve at high levels and support other team members when group membership exists." The overall consensus is that a sense of belonging to a group is necessary to foster and promote individual motivation.

So, the short story is that the motivation of your students is ultimately tied to the concept of an invitational classroom. Invitational classrooms create the conditions that encourage, enhance, and promote student motivation. In "non-invitational" classrooms students tend to be more competitive and combatant and, as a result, less motivated.

3. A Value on Learning

The third element that contributes to the motivation of students is whether or not students see a value in what they're learning. The predominant question in the back of every learner's mind is, "What's in it for me?" Learning something is one thing, but knowing why you need to learn something is quite another.

For motivation to occur, students must know the reasons, rationale, and whys of any learning task. Your students will be more engaged and more motivated when you provide them with specific reasons for learning something. To do that, relate the learning directly to their lives. When students see a connection between what they learn in the classroom and their lives outside the classroom, they'll be motivated to actively participate in the learning process. Try the following suggestions:

- "Let's take a look at how this idea of friction might affect our performance on a skateboard."

- "We know Andrew likes to collect baseball cards. If he wanted to add twenty-five new cards to his collection and each one was priced at $1.79 each, how much money would he need?"

- "Remember the fight on the playground last week? How was that confrontation similar to or different from the conflict between the North and the South?"

- "I know you're all familiar with this rap song. I wonder if we can take the 'food pyramid' and turn it into our own rap song."

It's also important that you provide your students with opportunities to make their own choices. Making personal choices helps develop a sense of ownership and can be a powerful motivational strategy. Students can select various ways to complete an assignment, the due date of an assignment, or the complexity of a learning task. These kinds of decisions offer students a measure of control over their academic lives. More control = more motivation.

Locus of Control

How can we provide the conditions that will stimulate students to be more motivated to learn? Many educators say it comes down to a question of locus of control. In essence, locus of control refers to the degree to which individuals perceive they are in control of the factors that affect their lives. By in large, "external individuals" feel they are strongly influenced by others (parents, teachers, peers). "Internal individuals" feel they are primarily responsible for the events that happen to them.

It's important to view the concept of locus of control as a continuum. That is, people aren't 100 percent external or 100 percent internal; they fall somewhere along a continuum line, with a predisposition to one side or the other. Here's what it looks like:

External...Internal

Interestingly, students who are more internally motivated demonstrate higher levels of academic achievement. On the other hand, external students tend to exhibit lower levels of academic achievement. Thus, it stands to reason that if we can help students achieve a more internal locus of control, we can assist them in achieving higher levels of scholastic achievement. One of the ways teachers do this is through the use of positive reinforcement. Yet, consider for a moment the following research:

- About 90 percent of the positive things students do in a classroom go unrecognized.

- On average, only about 2 percent of a teacher's day is devoted to any kind of positive reinforcement.

It should be obvious that we often don't take the time to celebrate the work or efforts of our students. The reasons may be numerous: we get too busy, we need to cover an expansive curriculum, there's too much paperwork, grades are due, lesson plans must be written, and a host of other reasons and excuses. Yet, if we don't recognize our students, we deprive them of a powerful motivational incentive for any and all learning tasks.

The two "classics" of positive reinforcement are praise and encouragement. But, be cautious here, they are not the same thing, nor do they have the same effect on students. First, let's clarify the two concepts with brief definitions:

- Praise: to express a favorable judgement.

- Encouragement: to inspire one to do better.

Look carefully at those two definitions and you'll notice something. That is, praise is something that is done to someone else. That is to say, praise is when one person says something positive to another person ("You are doing a good job in math today, Jason."). On the other hand, encouragement is when one person moves another towards some type of favorable outcome ("What else will you need to do to continue your success in the chess tournament?"). But here is the most important and most significant difference between these two concepts: praise and encouragement are at either end of the locus of control continuum. Praise tends to foster an external locus of control, while encouragement fosters an internal locus of control. Please take a look at the chart on the next page to see how everyday teacher comments can influence a student's locus of control.

This is not to say we should eliminate all praise and concentrate solely on encouragement. Rather, we need to emphasize more encouragement than praise to help students achieve a more internal locus of control. We also need to take time regularly and consistently to recognize the effort or work of our students. No one likes to do work without recognition—you don't, I don't, and your students don't.

Praise	• Recognizes the doer. ("You got an A on the test.") • Is control from the outside. ("You are good when you follow all my class rules.") • Is evaluation by others. ("I was very happy when you picked up all the pencils.") • Focuses on the finished, well-done task. ("You did your homework which is what I expect you to do every day.") • Emphasizes personal gains. ("You came in first place, which means you are a winner.")
Encouragement	• Recognizes the effort of the doer. ("All of your hard work is to be celebrated.") • Is faith that the individual can control herself or himself. ("You are learning because of your own efforts.") • Promotes self-evaluation. ("How do you feel about your work so far?") • Emphasizes effort and progress of a task. ("You must be pretty proud of all the improvement you have made.") • Emphasizes appreciation of contributions and assets. ("Your efforts helped us have a good science fair.")

Praise and encouragement, in measured quantities, can be powerful elements in any successful teacher's classroom. But you must remember some major considerations if your verbal comments are to be effective:

- You must use positive reinforcement consistently. It cannot be used every once in a while or randomly. And it cannot be used just for the good students and not the underachieving students.

It must be a regular element for every student in every learning activity.

- It's generally acceptable to recognize students in front of other students at the elementary level. At the middle school and high school level, positively reinforce individuals privately.

- You must be honest with the positive reinforcement. It must acknowledge the learner's true achievement, rather than any fake or made-up accomplishments ("Wow, Bobby, this time you let the earthworm live.").

- You must be specific. General statements such as "Good," "Great," or "Cool" are too general to have any meaning. Provide a very specific reference for a student. ("You must feel very proud about the work you did on your Civil War project.")

- The feedback must always be immediate. It has to occur soon after the event or task is completed, or it will be meaningless. One of my own self-made rules is to return any written assignments within one week of submission—no exceptions! Writing encouraging statements on a term paper and then waiting three weeks to return that paper defeats the whole purpose and practice of positive reinforcement. The words are hollow.

What a Great Idea!

- Positive recognition should be done in a casual manner.
- It should require no more than eight to ten words.
- It should last no longer than three to five seconds.

A word of caution is in order here. Many teachers, particularly novice teachers such as yourself, tend to fall into a perilous trap: false and excessive praise. We want to be friendly with our students, we want to let them know that we support all their academic efforts, and we want them to have good and positive experiences in our classroom. So, we hand out lots of praise—lots and lots of praise for anything and everything. The problem comes about when we praise students for minimal effort and achievement ("Oh, wow, Sonya, you got problem number 27 correct.

What an absolutely terrific job!"). The message to the student is clear: I can get some recognition and commendation with very little work. In other words, less than my best work is good enough. What happens is that students quickly get a message that minimal effort is perfectly acceptable (Because even some minimal effort will get me some kind of praise.). In short, excessive praise not only fosters an emphasis on external controls, it "unmotivates" students.

There's another common practice teachers use to try and motivate their students: tangible rewards. These include things like stickers, smiley faces, coupons, patches, gold stars, and the like as motivational tools. The practice of providing these tangible rewards has been a consistent one in education. But there are some controversies surrounding the use of tangible rewards:

- They are a form of external control; one person controls the behavior of another.

- They do not foster an internal locus of control.

- They are a form of bribery or coercion.

- The more rewards teachers give, the more rewards students come to expect.

- Students often do work for the rewards rather than for the learning that may occur.

- Rewards are a way of manipulating and controlling people. It's similar to the way we train animals: do a trick and get a treat.

Here's an example: your students are participating in a field day (an all-school athletic competition, usually conducted at the end of the year). Let's say they all do well and the team gets second place overall. You announce that you're going to give the class an ice-cream and cake party. That's a celebration because it was unexpected and wasn't a condition of the event. However, if you say to your students, "If you do well at the field day tomorrow, I'll give you all an ice-cream and cake party," that's a reward because you tried to influence their behavior or performance with an external premium.

Think carefully about the value of rewards in your classroom. Am I "dead set" against them? No! But, I do believe they are used to an excess and as an easy substitute for more effective methods of long-term motivation. The problem, as I see it, is that rewards are often based on criteria established by teachers, not students ("You will get <u>this</u> if you do <u>that</u>."). If, as current research strongly supports, there is a strong connection between an internal locus of control and positive scholastic achievement, then it behooves us as teachers to emphasize practices that enhance personal responsibility, self-determination, and internality. Tangible rewards won't do that!

But They're Not Motivated!

Every teacher gets them. So will you! They are the unmotivated students, those who could care less about the lesson, the class, or the whole school experience. How do you deal with the unmotivated? You might consider these ideas:

- Create an atmosphere of puzzlement and novelty in your teaching. Tap into students' natural curiosity with unusual events. ("Has anyone ever seen a creature covered in slime? I have one right here in this box.")

- Use a combination of both individual and group projects. Provide opportunities for students to share and discuss in groups as well as opportunities to work on their own.

- Periodically invite students to meet and discuss any barriers to their learning (time, textbook, teacher, rules, etc.).

- Ensure numerous opportunities for students to set their own goals. Keep those goals realistic, and be sure to start with tiny steps before moving to larger goals.

- Be especially vigilant for opportunities to encourage (more so than praise) learning accomplishments.

- Model your enthusiasm for learning. Let students see your excitement for a task or assignment. (This, I have discovered, is perhaps the best motivator of all!)

- It's critical that students know you're working for their benefit, not for a paycheck. Be encouraging and supportive in all your contacts with an unmotivated student. As soon as you give up, so will the student.

- Relate academic tasks to a student's life. They might never ask you why they have to learn something, but you should always give them the answer.

- Provide frequent offers of help ("I don't know; let's see what we can discover together").

- Be willing to accept (and celebrate) different viewpoints ("That's not what I had in mind; could you please explain your position?").

- Students who are turned off to learning are often turned off to authority. Don't be dictatorial or authoritative. Create an invitational, cooperative climate in your classroom, one without intimidation or threats.

- This is a "must": Be sure to call on every student every day— **every day**. Each student in your classroom deserves your attention. It's quite easy to pass over or ignore the typically unmotivated students. But in doing so, we create a "snowball" effect that spirals way from us and reinforces the fact that certain students are clearly unmotivated and will continue to be unmotivated—particularly since we aren't devoting any time to them.

- Engage students in lots of collaborative assignments. Group work on a regular basis provides you with an opportunity to expose students to several positive role models in the class. So too, does it reinforces the concept of an invitational classroom, one that supports and encourages all members.

- I have found that the asking of lots of open-ended questions is a great way of motivating students. As you'll remember from Chapter 15, too often, students are asked questions that have a single right answer ("How many square feet in an acre?"). If they get the wrong answer, and consistently get the wrong answers, their motivation suffers. But, by asking a plethora of open-ended questions—questions for which there is no single correct answer ("Why do you think he went into the cave?", "What do you especially like about this painting?") and acknowledging the responses—you can contribute mightily to the level of positive motivation in your classroom. In short, lots of open-ended questions virtually guarantee student success. Trust me on this one, you'll see a pronounced and decided difference in the overall level of classroom motivation.

Motivation is a critical element in any successful classroom. Weaving it into and through all your lessons and all your interactions with students may be one of the most positive things you can do as a new teacher. It is, in so many ways, a "main ingredient" of the invitational classroom.

A Word of Advice

"Motivation comes from being inspired. Remember why you chose this profession. You have a passion that needs to be shared with each student. Sometimes you can motive the whole, sometimes you must connect with the individual. Find a way to touch each student."

—Donna Cherry, current secondary teacher

Part V

"Yes, I'm Ready!"

Chapter 20

<u>Under the Microscope: Formal Observations</u>

October _____, 20 _____

Dear Diary:

OMG—I'm freakin' out! Tomorrow Mrs. Lupinski [the principal] is coming into my classroom for my first observation. I am sooooo scared!!! What if Jasmine has a total meltdown? What if Miranda has one of her classic "hissy-fits"? What if Derek and Tyrone get into some kind of big fight? What if the water experiment gets all over the classroom and the custodian has to come in and mop everything up and all the kids are laughing and having way too much fun and Lupinski gives me a lousy grade and I never get tenure and my career as a teacher is over, over, over? Why, oh why, did I ever decide to schedule the unit on "Water" for this week? What a stupid, stupid idea that was! Now Lupinski's going to see me at my absolute worst. OMG—I'm having nightmares already and it's only 6:00 PM. I am just so freakin' out over this.

Maybe I could get sick. Maybe I could just call in sick and have some sub take over the class for the rest of the week and use that time to get my head together to work on a lesson that won't over-stimulate the kids and help me keep my sanity and show Lupinski what I can really do. Yeah, that's what I should do. I just need more time, more time, there's just not enough time. What am I going to do! **WHAT AM I GOING TO DO!**

It's inevitable! Sometime during your first year of teaching, the principal or some other school administrator will come into your classroom and do one or more formal observations. Depending on the regulations in the state or district in which you teach you may also have several informal observations during the course of your first year.

Please don't freak out!

You, like every other teacher in your school, will be subjected to these evaluations. You may fret over them, worry about them, concern yourself over them, and lose a few hours of sleep over them (you may give up sleep altogether). You experienced them several times during student teaching and now you're going to experience them throughout your teaching career. They are as inevitable as the sun rising and the payment of income taxes.

Many first year teachers excessively worry over these visits because they have the mistaken belief that the administrator is there to find out what they are doing wrong. Nothing could be further from the truth! A good formal observation is a collaborative effort aimed at ensuring that students are afforded a positive and successful educational experience. You were hired because several people in the school or district believed you had the skills, talents, and temperament to make an academic difference in the lives of students. In other words, you were seen as a very positive addition to the overall school climate—you were NOT hired because you had a plethora of faults, liabilities, or imperfections.

Does that mean you're perfect? Of course not! No first year teacher ever hired anywhere in the world ever is. We are all, as a friend of mine puts it, "works in progress." There are many areas in which we excel. It is likely I have some teaching skills that you may not. It is equally likely that you have some talents and experiences that I do not (say, in the area of social media as a teaching tool, for example). That's OK. The point of a formal observation is to highlight your strengths and point out some of your weaknesses so that they, too, can be improved and strengthened. Growth as an educator must be a continuous process throughout your teaching career - it never ends when you graduate from college. The people who observe you are there as your professional assistants and personal trainers—offering advice and counsel to keep you growing and improving.

Although standards and regulations vary from state to state and from school district to school district, you can usually expect to be formally observed by your school administrator from two to four times during your first year. So, too, is there considerable difference in the evaluation standards used among various states and districts. Nevertheless, the following four domains (and accompanying standards) are typically used in most teacher evaluation protocols:

1. **Planning and Preparation**: State standards, Objectives, Knowledge of content, Lesson plans, Differentiation, Resources, Technology, Assessment of learning, Level of instruction

2. **Classroom Management**: Physical environment, Behavior management, Interactions, Routines and procedures, Rapport, Focus, Engagement rate

3. **Instructional Delivery**: Congruence, Communication, Strategies and techniques, Content, Engagement, Transitions, Questioning, Pacing, Feedback, Assessment, Integration, Reinforcement, Higher order thinking

4. **Professionalism**: Integrity, Judgment, Respect, Peer interaction and communication, Journaling and reflectivity, Procedures, Participation, Student records, Relationships, Awareness of professional growth opportunities, Commitment

A Word of Advice

"Always remember: you are a teacher of so much more than your content area or area of specialty!"

—Bryan Quibell, current secondary teacher

Preparing for an Observation/Evaluation

Observations and evaluations will have some degree of stress associated with them—that's inevitable. But, you can counter this stress by preparing beforehand. Doing your homework in advance of an evaluation will make the entire process considerably smoother and productive. Here are some tips to consider.

1. Get a copy of the observation form the administrator will be using. As a new teacher you may have been provided with a copy of the state or district form as an element in an orientation packet you received just prior to the start of the school year. Review this form and know the specific elements that will be reviewed during your lesson.

2. If permitted and convenient, I always suggest a pre-visit meeting with the administrator. This should be an informal conversation between the two of you about what will be observed, things to look for, and any special circumstances. This would also be an opportunity to review the standards enumerated on the formal observation document. It is always appropriate to ask, "What will you be looking for?

3. Plan to teach a lesson that is simple in design and relatively uncomplicated. Administering an exam, viewing a YouTube video, conducting an elaborate experiment, or scheduling a guest speaker would all be inappropriate. Make sure there is a distinct beginning and end to the lesson, rather than a lesson scheduled over a three-day time frame.

4. Think about doing a trial run of the lesson at home or in your dorm or apartment. If you can recruit some individuals (roommates, family members, boyfriend or girlfriend, unsuspecting neighbor) all the better. I know this is going to sound crazy, but I like to do my trial lessons in front of the bathroom mirror. That way, I can see how comfortable I am with my pacing, delivery, timing and presentation. (NOTE: I used to get lots of strange looks from the family cat when I first did this, but he's able to deal with it much better now.).

5. Get your students involved. Let them know that a visitor will be in the classroom to observe you (not them). It would be a good idea to review behavioral expectations and any necessary classroom procedures.

6. If you don't already do so, post the objectives for the lesson in a prominent place in the classroom. Make sure you review those objectives at the start of the lesson (you may want to re-read Chapter 13) as well as at the end of the lesson.

7. Prepare and provide a packet of information for the observer. These may include some or all of the following items: class list, seating chart, classroom procedures, a copy of the actual lesson plan, a textbook, and any special instructions or events. As necessary, you may wish to provide a copy of the previous

day's lesson or specific samples of student work as background preparation for the lesson you are about to teach.

8. The day before the lesson spend some time to get all necessary materials, equipment, supplies in order. Five minutes before your principal shows up is not the time to discover that your laptop can't access the school's Wi-Fi for some strange and mysterious reason. Check everything out beforehand not once or twice, but three times! Many years ago, I was being formally observed in fourth grade. The lesson was one on a specific reading comprehension strategy. I had planned to start the lesson with a read-aloud—something I did with every reading lesson. The principal sat in the back of the room, pen and evaluation form at the ready, and I reached over on my desk to pick up the incredible and amazing book I had planned to read to the students. It wasn't there. In my rush to get to school early that day, I had left the book on the kitchen table at home that morning. Needless to say, I received (and deserved) a small post-lesson lecture about preparedness (Gulp!).

9. Start off the lesson with a great motivational opening: something exciting, dramatic, and engaging. Ramp up the enthusiasm level so that your students are eager and motivated. By the same token, be sure your lesson conclusion is equally rousing and stimulating (NOTE: In observing hundreds of student teachers over the years, it has been my experience that the conclusion is, quite often, the weakest part of a lesson. Plan to spend some extra time to ensure that yours is powerful and robust.).

10. Time, time, time. One of the big advantages of doing a trial run of the lesson to be observed is to make sure that sufficient time is devoted to each and every component of that lesson. The ability to manage your time will be one of the elements of the formal evaluation; so it is critical that you allow sufficient time for the lesson as a whole as well as sufficient time for each component within the lesson.

11. As you're teaching the lesson, be your natural self. Don't try to be someone you're not. If you are not normally demonstrative, don't try to be demonstrative just because you think it will

make a better impression on the administrator observing you. In almost every case you'll come across as "fake." Be normal, be natural, be yourself—anything else will just put unneeded stress on you.

12. Don't try to teach the "perfect lesson." Rather, teach the best lesson you can in the best way you can. Keep in mind that you're in your first year of teaching—the administrator knows that and certainly doesn't expect that you will have "all your ducks in a row" just yet. Know that there might be one or two miscues or one or two "hiccups" during the course of your lesson. And, that's OK. They might also give you something to laugh at with your students or with the administrator in your post lesson review session. As you might expect, those "boo-boo's" are always a good way to engender rapport.

Most administrators will want to meet with you shortly after the formal observation. This debriefing session will give you an opportunity to get some feedback on how well you addressed each of the four domains listed earlier in this chapter. It is critically important that you go into these conferences with a positive attitude. This is a terrific opportunity to learn about some of your strengths (from an impartial observer) as well as some areas that might need a little strengthening. Coming to the meeting with a defensive attitude will do you more harm than good. The ultimate goal is to help you become a better teacher; that's something very difficult to do if you erect lots of defensive walls around yourself.

The key to a good debriefing session is to do more listening than talking. If you are the one taking over the conversation, then you're probably offering lots of excuses, unnecessary explanations, and lots of defenses. Sure, you may hear some negative stuff, but that's designed to help you establish some improvement goals—goals that will result in better teaching. Instead, listen objectively and be open-minded about what you might do better next time. So too, will you hear about the "good things" you did during the lesson - again, you want to listen carefully to these items; they too are a part of who you are as a teacher.

What a Great Idea!

Actually, two great ideas:

1. After you conference with the administrator, plan to send a thank you note, letter, or e-mail. Extend your appreciation for the time she or he took to come and visit you. Also, thank the individual for the ideas and suggestions proffered in the debriefing session. This may sound old-fashioned, but it will make a difference.

2. Within one week of the debriefing session make up a "plan of attack" as to what you will do regarding each of the areas for improvement. Use any notes you took during the debriefing session listing specific areas of weakness as well as specific strategies you plan to implement to address each of those areas. Send a copy of this "Improvement Plan" to your administrator so that she or he is aware of your intensions. BONUS: Provide an extra copy of this plan to your administrator in advance of the next formal evaluation session. Invite the administrator to look for improvements in any of the designated areas. Make sure you talk about those in the follow-up debriefing.

A Self-Evaluation

Each semester I supervise at least one student teacher. Each week I visit the student teacher's classroom and observe her or him "in action." After each observation, I sit down with the student teacher and begin the review session with two very critical questions:

1. "On a scale from 1 (low) to 10 (high) what number would you assign yourself for the lesson you taught today?", and

2. "As you look back on that lesson, what would you need to change in order to give yourself a higher score?"

Student teachers always find those two questions very challenging, often because it is, usually, the first time they have had to self-evaluate a lesson they have taught. Self-evaluation is not something we do very often, but it can be one of the most powerful and productive ways we can grow as teachers. A regular self-evaluation helps us understand some of our weak points, some of our strong points, as well as strategies that might help us continue to learn and grow as teachers.

The evaluation process is one more thing on our professional agenda; but, it is definitely necessary! Although you will be formally evaluated throughout your first year, you can also add to that process by engaging in regular and sustained self-evaluations. These would be important throughout, not only your first year of teaching, but throughout your entire career (I still do them after forty-seven years in the profession.).

QUOTABLE QUOTE

"All of us have two educations: one which we receive from others; another, and the most valuable, which we give ourselves."

—John Randolph

What you will discover below is a professional paradigm for teacher evaluation. It is similar, in many respects, to the teacher evaluation forms used by principals in many school districts throughout the country. I have modified it somewhat so that it is now a self-evaluative form, one that can offer personal insights into how you are doing and what areas you may need to strengthen. I would suggest that you self-administer this form at regular intervals throughout the school year (perhaps at four evenly spaced junctures during the entire school term). I would also suggest that a self-evaluation using this form might be something appropriate to complete in advance of the more formal evaluation done by your school principal. That way, you will have two views of your performance. And, that way, you can identify and address any misperceptions that may exist between those views.

A Self-Evaluation Paradigm

Directions: The paradigm outlined below can be duplicated and used at any time during your first year. For each of the four domains (Planning and Preparation, Classroom Management, Instructional Delivery, Professionalism) you are invited to do a self-assessment. Read each statement and indicate your perceived level of competence according to the box below:

Masterful (M) - Consistently exceeds expected levels of performance with a high degree of skill.

Proficient (P) - Consistently meets expected levels of performance.

Basic (B) - Usually meets expected levels of performance and would benefit from continued growth to achieve greater consistency and effectiveness.

Unsatisfactory (U) - Usually fails to meets expected levels of competence and performance.

Today's Date: _____

Date of Previous Evaluation: _____

1. Planning and Preparation: The teacher demonstrates thorough knowledge of content and pedagogical skills in planning and preparation. The teacher makes plans and sets goals based on the content to be taught/learned, knowledge of assigned students, and the instructional context.

	M	P	B	U
I am knowledgeable about content.				
I am knowledgeable about pedagogy.				
I am knowledgeable about (name of state)'s academic standards.				
I am knowledgeable about students and how to use this knowledge to impart instruction.				

	M	P	B	U
I use resources, materials, or technology available through the school or district.				
I use instructional goals that show a recognizable sequence with adaptations for individual student needs.				
I use assessments of student learning aligned to the instructional goals and adapted as required for student needs.				
I use educational psychological principles/ theories in the construction of lesson plans and setting instructional goals.				

2. Classroom Management: The teacher establishes and maintains a purposeful and equitable environment for learning, in which students feel safe, valued, and respected, by instituting routines and setting clear expectations for student behavior.

	M	P	B	U
I have expectations for student achievement with value placed on the quality of student work.				
I give attention to equitable learning opportunities for students.				
I appreciate interactions between teacher and students and among students.				
I have effective classroom routines and procedures resulting in little or no loss of instructional time.				
I have clear standards of conduct and effective management of student behavior.				
I give appropriate attention to safety in the classroom to the extent that it is under my control.				
I demonstrate the ability to establish and maintain rapport with students.				

3. Instructional Delivery: The teacher, through knowledge of content, pedagogy and skill in delivering instruction, engages students in learning by using a variety of instructional strategies.

	M	P	B	U
I use my knowledge of content and pedagogical theory through my instructional delivery.				
My instructional goals reflect (name of state)'s K-12 standards.				
I communicate procedures and have a clear explanation of content.				
I use instructional goals that show a recognizable sequence, clear student expectations, and adaptation for individual student needs.				
I use questions and discussion strategies that encourage many students to participate.				
I engage students in learning and adequate pacing of instruction.				
I provide feedback to students on their learning.				
I use informal and formal assessments to meet learning goals and to monitor student learning.				
I am flexible and responsive in meeting the learning needs of students.				
I integrate many disciplines within the educational curriculum.				

4. **Professionalism:** The teacher demonstrates qualities that characterize a professional person in aspects that occur in and beyond the classroom/school.

	M	P	B	U
I am knowledgeable about school and district procedures and regulations related to attendance, punctuality and the like.				
I am knowledgeable of school or district requirements for maintaining accurate records and communicating with families.				
I am knowledgeable of school and/or district events.				
I am knowledgeable of the district's professional growth and development opportunities.				
I exhibit integrity and ethical behavior, professional conduct in accordance with local, state, and federal laws and regulations.				
I use effective communication, both oral and written with students, colleagues, paraprofessionals, related service personnel, and administrators.				
I exhibit the ability to cultivate professional relationships with school colleagues.				
I am aware of (name of state)'s requirements for continuing professional development and licensure.				

After you have evaluated yourself on all four domains, review the chart and note any areas in which you placed a check in the "Basic" or "Unsatisfactory" boxes. I would strongly suggest that you share that information with a mentor or other colleague in your school. Invite that individual to offer some ideas or suggestions on how you could improve on a specific item with a domain or how you might address several concerns within an entire domain.

A Word of Advice

"You're going to have good days and bad days. The bad days may be really bad days. Use those days to reflect on what is happening, work to find the root cause, as well as other ways you can approach the situation. Keep searching for an approach that works."

—Kim Dunlap, current elementary teacher

You will also find it beneficial to share this self-evaluation with your building principal. In doing so, you are sending a very clear message that you most interested in becoming the best possible teacher you can. You are also inviting your principal as a partner in that journey—a collaboration that can benefit you tremendously, not only in terms of professional growth and development, but also in terms of striking a positive and effective relationship with your administrator.

Keep an on-going record of these self-evaluations. At the conclusion of your first year of teaching you should sit down with all your charts and:

1. Note any trends over time. What comes most easily for you? Are there habits or procedures that are challenging for you? What has been frustrating? What has been most rewarding?

2. What were some of your most effective changes? What were some possible ineffective changes? Why were some elements a struggle and others not so much?

3. What do you need to do (in terms of professional growth and development) over the summer months to improve in any area? Make a plan. What web sites can you consult? What books (including this one) or articles can you read? What professional meetings or seminars can you attend? What on-line discussion groups can you join? What colleagues can you talk with for self-improvement ideas?

Regular evaluations will be part and parcel of your life as a professional educator (just like death and taxes are a part of regular life). Viewing them as positive additions to your career can be a most refreshing way to help yourself improve and, in so doing, eventually help your students improve both academically and personally. Your attitude about evaluations will also be the attitude you take into the classroom, an attitude that can truly make a difference.

Teacher evaluations: Please don't freak out!

Chapter 21

<u>Stress Management 101</u>

Intercom: *Miss Smith?*

You: *Yes!*

Intercom: *Mrs. Jones* [the principal] *would like to see you after school today.*

You: (heartbeat increases, breathing becomes shallow, perspiration beads on your forehead) *Did she say what she wanted?*

Intercom: *No, she just said she wanted to see you.*

You: (heart is beating faster, breathing is more labored, sweating is profuse) *Did she say what time?*

Intercom: *Right after student dismissal.*

You: (nervousness increases dramatically, body functions are in total disarray, and serious questions are being asked ["OMG—What did I do now?"]) *OK, I'll be there. Thanks.*

Stress—it's a part of life! Ever since the first wholly mammoth began chasing the first cavewoman or caveman, stress has been a constant element of human life. Although we often think all stress is bad, believe it or not, there is also something known as good stress. Good stress is the anticipation of a first kiss, waiting for a loved one to come back from a long journey, or drawing to an inside straight in a game of poker. Good stress is what propels us to satisfactorily complete a task.

But much of the stress we encounter as teachers is not good stress. It is the stuff that affects us physically, mentally, emotionally, spiritually, and professionally. It's the stress that has a negative impact on our attitudes, personality, and work performance. Defining the stressors of our lives is important; even more significant is how to deal with those inevitable events.

What Is Stress?

Interestingly, there's no universal agreement or exact definition for stress. For years, psychologists have disagreed on a precise definition, probably because stress appears in so many forms and is caused by so many factors—both good and bad. That said, here is a definition I find to be particularly appropriate for teachers: stress is what people experience when an event or situation challenges their ability to effectively cope with that event or situation. It is the difference between the demands of a situation and your perception of how well you will be able to deal with that situation.

Let's take that definition one step further. For the following three statements, put a number 1 in front of the situation that would cause you the most stress, a 2 in front of the situation that would cause you moderate stress, and a 3 in front of the statement that would cause you little or no stress:

_____ While you're driving, a cop pulls you over.

_____ The cop wants to sell you tickets to the upcoming local police ball.

_____ The cop gives you two all-expenses-paid airline tickets to Cabo San Lucas because of your outstanding driving record over the years.

I think you might agree that these examples represent three differing levels of stress. One is severe, another is moderate, and the third is mild or minimal. Not surprising, each of us envisions stress in different ways. Throughout each and every day, many stressors impact our lives. As humans, we tend to automatically and arbitrarily categorize those stressors depending upon our perception of their severity.

If, for example, we categorize many events in our daily schedule as severe stressors, we have a very stressful day. On the other hand, if we group most of the events of our day as mild stressors, we tend to have a minimally stressful day. How we perceive stress will frequently determine how much that stress affects us now and into the future.

A Model of Stress

Here's a good way of looking at stress. Proposed by the noted psychologist Albert Ellis, it's called the ABC model:

A + B = C

- A is the activating event or potentially stressful situation.

- B stands for your beliefs, thoughts, or perceptions about A.

- C is the emotional consequence or stress that results from having these beliefs.

Here's another way of translating that equation:

A potentially stressful situation + your perceptions = your stress (or lack of stress)

Here's an example: you get a note from the principal for an after-school meeting to talk about the results your students got on the latest round of standardized tests.

A: Having to go to the principal's office + B: She's going to yell at me for some of the low scores = C: I have an upset stomach and a migraine headache, and I'm perspiring heavily.

The key part of this equation is B—your thoughts, views, ideas and interpretations. Your perceptions are the key to determining how much stress you will feel. Here's what's important: what you think about the stressor (or stressors) will either increase or decrease your level of "uncomfortableness." If we perceive an event or situation as beyond our control, our stress level goes up. If we perceive ourselves to have some degree of control over the event or situation, our stress levels go down.

The Causes of Stress

With all teachers have to do, it might be easy to see the major causes of stress in a teacher's life. Teachers from around the country have reported the following as significant and frequent stressors:

- Isolation. Many teachers, particularly elementary teachers, point out that isolation (from other adults) is one of the major stress factors in their lives. Working with students all day long without significant adult conversation or interaction is a leading cause of teacher stress.

- Low status of the teaching profession. The public is often seen as uncaring or noncommittal toward teachers and the work they do. Many classroom teachers report that the public's negative attitudes or perceptions have a major impact on their stress levels.

- Work overload. Teachers are being asked to do more and more, often with less and less time available to do it. New materials, new regulations, new curricula, new regulations, and a host of other new stuff keep getting added to the pile, and there is often no relief in sight.

- Standards/Common Core. The move to standards-based and/or Common Core education, in which teachers often feel as though they are accountable for every tidbit of information presented in a classroom, is also seen as a burden. The pressure to have all kids perform well on all tests is frequently cited as a significant stressor.

- Unruly, disruptive students. Students who are undisciplined, disrespectful, and negative add a personal and professional burden to the lives of many teachers. Teachers frequently mention the increased numbers of children (elementary and secondary) who come to school with an "attitude."

- Lack of parent support. Parents who don't take (or who have never taken) an active role in the scholastic and academic lives of their children are another frustration for many teachers.

- Unsupportive administrators. Often principals and other administrators are often seen as the "enemy." Teachers mention that there sometimes seems to be little support (for classroom management and curriculum change) from the front office and little encouragement for the daily grind.

- Evaluations. The annual or semi-annual evaluative process for teachers has been (and will always be) a source of stress, as it is for most workers.

Stress Relief for Your School Life

Stress is a normal and expected part of your life as a first year teacher. Below you will discover a collection of proven and validated strategies from experienced teachers around the country. Several of these suggestions are mental; others are physical. These ideas will help you reduce your levels of stress at school and help you approach each day with a refreshed mind and a more relaxed perspective.

- One of the most important lessons I have ever learned came from my father. He used to say, "Give the other person the right to be wrong." This includes students, colleagues, friends, and relatives. Allowing others to be wrong requires a great deal of patience and self-restraint, but it can result in significantly reduced levels of stress.

QUOTABLE QUOTE

"No one has the right to determine what kind of day I'm going to have."

—Eleanor Roosevelt

- Set up lots of short-term goals for yourself, and work toward satisfying those. Often, we focus on too many long-term goals (redesigning the entire math curriculum, for example) rather than a series of short goals (cleaning out the top desk drawer). An accumulation of long-term goals becomes mentally overwhelming and stressful.

- Interact with adults in your school community outside the classroom. Start a book club; talk over a cup of morning coffee; meet for dinner once in a while. Get together with colleagues to see a movie, volunteer, or just talk about things other than school.

- Take a look at your classroom environment and jazz it up! Your classroom is where you spend most of your days. Make it a place that is both pleasing to the eyes as well as relaxing. If you're so inclined, get a book on *feng shui* and make your room compatible with your personality. What your workplace looks like has a major impact on your mental state.

- Never try to "please all the people all the time." Trying to make everybody around you happy will frustrate you (and stress you) to no end. Some people just want to be grouchy; and will continue to be grouchy no matter what you might do. Let them be.

- One of the most influential books I've ever read is *Last Child in the Woods* by Richard Louv. When you read it you'll see what a daily or regular experience in nature can do for your psyche and your overall well-being. You will discover, as I have, that a regular exposure to the natural world does wonders in significantly reducing your stressors in addition to keeping you on an emotional even-keel. And you'll definitely want to read about the incredible benefits for your students!

Stress Relief for Your Personal Life

This assembly of techniques, ideas, and proposals can reinvigorate your life and help you more effectively deal with the stressors that are a normal and natural part of your everyday life. Some of these will be passive; some active. Use these, modify them to your own needs, and make them a part of who you are as an individual. You may discover heightened motivation, increased awareness, and a more even temperament.

1. Accept your imperfections. Realize that you can't be all things to all people. Embrace your imperfections, and celebrate them.

2. Every so often (once a week, for example) stop and give yourself a much-needed pat on the back.

3. At the beginning of each week, take a few minutes to list five things you like about yourself. Put the list in your desk drawer, and peek at it every so often.

4. Teachers spend a large part of their lives trying to make other people happy. It's equally important that you take time, each day, to recognize and celebrate the things that bring you joy and happiness.

5. Take time, each day, for yourself—no one else, just you!

What a Great Idea!

Many teachers have discovered that mindfulness meditation, done ten to twenty minutes each day is a wonderful way to deal with the inevitable stresses of teaching. With mindfulness, many teachers have learned effective ways of dealing with anxiety, exhaustion, and pressure. In an interesting study conducted with hundreds of teachers in thirty-six different schools in New York City, it was discovered that educators who received mindfulness training were significantly better at handling their own stress. Interestingly, the benefits appeared to spread to students as well. As a result, teachers participating in the training were able to foster a more productive environment for learning and were increasingly more sensitive to their students' needs. For further information on mindfulness, you may wish to consult the following recommended books:

- Mindfulness: An Eight-Week Plan for Finding Peace in a Frantic World by Mark Williams & Danny Penman. (My personal favorite)

- The Little Book of Mindfulness: 10 minutes a Day to Less Stress, More Peace by Patricia Collard.

- Wherever You Go, There You Are by Jon Kabat-Zinn

- Mindfulness: A Practical Guide to Awakening by Joseph Goldstein

6. Take a non-education course at the local junior college, enroll in an art workshop, or participate in a conference or convention. Keep learning new stuff; keep your mind active and engaged.

7. Take a daily walk or run. Use this time to get away from the pressures of your job or life. Use this time for self-reflection and self-renewal.

8. Take a mini-vacation. Find someplace within an hour's drive

of where you live, and spend some quality time there. Look for some of the following places:

- An airport, gallery, or planetarium
- An aquarium, garden center, or quarry
- An arena, greenhouse, or river
- A ballpark, hiking trail, or rock formation
- A beach, historical area, or small cafe
- A bicycle path, hobby shop, or stable
- A botanical garden, home center, or state capital
- A mountain, ice rink, or swamp
- A cave, lake, or theater
- A coffee shop, library, or tide pool
- A country inn, lumberyard, or train station
- A county fair, swimming hole, or bowling alley
- An ethnic restaurant, museum, or winery
- A farm, nature park, or zoo
- A flea market, ocean shoreline, or toy store
- A forest, orchard, or home goods store

9. Play. No, seriously. When was the last time you played? Make regular time to do a crossword puzzle, play a game of cards, paint a picture, play pool, play a board game, or participate in a frivolous activity.

10. Each day, schedule time for yourself. Write down a time in your calendar to be spent on you. This may be a period of time when you read a chapter of a trashy novel, listen to your favorite music, engage in some mental imagery, or simply look out the window and enjoy the view.

11. Stretch it out. One of the ways we can recharge and re-energize ourselves is to take five or ten minutes in the middle of the day to engage in simple stretching exercises. These will get you started:

- A leg up. Sit in your chair with your back straight and your feet firmly on the floor. Slowly lift both legs until your body forms an L shape. Hold that position for a count of ten. Lower your feet to the floor. Repeat ten times.

- Necking. Reach up with your right hand, and place it on the left side of your head. Slowly pull your head down to your right shoulder. Straighten your head, and repeat ten times. Repeat the procedure with your left hand and pull your head down to your left shoulder. Repeat ten times.

- Chest stretch. Stand up straight. Bring your arms straight behind you, and clasp your hands together behind your back. Raise your shoulders slowly up and then slowly down. Repeat ten times.

- Twist and shout. Stand straight up. Touch your right shoulder with your right hand and your left shoulder with your left hand. Slowly turn your upper torso to the left. Return to the starting position, and slowly turn your upper torso to the right. Keep your feet in the same place each time. Repeat ten times.

- Push off. Stand approximately two feet away from a wall. Fall toward the wall with your hands firmly on the surface. Do a simulated push-up from the wall (let your head come close to the wall then push off with your hands). Repeat ten times.

A Word of Advice

"Take care of your health - physical and mental. If you're sick, stay home. Find a way to exercise. You'll be very busy, but you need time with your friends and family. It can't be all work."

—Vicky Lynott, former middle school teacher

12. Carve some time out of your day to tell someone how much you care. A phone call, an email, a letter, a text message, a greeting card, or even a simple hug will bring something special into that person's life, as well as your own.

13. Interact with adults away from the school. Foster relationships with adults who are not educators (you don't want to "talk

shop" all the time). Participate, enroll, and contribute to volunteer organizations and service clubs. Join a church group, a community association, or a gym. Join the community choir, a theater group, a bowling league - anything you'd enjoy in the adult community outside school. It's important to participate in a variety of non-school-related functions.

14. Sometime, early in the day, engage in a period of time in which you close off the rest of the world to meditate, write in a journal, or simply daydream. Take some time each morning to create a positive image of your day.

15. Pace yourself. Don't try to be Superwoman or Superman! Don't try to implement every idea, strategy, or technique you've ever learned about teaching into the first week.

A Word of Advice

"Build a work/life balance. Leave planning and grading at school. Make one weekend day work free. Don't forget to do the things you enjoy (yoga, running, painting, leisure reading, etc.). Your body and mind will benefit and so will your teaching."

—Nicole Hesson, former middle school teacher

Love Yourself

A former student of mine, who now teaches in a nearby school district, has this philosophy of life: "Love the kids, love the job, but take time to love yourself."

After 20 or 30 years in the classroom, how are some teachers able to approach each day with the same vigor and energy they had when they first started teaching? How are they able to continue to create exciting lesson plans and dynamic units that inspire their students week after week and month after month? How are they able to achieve balance in their personal and professional lives?

These are all good questions, and they all engender the same response. The key to success as classroom teachers lies in our ability to take care of ourselves. Devote time and energy to your own well-being, self-renewal, and personal objectives. Caring for yourself does not mean you become self-centered or selfish. Caring for yourself is a significant factor in the physical, emotional, and mental balance you need to maintain your stamina.

It all boils down to this: you cannot take care of others until you first take care of yourself. Teachers who give so much to others that they have little left for themselves begin to burn out. They lose touch with the core of their existence and with the magic of self-renewal that is within all of us. When you commit yourself to becoming the best you can be, you will discover a new energy, a new serenity, and a new spirit of giving that will empower you to help others. As you empower those around you, you will become a better teacher and a better human being!

A Word of Advice

"You will have rough days—especially in your first year. Even after that, as a veteran teacher, I have rough days. It happens to the best of us, but always remember something positive about every day you have. Take the positive with you, and it will help you remember why you do what you do."

—Ashley White, current elementary teacher

A Word of Advice

Making a Difference: 1001 Ways to Reduce Your Stress, Increase Your Happiness, and Influence the World
(Kindle Edition)

by Anthony D. Fredericks

Making a Difference is a collection of 1001 proactive suggestions to improve your life and to calm down in the midst of your incredibly hurried life. You will discover dynamic and exciting ideas that will have a positive influence on how you approach each day. You'll learn how you can significantly change your life, and the lives of those around you, for the better.

Chapter 22

How to be an A+ Teacher

In this final chapter, I'd like to share three guideposts that are essential characteristics of effective teachers. These three overarching behaviors are easy to remember and equally easy to implement into your personal development plan. And, it doesn't make any difference what grade or what subject you teach or where you teach; any first-year teacher, by this point in the book, will be able to implement these with ease. In so doing, you will set yourself up to be an A+ teacher—one who will truly make a difference!

In fact, it's as easy as A-B-C!

1. **A**lways the Learner

Early in my teaching career I adopted a philosophy that has guided and nurtured me through more than forty-five years of teaching. I embraced it as an elementary and secondary classroom teacher, a district reading specialist, and as a college professor. It has been both my light and my destiny and I have freely shared it in almost every college class I have ever taught. It is, for me, one of the most powerful statements I could ever share with the next generation of teachers. It has never failed me as an educator and I share it with you as perhaps the most significant piece of advice I could pass along within the pages of this book;

The best teachers are those who have as much to learn as they do to teach.

By the time you read these words, I will have formally retired from full-time teaching, but I am still a teacher! Why? Because somewhere along the line I got this notion that if I'm going to be an academic force in the lives of students I need to model the kind of learning I'm advocating. That is to say, I cannot in all good conscience tell people how to be a good teacher if I don't model one of the basic and fundamental truths about what good teachers do.

Do I plan to stop learning during my "golden years?" No Way!!

A Word of Advice

"The best advice I ever received as a first year teacher was to start a journal. Keep a notebook and use it to reflect on your lessons, jot down ideas, work out problems, and set goals. This can help you track the progress you've made over time, and it is a great way to see how far you've come. Be sure to record at least one positive interaction every day. In the end, you'll have a journal full of wonderful memories, innovative ideas, and invaluable reflections."

—Darian Kiger, current secondary teacher

Throughout my professional life as an educator I have been pleased and honored to have written a diverse, eclectic, and expansive list of books. Each book I've written has taught me something new - something I didn't know before or something I was curious about.

Many of my published books have been education titles. When I wrote *The Complete Phonemic Awareness Handbook* I had just a sprinkling of knowledge (from my college classes) about the dynamics of this foundation of beginning reading, but I wanted to learn more simply because the teachers I was working with wanted to learn more. I wrote *MORE Science Adventures with Children's Literature* because I was curious about how children's books could be used to promote and extend the science curriculum in new and exciting ways. And you know what? I discovered, not just a handful of innovative strategies, but hundreds of new ways to expand science learning in fascinating ways.

The same zest for learning has propelled me through a most successful career as a children's author. As a specialist in nonfiction literature, I continually find myself asking lots of questions about things I know very little about. To learn, I then go out and try and discover the answers on site or from the experts. Having attended school in Arizona, I was curious about the different kinds of animals—nocturnal and diurnal— that inhabited the Sonoran Desert. What I discovered resulted in one of my all-time best-selling children's books: ***Desert Night, Desert Day***. My curiosity got the better of me another time when I wondered what could possibly be living under a single rock. The result was my award-winning children's book: ***Under One Rock***.

I've also been fortunate to write adult non-fiction books that have offered me unique (and extended) opportunities to discover answers to questions about the natural world. For example, I love to eat clams, but had no knowledge of these magnificently delightful creatures, so I went and wrote **The Secret Life of Clams** (Did you know that clams have been around for 510 million years?). Another literary venture propelled me up and down the east coast in order to satisfy my curiosity about some enigmatic critters—***Horseshoe Crab: Biography of a Survivor***—another 5-star (and award-winning) adult non-fiction book.

And, I have hundreds of additional questions that still need to be answered.

Although you have graduated from college you have not completed your education—in fact, you have just started. That's simply because education is never a product, it's always a process. That is to say, it is always going on, always taking place, always in motion. To stop learning is to stop growing. And when you stop growing you stop living.

I frequently tell my undergraduate students that the courses they take in college will provide them with only about one-half of their education. The other half will come from the students they teach—those they will teach during student teaching, those they will teach in their first year, and those they will teach throughout their entire career as a professional educator. I have never had a group of students—either elementary, middle school, high school, or college—who have not taught me something, have not added to my repertoire of teaching strategies or improved my outlook on what works and what doesn't. In short, my students have always been my best teachers. By listening carefully, I have become a much better educator than I ever was when I began many decades ago.

QUOTABLE QUOTE

"If everyone is thinking alike, then somebody isn't thinking."

—George S. Patton

Putting It into Action:

1. Create your own teaching portfolio. Continually add your best lesson plans, letters from students, regular evaluations by your principal, photos of special projects or displays, article read, and notes from conferences or in-service programs. Occasionally review the portfolio for potential weak areas in addition to celebrating your ongoing accomplishments.

2. Maintain a reflective journal. Keep an inexpensive notebook in your desk and write a comment, reflection, observation, or critique of your day or week. Do this on a regular basis and review your notes periodically.

What a Great Idea!

Here are three questions I ask myself at the end of each week. This form is duplicated and the sheets kept in a binder in my desk.

3 - What are three things my students learned this week:

2 - What are two things I still need to improve:

1 - What is one piece of research (article, video, colleague, web site) I'd like to explore:

3. Keep a diary of your thoughts and ideas. You may wish to sit down with other teachers periodically to discuss those thoughts and share some mutually supportive responses.

4. Begin an action research log. Action research is research that comes directly from a question you pose in your own classroom about your own students.

5. Read lots of educational magazines and professional journals. Take notes and keep an ongoing journal of some of the best ideas culled from those resources. Consider reading an education blog on a regular basis.

6. Be sure to attend any local, regional, or statewide conferences in your subject area or at your grade level. These can be wonderful opportunities to network with other teachers in addition to "rubbing elbows" with some of experts in your field. Consider joining and participating in some of the professional organizations in your area.

When we acknowledge the potential for growth in our lives, then we can celebrate the possibilities for self-improvement and self-development. People who resist change and say, "That's the way I've always done it," frighten me. The implication is that if it worked in the past, it will surely work in the future. Coping with the world by clinging to the past makes life static, stagnant, and unrewarding. There is real value in realizing our capacity for growth and development. Growing, changing, and becoming do not end with graduation and certification as a teacher. They are part of a lifelong process to be pursued and celebrated.

It is not the destination that is important, but rather the journey.

A Word of Advice

"Read something no one else is reading, think something no one else is thinking, and do something no one else is doing. To be an interesting teacher, you must be an interesting person first."

—Susan Fetner, former classroom teacher

2. **B**eing a Positive Role Model

When I was growing up, one of my childhood heroes was Davy Crockett. I was enamored of his bravery, his ability to set a course of action and stick to it, and of his determination to face problems head on. I was an ardent fan of the TV series based on his life which ran from 1954-1955. In addition, I made absolutely sure I had a Davy Crockett lunch pail, an official Davy Crockett shirt (with authentic fringe), and the requisite coonskin hat (which, if I had kept it, would now be worth about a gazillion dollars on E-bay). In so many ways, Davy Crocket epitomized what I believed a hero was: fearless, determined, and honest.

Over the years, my heroes have evolved. I've admired many different women and men – not only for who they are, but also for what they believe or think. As I've grown older (and, hopefully, wiser) I've embraced intellectual heroes more than the action heroes of my youth. I've looked to artists, explorers, scientists, and inventors for their dynamic leadership, innate sense of curiosity, limitless imagination, and infectious creative spirit. I admire those who buck the status quo (intellectually speaking), those who think well "outside the box," and those who chart thoughtful investigations far beyond their contemporaries.

Take a few moments and think of some of your heroes—not the Wonder Woman or Incredible Hulk of your youth, but rather those people, living or dead, who have shaped (or are in the process of shaping) who you are as a fully cognitive person. Who makes you think? Who sparks your creativity or stimulates your curiosity? Who asks the questions no one else is asking? Who are the intellectuals you admire most?

You and I and a few billion other people in the world look up to others as heroes. These are the people who epitomize what we aspire to. These are the people who "set the standard" for behavior, achievement and discovery. These are the people we admire as role models for our own lives because they do what is right, and just, and necessary. However, I'm certainly not suggesting that media stars or celebrities are heroes, they just have the "limelight" for a brief moment in time. They often do not endure, and when they do, it's frequently for all the wrong reasons.

What I am suggesting, however, is that as teachers we carry a very powerful responsibility. We are role models for our students. How we behave, how we act, what we say, and what we do are 'behavioral standards" for our students. Walk into any classroom and you will quickly discover how well a teacher is serving as an appropriate role model by the class. By example, we serve as an exemplar of how to behave, think and act in a classroom environment. Our students look to us for cues as to how they should act; they see us as models of behavior for the simple reason that we are adults and we are supposed to know what to do in any number of social situations.

Here are some suggestions:

Putting It into Action

1. Model the positive choices you make during the course of the school day. As you contemplate a decision or instructional choice, let students "see inside your head" (e.g. practice metacognition out loud). For example, as you consider two or three different books to share with your Kindergarten students, talk out loud about what is going on in your mind. As you consider two separate YouTube videos to share with your eleventh grade history class, talk out loud to your students and let them "see" what goes on during this decision-making process. These "models of thinking" are easy to implement, take very little time, and, most important, serve as very positive role models for the thinking you want your students to engage in throughout the year.

2. Celebrate your mistakes. Yup, you and I and a trillion other people throughout the world make mistakes. It's all part of the learning process. Please don't assume that just because you're now a teacher that you're not allowed to make mistakes. You will—GUARANTEED! I do all the time. But, what is critical is that students see what happens when you make those mistakes. How do you behave? How do you react? How do you deal with the situation? You need to feel free to 1) make mistakes, and 2) admit to those mistakes in the presence of your students. Apologize, admit your mistake, and fix the error. In so doing you will be demonstrating to your students a most important behavior. You will also be helping to establish a classroom in which students can feel free to take some risks—to branch out

into new territories and new adventures without the expectation that they must always be right. The freedom to make mistakes may be one of the most important academic skills we can pass along to our students. Equally important is what they do when those mistakes happen. They need models (like you) to show them the way.

3. Follow through on your promises. If you tell students they must be on time for class, you must be on time for class. If you start a difficult task, make sure you finish that difficult task. If you tackle a problem, make sure you work through that problem to the end. One of the most important things we can do as instructional role models is to follow through on our actions, stay with our commitments, and keep our promises. As role models we must consistently demonstrate to our students that there are also consequences to our personal procedures, too. If we say one thing and then do something else we are telling our students that we don't place any importance on our commitments. To use the vernacular, "If we talk the talk, we must walk the walk!"

4. Most important: Every day, model the joy, happiness, and excitement of the teaching/learning paradigm.

I know this may sound intimidating, but we need to remember that our students are observing us all the time. They are looking for cues on how they should behave based on the behaviors of their teacher. By showing them constant respect, demonstrating the thinking process, following through on our promises (all the time) we are giving them a positive role model for their own lives as well as the life of the classroom.

QUOTABLE QUOTE

"One looks back with appreciation to the brilliant teachers, but with gratitude to those who touched our human feelings. The curriculum is so much necessary raw material, but warmth is the vital element for the growing plant and for the soul of the student."

—Carl Jung

3. **C**ultivate the Affect

A long, long time ago—when I was a doctoral student—I decided to do my dissertation on an element of teaching that had always interested me. For the longest time I wondered how much a child's affect (e.g. feelings, emotions, sentiments, belief in self) influenced her or his academic development. Specifically, I wanted to find out if there was any kind of correlation between how well students learned to read and some carefully selected affective factors.

What I discovered was eye-opening. In a nutshell, I learned that as much as 25 percent of a student's academic growth and development was influenced by affective factors. That is to say, those students who made satisfactory progress in learning were those who also has elevated levels of selected affective factors (e.g. self-concept, locus of control, etc.). On the other hand, and not surprisingly, students who frequently struggled with academics were those who tended to have depressed levels of selected affective factors. I concluded (and the research continues to support this belief) that if teachers integrated more affect into their lessons and classroom management plans they could make a very positive difference in how well students could learn. To put it another way, cognition without affect is an incomplete education; learning without an emotional connection is ineffective.

Since then, I have worked hard to incorporate affect as a critical element in every class or course I've taught. As a result, I've noticed some very positive results (both empirically as well as anecdotally) in student achievement. Conversations with colleagues as well as with educators across the country have also proven the value of an academic program steeped in affective objectives as natural elements of the overall curriculum.

QUOTABLE QUOTE

"People don't care about how much you know until they know how much you care."

—Theodore Roosevelt

By definition, educators look at affect as the manner in which we deal with things emotionally. This would include things such as feelings, values, appreciation, enthusiasm, motivation, and attitudes. In Chapter 19 we learned about ways to help your students become more motivated. In so doing, we examined a fundamental element of good instruction; that is, teaching is not just about imparting knowledge, it is also about making personal connections with that knowledge. If we don't care about something, then it is highly unlikely that we would take the time to integrate that knowledge into our schema (mental database). For example, if we have absolutely no interest in Renaissance painters, then it is highly unlikely that we would invest any time in learning about artists such as Raphael, Botticelli, or Bosch. On the other hand, if a teacher was able to demonstrate to us the connection between foreshortening (the shortening of lines in a painting to create the illusion of depth) —a Renaissance painting technique—and our interest in computer game design then she will have created an affective connection. We may be more inclined to invest some learning time in European painters of the fifteenth and early sixteenth century.

A Word of Advice

"Be true to yourself and never stop learning. Don't settle for mediocre. Know who you are as a teacher and what you want for your students (I strive to be the kind of teacher I'd want for my own child.). Always be willing to try something new...and keep growing."

—Ashley White, current elementary teacher

Here are some ideas to implement:

Putting It into Action

1. Give students the opportunity to select their own assignments. For younger students you might want to ask, "Which of the following two homework assignments do you think would be most appropriate in helping you master this concept?" For older students you might consider posting a list of three different

follow-up assignments to a class lecture. Students form groups and each group selects an appropriate assignment.

2. This will sound familiar! There is considerable research to support the value of group work as a way to help students master important concepts AND develop positive attitudes about learning. In fact, I am so convinced of the value of group work that I include it in almost every class I teach. Students grow and expand their knowledge base when they have active opportunities to share that knowledge with their peers. It's that sharing process that allows students to see different and varied interpretations of information that is so effective. That group investment, as we have seen earlier in this book, is also critical in establishing and maintaining an invitational classroom.

3. Take the time to learn more about each of your students' personal lives. What do they like to do on the weekend, what are their hobbies or free-time interests, where do they go with their friends, what kinds of books do they like to read, who are their favorite singers, musical groups or sport teams, and what kind of television programs do they watch. Whenever possible, include some of those personal factors in your daily conversations with students ("Hey, Jeremy, I see that the Broncos and Patriots are going to play this Sunday. Who do you pick to win?"; "Simone, have you had a chance to listen to the latest song by _____?")

4. As we discussed in Chapter 19, be sure to use lots of intrinsic comments and questions with your students ("How do you think you're progressing with this new unit on 'The Role of Women in Politics', Samantha?"). Keep praise to a minimum and focus, instead, on giving students an opportunity to develop more self-awareness and higher levels of self-worth.

5. Make sure students understand why they need to learn a new concept or principle. How does that information relate to their daily or personal lives? What is its direct value to them? How will it make them a better student or better person? When students "see" the connection between what is taught in the

classroom and their everyday lives, they will be more directly involved in the learning process.

6. Provide frequent and consistent opportunities for students to be successful every day! It may be something simple as thanking a student for hanging up her coat correctly in the coat closet or something a little more complex such as reaching a self-initiated objective in terms of a midterm grade on an exam ("Congratulations, Emily, it looks like you obtained your stated objective of a 85% on the trigonometry test."). We all need regular successes in life (that's part of our self-concept); but, more important, we need to be recognized for those successes by others.

7. Engage students in regular self-reflective opportunities ("What do you think about your progress so far, Juan?"; "Why do you think your argument is valid, Heinz?"). Opportunities to reflect are critical to academic success and personal identity. Make them part of your everyday activities.

Being an A+ teacher is something you can do from the very first day you walk into a classroom. It doesn't take years of experience, lots of graduate courses, or considerable reading of educational journals. It simply takes a sense of commitment—a belief that you have some incredible potential and equally incredible things to share with your very first class of students. It's a belief that good teaching can, and should, begin from the very first day of your career.

And, you know what, it's as easy as **A-B-C**!

QUOTABLE QUOTE

"The mediocre teacher tells.
The good teacher explains.
The superior teacher demonstrates.
The great teacher inspires."

—William Arthur Ward

Postscript

<u>The Best Advice</u>

Every year I give a short speech to my undergraduate students, something like this: "The absolute worst thing I can do for you is for you to walk out of this course with my philosophy of education; my philosophy of teaching. My philosophy works for me—it's been developed and refined over more than forty years of teaching. It works for my personality, style, attitude, and perception. BUT, and this is a very big BUT, not everything may work for you in the same way it has worked for me. Sure, take some bits of it, borrow some elements, steal some principles, run away with some ideas, pilfer some thoughts, abscond with some pieces, and swipe some procedures, but, and this is the big BIG but, it is essential you create your own philosophy of teaching."

Here's the key: Please don't try to become me, or your favorite classroom teacher, or your high school coach, or even some actor you've seen in a "Teacher" movie—it just won't work. Take the time to become you. That process will not happen overnight, it is evolutionary, it will take time. It's not something that will happen in your first year, or even your second. It may take a few years before your style begins to emerge from all the theories, techniques, and strategies you have been exposed to throughout your undergraduate career, all the field experiences you had in your methods courses, all the ups and downs of student teaching, as well as all your experiences as a first year teacher. Let it happen, let it grow, let it evolve. It will take some time, but the time it takes will be worth it.

A Word of Advice

"Be the teacher you always dreamed you would be, don't try to emulate others. Hint: Ask yourself why you went into teaching in the first place."

—Steph Crumbling, current elementary teacher

Keep in mind that when you blindly use the ideas and procedures of other experts without enveloping them in your own way of doing things, then all you are doing is manipulating students into a way of doing things that worked for someone else, but which do not have your own personality, belief, and passion woven into them. Think of all that stuff you learned as a pre-service teacher (and in this book) as a <u>scaffold</u>: a basic structure for how teaching works, but not necessarily an inviolable blueprint for how teaching will work for you. Just because I suggest that you should use something, doesn't necessarily mean it is the best (or only) thing for you. It is merely a suggestion; much like a coloring book waiting for someone to take a bunch of crayons and color it according to their own perceptions, their own ideas, and their own interpretations of how a particular illustration should look. If you and I have identical coloring books, it is quite likely we will color in the same illustrations quite differently.

Please don't make the mistake of accepting the suggestions in this book blindly. These are my suggestions, in combination with more than four decades of teaching experience and in concert with the latest research into the standards and expectations of good teaching. They are equally based on the "best practices" that hundreds of thousands of teachers have found to be successful during their work with elementary, middle school, and secondary students. But (again, the "big but"), using other people's ideas because they said it would work, rather than because it is something you believe in, may result in frustration. Instead, you should spend less time trying to make someone's else's lessons or strategies work in your classroom and more time focusing on developing a philosophy of teaching that will work for your students and their academic success.

Yes, it's OK to beg, borrow, and steal ideas from other teachers. But, keep in mind that a strategy that worked exceptionally well for one teacher may not work equally well for you, particularly if it's something you're simply replicating in your classroom, rather than something you have passionately embraced your own. Don't automatically insert one of the ideas in this book into your classroom just because I, or your college professors, or a couple thousand other teachers said it was a good idea. Instead, you need to ask yourself some critical questions. Your answers to these queries will inform you as to the appropriateness of a strategy in terms of your own teaching philosophy and personal beliefs.

- Is this strategy a fit for my philosophy?
- How will this technique improve my teaching skills?
- In what ways will this be instructionally beneficial for my students?
- In what ways is this compatible with my teaching style?
- Why is this something I believe in?

<u>Here's the bottom line</u>: don't use a technique or strategy because it's something someone else says is good; use it because it is something in concert with your philosophy. What you believe in will ultimately be more successful than what you simply borrow from someone else.

<u>Bottom, bottom line</u>: Good teaching is always a reflective and philosophical endeavor—not simply a process of duplicating the work of others.

What a Great Idea!

If you would like to keep up on some of the latest teaching resources, children's books, blogs, videos, and other informational materials, please include my web site as one of your "Favorites":

www.anthonydfredericks.com

Index